Hami Inan Gümüs
American Missionaries in the Ottoman Empire

To my mother Canan, my father Ercan, my partner Carolin, and my sister Feride.

Hami Inan Gümüs (PhD) is an associated post-doc at the Graduate School Society and Culture in Motion, Halle, Germany. His current research focuses on American missionary activities in the Ottoman Empire.

Hami Inan Gümüs

American Missionaries in the Ottoman Empire

A Conceptual Metaphor Analysis of Missionary Narrative, 1820-1898

[transcript]

Bibliographic Information published by the Deutsche Nationalbibliothek
The Deutsche Nationalbibliothek lists this publication in the Deutsche Nationalbibliografie; detailed bibliographic data are available in the Internet at http://dnb.d-nb.de

© 2017 transcript Verlag, Bielefeld

Cover concept: Kordula Röckenhaus, Bielefeld
Cover illustration: A group photo of professors at Anatolia College, Marsovan (Merzifon, Turkey), 1912, © in SALT Research, Records of the American Board of Commissioners for Foreign Missions, affiliates, and successor organizations. Photographs and other Visual Materials. By permission of the American Research Institute in Turkey.
Printed by Majuskel Medienproduktion GmbH, Wetzlar
Print-ISBN 978-3-8376-3808-0
PDF-ISBN 978-3-8394-3808-4

Contents

Acknowledgments

Foremost, I would like to express my gratitude to my doctoral advisor Professor Dr. phil. habil. Werner Nell for his constant support, motivation, and patience. His guidance illuminated my path throughout my doctoral studies and I cannot think of a better doctoral supervisor. I would like to thank Professor Dr. Eric Redling for accepting to be my second supervisor despite his busy schedule. I would also like to thank my mentor Dr. Daniele Cantini for offering his help when I was stuck as well as contributing with knowledge and insight to the supervisory meetings.

This research was supported by the "Graduate School Society and Culture in Motion" of the Martin Luther University, Halle-Wittenberg. Being a member and stipend holder of the Graduate School was a privileged and enriching academic experience. I would like to thank PD Dr. Ralph Buchenhorst, Dr. James M. Thompson, and Dr. Daniele Cantini for providing an excellent academic environment enriched by their outstanding contribution as senior research fellows of the Graduate School. I am grateful to Dr. Hagen Findeis, former academic coordinator of the Graduate School, for his motivating support. I thank Ms. Yvonne Hellwig for her help as the former secretary of the Graduate School. I also want to express my thankfulness to Mr. Oliver-Pierre Rudolph, M.A., for his constant assistance as the administrative secretary. Special thanks to my fellow PhD students. They have contributed a great deal to my project by their comments and discussions.

I am grateful to my friends Caner Can, Gözde Kıral, İlker Şatıroğlu, Onur Kır, Özgür Uçar, and Parvin Zare. They have not only provided a lovely friends circle in Halle (Saale) but also contributed to the development of my ideas with their excellent academic and intellectual input. Special thanks to GALATA band, the members of which intersect with the above mentioned friends; as one of its co-founders I enjoyed an extremely enriching musical experience, which also reflected on my academic creativity.

I would like to thank Altuğ Dural for being there for the last quarter century with invaluable and wise insights whenever I needed. I am thankful to my friend İlke Tuğrul for offering his enriching ideas and friendship. I am grateful to my friends Ayşe Koca Caydaşı and Hakan Caydaşı for their friendship and constant support. I thank İbrahim Umut Sönmez for his friendship and our never-ending talks on a great range of subjects.

I want to thank my partner Carolin Elisabeth Liebisch for her invaluable contributions to my project, for her encouragement, for enduring the hardships together with me I went through in the process of writing, for being next to me. I am grateful to my mother, Canan Gümüş, for believing in the path I took and for constantly expressing her support together with offering her contributions. I would like to thank my father, Ercan Gümüş, for his understanding and support. I want to state my thankfulness to my sister Feride Gümüş Küçükoğlu who has been a good, patient and motivating listener, and an excellent mentor. I would like to thank my brother in law Erhan Küçükoğlu for his assistance. I also want to thank my niece Defne Küçükoğlu for being a constant source of inspiration. I appreciate their loving support.

Introduction

> It is one thing [...] to make mention of the trials of a missionary, and quite another thing to experience them.
> (Missionary Levi Parsons to Mr. Cyrus Byington)[1]

The story of the establishment of American overseas missions began when five Williams College students took shelter under a haystack to protect themselves from the imminent danger of a thunderstorm in August 1806. Under the stack, the students, led by Samuel J. Mills, talked about the "moral darkness in Asia," and Mills proposed to start an overseas mission in order to send the gospel to that "dark and heathen land." All of the students except one took to the idea. That one opposed the idea on the premises that it would be a premature attempt, that the missionaries would be murdered and "Christian armies must subdue the country before the Gospel could be sent to the Turks and Arabs." In his reply, Mills told him that the work would be carried out and the Roman adage would prove true, "Vox populi vox Dei." After the discussion, he supposedly told the others "let us make it a subject of prayer, under this haystack, while the dark clouds are going, and the clear sky is coming."[2] The Haystack Meeting soon bore fruit

---

1 Levi Parsons. "Palestine Mission: Letter from Mr. Parsons to Mr. Cyrus Byington." *The Missionary Herald*, April (1822): 109.

2 The story was told by an eyewitness, Byram Green, who was present at the haystack meeting, and his account was quoted by Arthur L. Perry. (Arthur L. Perry.

in the foundation of the first American overseas missionary organization, the American Board of Commissioners for Foreign Missions (ABCFM). Today, a twelve-foot monument marks the sight of the haystack prayer meeting. There is a stone globe representing the Earth on top of the monument, and an inscription underneath reads "The Field is the World." The surrounding area, which at the time of the incident was called Sloan's meadow, was later named Mission Park.

The founding myth of the Board points to a vivid imagery that can also be seen in the seal of the Board. On the seal, a white man standing in an opening or a field stretches out his arm and offers the Bible (the Word) to a kneeling, half naked indigenous person, under rays of light diffusing from above. There is also a plant behind the kneeling person. The inscription around the seal is a quotation from the Bible, Mark 16:15: "Go ye into all the world, and preach the gospel to every creature."[3] The light implied in the story of Samuel J. Mills via reference to clear skies after a dark sky is shown in the seal, along with the references to the 'field' and 'growth' (the plant).

The activities that the American Board of Commissioners for Foreign Missions conducted in the Ottoman Empire constitute an interesting part of the entangled history of the United States and the Middle East. The American Board started the first American Protestant mission in the Ottoman Empire, and up until the collapse of the Empire remained one of the most widespread and effective missionary societies. This work is a conceptual metaphor analysis against the backdrop of the history of a cultural encounter, which also makes it a history beyond the idea of two self-contained histories at a transcultural and transnational level. Moreover, the study of missionary texts is an opportunity for evaluating outstanding travel writing. The missionary establishment is such an essential part of both Turkish and American histories that during his visit to Turkey, Barack Obama referred to Robert College, a school in Istanbul founded by the missionaries of the

---

Williamstown and Williams College. New York: Charles Scribner's Sons (1899): 361-362.)

3 Douglas K. Showalter. "The 1810 Formation of the American Board of Commissioners for Foreign Missions." *The Role of the American Board in the World.* Eds. Clifford Putney, Paul T. Burlin. Eugene: Wipf & Stock (2012): 7.

American Board of Commissioners for Foreign Missions in 1863, as follows:

So as President, I'd like to find new ways to connect young Americans to young people all around the world, by supporting opportunities to learn new languages, and serve and study, welcoming students from other countries to our shores. That's always been a critical part of how America engages the world. That's how my father, who was from Kenya, from Africa, came to the United States and eventually met my mother. It's how Robert College was founded so long ago here in Istanbul.[4]

The present work ascertains the network of kindred allusions as presented in official missionary texts from the field of the Ottoman mission in the official magazine of the Board, *The Missionary Herald*. The study detects how the American Board of Commissioners for Foreign Missions articulated, and appropriated the discursive formations and academic and intellectual production of Congregationalist American Protestantism in the Ottoman Empire in the years 1820-1898. It also examines and explains a specific discourse originating from 'liberal' American Protestantism, which was adopted, appropriated (or re-invented) and diffused by the missionaries with the intention of civilizing the 'corrupted Christians' and 'the heathen,' and which was received and countered by both the Ottoman State as well as other religious groups.

The allusions involved here are metaphorical by nature and display a conceptual trait. There is something more to the texts in terms of conceptual background than meets the eye. It is suggested that there are conceptual metaphorical networks inherent to the official missionary discourse, that the missionary discourse constitutes a narrative, and that those networks constitute a core structure in that narrative. Moreover, it is claimed that the conceptual metaphorical formations contribute as a key element to the rise and formation of a missionary narrative.

The assumption is that the detection and explication of such networks will uncover the ways the missionaries:

1. Defined and depicted themselves and their organization,

---

4   "Remarks of President Barack Obama at Student Roundtable," 2 May 2009, URL = http://www.whitehouse.gov [view date: 24 June 2015].

2. Defined and conveyed their actions, activities and purpose,
3. Managed their institutional sense-making through a coherent narrative,
4. Defined and depicted the 'other', including individuals, groups, peoples, geographical locations, political entities and systems, religious and political opinions, cultural formations, and actions,
5. And how they brought all these constituents together in a coherent narrative without missing the point that the Board was a purposeful organization conducting a transnational operation.

As the narrative does not occur in a vacuum, the study at the same time stresses and examines three historical processes that form the background. These processes are the historical Congregationalist background, the history of the ABCFM in the Ottoman Empire, and the question and implementation of modernity by the missionaries and the Ottoman state, as well as the Ottoman state's reaction to the ABCFM against this background.

The first chapter is a historical survey of the ABCFM in the Ottoman Empire. The chapter starts with the preceding historical background information on American Congregationalism, with the focus on the ABCFM's activities and establishment. The commencement of the mission, important events and turning points in mission history, its work in printing, education and the medical field, and the transformation of the mission establishments in the Republic of Turkey to this day, are all examined with factual data and figures.

The second chapter focuses on the theory and methodology, and also poses several research questions. In the light of these questions, the issue of conceptual metaphor is introduced. Since the missionary texts are considered to constitute a narrative, a narratological examination and theoretical background is provided. The chapter proceeds with the discussion of these conceptual and narrative elements as components of a narrative with story and discourse components and Blending Theory is proposed and presented as an analytic tool.

In the third chapter, the conceptual metaphor networks are presented from the first ten years of the Ottoman mission. It is believed that the founding years are representative of missionary discourse and that the ten-year period is adequate to provide the reader with representative data on its conceptual formations. The chapter starts with the relevant Congregationalist history and proceeds with the discussion of metaphor networks. A section on the non-metaphorical linguistic use of invectives is also added to display the complete imagological extent of missionary discourse.

The fourth chapter dwells on the application of the metaphors and the conceptual domains of the founding years in different settings and periods. For this purpose, two case studies have been chosen. The first study focuses on the failed attempt at proselytization among the Muslims, 1856-1865. The second study is on the missionary responses to the Armenian Massacres of 1894-1896. Both time periods are discussed with reference to the historical and political background and the use of missionary conceptualizations are scrutinized in detail.

Fifth chapter deals with the notion of modernity as a greater background for the missionary narrative. In this chapter, the notion of modernity, missionary and Congregationalist stances regarding the notion, and the reaction of Ottoman state against the missionaries in the context of modernity are scrutinized.

In the conclusion, the data discussed in the previous chapters are presented collectively and the use of conceptual metaphors and other conceptual tools at different periods are discussed comparatively. In addition, the real world repercussions of missionary activities and the ability of missionary discourse to cope with that reality is explained.

The work heavily relies on the analysis of issues of *The Missionary Herald* from the relevant period, since almost all of the references to the missionary discourse are taken from *The Missionary Herald*. The magazine contains correspondence, impressions, reports, and travel notes by the missionaries, editorial opinions and evaluations, and theoretical writings regarding missionary work. As a result, it is an invaluable source of primary material. Moreover, since the missionaries' correspondence and journals were edited prior to publication and only material approved by the Board was published, it can also be assumed that the magazine reflects the ideology of the Board in a strict sense.

Some important points should be noted regarding the quotations from *The Missionary Herald*: differences in punctuation, capitalization and the use of words that have become obsolete or old-fashioned are among the frequent elements in the quotations that may confuse contemporary readers. In addition, some proper names (especially those of cities) are written differently. Thus, for instance, Beirut was referred to as Beyroot or Beyrout. Other problematic points are the use of italics, punctuation, and anonymous remarks. When these points are kept in mind, the quotations can be regarded in their linguo-historical context. Furthermore, in many instances the use of commas after complementizers does not comply with modern English grammar.

Place names are predominantly given according to modern Turkish usage. Where the place names are clear in the missionary texts no further explanation has been given. To illustrate, the missionary use of Constantinople has not been corrected, but the name Istanbul is used in the dissertation.

The conceptual metaphors are displayed either in lower case bold characters or upper case bold characters in 12 points. Where the metaphors are subcases of a master metaphor they are written in lower case. Master metaphors are written in upper case. In order to detect the metaphors, the *Master Metaphor List* compiled by George Lakoff, Jane Espenson, Adele Goldberg and Alan Schwartz between 1989 and 1991 at the University of California at Berkeley has been used.[5]

This study aims at dwelling on the missionary narrative and discourse from a literary and comparative perspective by considering the historical background as well. Through this approach, the linguistic expressions of profound conceptual metaphor and parable networks are examined thoroughly.[6] The textual analysis enriched by a historical focus sheds light on a narrative that is created in the context of mobility of people and ideas as well as encounters related to these processes of motion in the nineteenth century. Research on American missionary activities in the Ottoman Empire has almost exclusively focused on its historical aspects and significance.[7] To date, no systematic investigation has examined the conceptual

---

5   George Lakoff, Jane Espenson, Alan Schwartz. *Master Metaphor List, Second Draft Copy.* Berkeley: University of California Berkeley, Cognitive Linguistics Group (1991).

6   Theory and methodology is discussed in the second chapter.

7   To name a few, Hans Lukas Kieser's *Nearest East: American Millenialism and Mission to the Middle East* (Philadelphia: Temple University Press, 2010) is a history of the ABCFM mission to Ottoman and post-Ottoman Middle East. Joseph L. Grabill's book *Protestant Diplomacy and Near East: Missionary Influence on American Foreign Policy, 1810-1927* (Minneapolis: University of Minnesota Press, 1971) approaches the missionary activities in terms of their diplomatic impact. James Field Jr. in a similar examines the missionary activities in

basis of American missionary narrative regarding the Ottoman Empire. This study fills that gap by analyzing the missionary narrative with literary, narratological, and linguistic tools in its historical context.

the general context of American involvement with the Mediterranean world in his influential work *America and the Mediterranean World 1776-1882* (New Jersey: Princeton University Press, 1969). *The Role of the American Board in the World* (Eds. Clifford Putney, Paul T. Burlin. Eugene: Wipf & Stock, 2012) is a compilation of articles focusing on the global impact of the ABCFM activities in nineteenth and twentieth centuries. Frank Andrews Stone's *Academies for Anatolia* (California: Caddo Gap Press, 2005) is the history of the educational establishments of the Board in Anatolia. Akşin Somel's article "Christian Community Schools During the Ottoman Reform Period" (Late Ottoman Society: The Intellectual Legacy. Ed. Elisabeth Özdalga. London: Routledge Press (2005): 254-273) and Benjamin C. Fortna's book Imperial Classroom (Oxford: Oxford University Press, 2002) deal with the issue of education in late Ottoman society. Ussama Makdisi's book *Artillery of Heaven: American Missionaries and the Failed Conversion of the Middle East* (Ithaca: Cornel University Press, 2008) offers original ideas on how the missionary activities contributed to the emergence of an Arab identity especially in Syria and Lebanon.

1 The History of the ABCFM in the Ottoman Empire

Before proceeding with the analysis of the metaphors in the light of the proposed theoretical and methodological framework, a historical survey of ABCFM and its activities in the Ottoman Empire is necessary for a better comprehension of the context in which the focus of the research, namely the metaphor networks and related narrative structures, is located. For this purpose, the impact of New Divinity as the intellectual forebears of the Board, the foundation of the organization, and a general outline of the Ottoman mission with particular emphasis on its commencement, its work for Armenians, key events that drastically shaped the way the missionaries became involved in proselytization, and the setting up of educational institutions, printing activities, and philanthropy as medical work are outlined to construct a thorough yet easily accessible historical account.

The aim of providing the reader with a historical survey is to give a better understanding of the world in which missionary discourse originated and with which it interacted. It should be noted that the survey takes ABCFM as its focal point. Consequently, it will be impossible to highlight every important event in nineteenth century Ottoman history, let alone depict them in detail. A more intricate examination of specific historical events is provided in the subsequent chapters in their immediate relation to the relevant metaphor networks.

1.1 THE BEGINNING: PRECURSORS AND FOUNDATION

Although there were numerous religious traditions that directly or indirectly affected the doctrines and foundation of the Board, New Divinity stands out as the most influential and dominant. Being one of the most important intellectual sources of eighteenth century Protestant thought in North America, New Divinity shaped subsequent thoughts and discussions on evangelism, the idea of the Millennium, and on domestic and later overseas missions.

Jonathan Edwards, one of the most important figures of New England theology, heavily influenced the New Divinity School. He mobilized his learning and intelligence for the defense, interpretation, and propagation of revivalist religion.[1] Sydney E. Ahlstrom defines New Divinity men as consisting predominantly of Yale graduates who acknowledged Edwards as their hero and settled in the Connecticut River valley in the second half of the eighteenth century.[2] He states that their efforts to disseminate their doctrine were rewarded by the Second Great Awakening and by extending New England theology, which was derived from Edwardsian theology: they "contributed creatively to the single most brilliant and most continuous indigenous theological tradition that America has produced."[3] It should be noted that New Divinity efforts were not the sole, or main, reason for the emergence of the Second Great Awakening. Edwards' approach to millennialism was among the most important constituents of New Divinity theology. For him the awakening was a sign of the approaching Millennium, the thousand–year Kingdom of Christ on Earth.[4] More importantly, Edwards was a postmillennialist and evaluated his time through a postmillennialist perspective.

Postmillennialism in New Divinity theology was articulated as a deeply theological, Biblical discourse with a discernible utopian quality prior to

---

1 Joseph A. Conforti. *Jonathan Edwards, Religious Tradition & American Culture*. Chapel Hill: University of North Carolina Press (1995): 2.

2 Sydney E. Ahlstrom. *A Religious History of the American People*. New Haven: Yale University Press (1972): 404.

3 *ibid*. 405.

4 Ruth H. Bloch. *Visionary Republic*: Millennial Themes in American Thought, 1756-1800. Cambridge: Cambridge University Press (1985): 12-14.

the Second Great Awakening. Eschatology became a central tenet in the propagation of the Gospel, and the prevalence of the intellectual approach to millennialism, in contrast to the political approach, along with a new sensitivity to global affairs made people believe in the possibility of the conversion of the world.[5] The belief in progress and in the gradual expansion of God's Kingdom determined the fate of later missionary activity.

The era of the Second Great Awakening, which lasted from 1790s to 1840s, also witnessed the rise of voluntary societies. Voluntary societies rapidly became important tools for evangelical millennialism during this period. They emerged as an important part of the campaign of assuming social responsibility in order to stem religious decline.[6] The American Board of Commissioners for Foreign Missions was founded as a voluntary missionary association in 1810, and it can be said that the Board embodied missionary, publication, educational, moral, and humanitarian interests in its range of activities.

According to Joseph Grabill, "[t]he Board arose out of various forces in New England society."[7] The Second Great Awakening and its theology about practical Christianity, a reaction to Unitarianism which gave dynamism to traditional Calvinism, and the necessity of missions for the moral renewal of the world were the principle factors in this.[8] The initial idea came from Samuel J. Mills in 1808. Grabill summarizes the foundation of the Board as follows:

Students at Williams College in Massachusetts, led by angular Samuel J. Mills, had conceived the idea for the American Board while praying by a haystack near the school. Mills and some of his fellows went to Andover Theological Seminary, which orthodox Congregationalists had begun as a counter to Unitarian influence at Harvard College. These Andover seminarians in 1810 made the initial move which persuaded Congregational and Presbyterian officials to found the American Board – the first organization in the United States concerned with missions abroad."[9]

---

5   *ibid*. 122-123.

6   Ahlstrom, *Religious History*, 422-428.

7   Grabill, *Protestant Diplomacy*, 5.

8   *ibid*. 5.

9   *ibid*. 5.

The foundation of the Board sprang from a complex historical background, and its activities in the Ottoman Empire up until the end of the 1914-1918 War should not be evaluated without bearing that background in mind. Eleven years after the foundation of the Board, their mission to the Middle East and consequently to the 'Bible lands' commenced.

The American Board of Commissioners for Foreign Missions was founded at Bradford, Massachusetts, by the General Association of Massachusetts on June 29, 1810.[10] The Charter was endorsed in 1812. As its name indicates, the Board was designed to act for others and it was created for "devising ways and means, and adopting and prosecuting measures, for the spread of the gospel in heathen lands."[11] At its first annual meeting, which was held in Bradford on September 5, 1810, it was declared that "[t]he object of this Board is to devise, adopt, and prosecute, ways and means for propagating the gospel among those who are destitute of the knowledge of Christianity."[12]

Their spirits were high and the Millennium seemed to be close. It was believed that the long expected day, namely the Millennium, was approaching and that the 'Lord' was "shaking the nations."[13] In the following year, the Board made an attempt to become associated with the London Missionary Society, in order to gain useful information they lacked in the field of missionary work and also to conduct joint operations. For that purpose, four missionaries were sent to London.[14] Although the idea of a joint operation was kindly declined by the London Missionary Society, the Board was influenced by the society's missionary activities in South East Asia. It was accepted that "[t]he Eastern world, especially Hindoostan, the Malayan Archipelago, and the Birman empire, presents most extensive fields for missionary labors; fields which appear to be fast whitening for the harvest."[15]

---

10 *Memorial Volume of the First Fifty years of the American Board of Commissioners for Foreign Missions*. Boston: Published by the Board (1863): 42.

11 *ibid.* 77.

12 *First Ten Annual Reports of the American Board of Commissioners for Foreign Missions*, with Other Documents of the Board. Boston: Crocker and Brewster (1834): 11.

13 *ibid.* 13.

14 *ibid.* 18-19.

15 *ibid.* 23.

The Board started six missions in the first nine years of its existence. The first mission was to Bombay. By 1818 they had started the Bombay, Ceylon, Cherokee, Choctaw, Arkansas and Sandwich Islands missions and founded a Foreign Mission School in Cornwall, Connecticut. The idea of starting a mission in Palestine was already ripe in 1818 and preparations started in 1819.[16]

The Middle East, or as the missionaries used to call it, Western Asia, was an important field of missionary activity for the American Board. There were several reasons to start a mission in the Holy Land and the Bible Lands:

These were the scenes of those great transactions and events, which involved the destinies of mankind of all ages and all nations, for time and eternity; the creation of the progenitors of our race - the beginnings of the sciences and arts, and of civil and political institutions the fatal transgression, which "brought death into the world and all our woe" the successive revelations of Heaven, with all their attestations, their light and their blessings the incarnation, labors and agonies of the Son of God, for the recovery of that which was lost and the first exhibition of that mighty and gracious power, which is to bow the world to his sceptre, and fill the mansions of immortality with his people.[17]

The millennialist belief that the conversion of the Jews was a prerequisite for the realization of the Kingdom of God was a further reason.[18] Conversion of the 'corrupted' Christians of the Middle East was yet another goal:

It is to be hoped, however, that among the Christians there, of various denominations, some might be found, who are alive in Christ Jesus; and who, were proper means employed for their excitement, improvement, and help, might be roused from their slumbers, become active in doing good, and shine as lights in those darkened regions.[19]

This aim was also considered as a step for the conversion of Jews and Muslims. The Board stated that those "who bear the Christian name, would

---

16 *ibid.* 210-250.
17 *ibid.* 229.
18 *ibid.* 230.
19 *ibid.* 230.

willingly and gladly receive the Bible into their houses, and do something towards imparting the heavenly treasure, as opportunities should be afforded, to the Jews, Mohammedans, and Pagans."[20] Indeed, the conversion of Jews and Muslims was of utmost importance for the fulfillment of prophecies and for the coming of the Millennium, and a matter of the prophecies of the Bible.[21]

1.2 ARRIVAL IN THE OTTOMAN EMPIRE

On January 17, 1820, Pliny Fisk and Levi Parsons arrived in Izmir.[22] They lost no time in setting to work. They were eager to explore their surroundings in order to attain the knowledge necessary for establishing a successful mission.[23] They were confronted with new lands and new people they only knew from books and second hand accounts. Soon they realized the hard way that the preconceived ideas and overambitious plans they had brought with them did not square with the reality. The challenge awaiting them was huge: acquiring the vernacular languages (Turkish, Greek, Arabic, Armenian), figuring out the complex political and cultural structure to evade problems and to penetrate the very fabric of the society, exploring the entire Eastern Mediterranean basin together with its hinterland (including the Caucasus and parts of Iran), finding the right way to conduct missionary activities such as delivering pamphlets or offering education by trial and error, and most importantly finding the right group of people as a promising target group.

Soon after they arrived, they spent five months at Chios in order to learn Greek and get acquainted with the archipelago in the spring and summer of 1820.[24] On November 1, 1820, they left Smyrna to visit the

---

20 *ibid.* 230.

21 *ibid.* 230.

22 Pliny Fisk, Levi Parsons. "Palestine Mission: Letter from Messrs. Fisk and Parsons, to the Cor. Sec. of A. B. C. F. M." *The Missionary Herald*, April (1820): 173.

23 *ibid.* 173.

24 Pliny Fisk, Levi Parsons. "Letters of Messrs. Parsons and Fisk to the Corresponding Secretary." *The Missionary Herald*, March (1821): 78.

countryside and do research.[25] During that journey, they traveled more than 300 miles, visited Ayvalık, Pergamos, Thyatira, Sardis, and Philadelphia, among other places, gave away 21 Bibles and Testaments and distributed 1,300 religious tracts.[26] The missionaries concluded that Izmir was the most promising place for a permanent missionary station due to its position as a busy seaport, its favorable climate, and the friendly attitude of the English consul.[27] In 1826, the Board sent Elnathan Gridley and Josiah Brewer to Izmir, meaning that Izmir became the first established missionary station strictly in Turkey.[28] As a result, the so-called Palestine Mission was re-named as the Western Asia Mission.[29]

One of the original fields of operation was Ottoman Syria, together with the region of Mount Lebanon. The Board conducted missionary work in Syria for a considerable amount of time. William Goodell and Isaac Bird arrived at Beirut on November 16, 1823.[30] Eli Smith joined them on February 18, 1827.[31] Because of the unrest created by the war between the Greeks and the Ottoman Empire, and the recent destruction of the Turkish armada at Navarino, Eli Smith, Isaac Bird and William Goodell departed from Beirut and embarked for Malta.[32] After a two year break, the missionaries returned to Syria in 1830.[33] Yet right after they started, the opposition of the Maronites, the outbreak of plague and cholera, and the disturbances of the Egyptian War interrupted missionary work. Despite these obstacles, the missionaries furthered their activities, particularly in the field of educa-

25 Pliny Fisk, Levi Parsons. "Letters from Messrs. Parsons and Fisk." *The Missionary Herald*, April (1821): 105.

26 *ibid*. 105.

27 William E. Strong. *The Story of the American Board*. Boston: The Pilgrim Press (1910): 83.

28 *ibid*. 86-87.

29 *ibid*. 86-87.

30 William Goodell. "Letter from Mr. Goodell." *The Missionary Herald*, July (1824): 214.

31 Eli Smith. "Extracts from a Letter of Mr. Smith to the Corresponding Secretary." *The Missionary Herald*, October (1827): 306.

32 Isaac Bird, William Goodell, Eli Smith. "Departure of Missionaries from Beyroot." The Missionary Herald, November (1828): 348-350.

33 Strong, *Story*, 98.

tion. Ten schools with three hundred pupils were opened by 1835 and, along with elementary schools, this period saw the beginnings of a boy's seminary. A girl's school, the first of its kind in the region, was opened as well. The missionaries established a new printing press and prepared new fonts which attracted the attention of Arabic scholars. In 1848, the first native church was established in Beirut and in 1850 another native church was opened in Hasbeiya.[34]

In 1860 civil war once again broke out between Maronites and Druzes in Syria. The turmoil did not abate until 1863, and thus hindered missionary activities. Despite the drawbacks, the Syrian Protestant College was opened in 1866 and a theological seminary was established in Abeih in 1869. The Syrian mission was taken over by the Board of Missions of the Presbyterian Church in 1870.[35]

1.3 WORK FOR ARMENIANS COMMENCES

After setting foot on the Ottoman Empire, the initial optimism of the missionaries diminished within a short space of time. Having stumbled upon unexpected hindrances, the missionaries continued to look for any opportunity that would enable them to start proselytizing. Jewish communities did not respond to missionary propaganda, as they had expected, and the Muslims seemed to be quite satisfied with their religion and the privileges that came with it. Moreover, the official position of the state authorities on mission work for Muslims was made clear from the very beginning.[36] Disheartened, they focused their attention on Christians. Being unable to grasp the religious fault lines and the autonomous position of religious communities under the Ottoman *millet* system, work for Christians caused even more friction, and these early problems soon evolved into a full-scale confrontation. The culmination was the imprisonment and death of Maronite convert Asad Shidiaq at the hands of the Maronite clergy.

---

34 *ibid.* 98; 99; 101.

35 *ibid.* 204-205.

36 Pliny Fisk, Jonas King. "Palestine Mission: Journal of Messrs. Fisk and King." *The Missionary Herald*, December (1823): 376.

As a consequence of this unexpected failure, Rufus Anderson visited the mission in 1829 in order to evaluate new opportunities and possibilities as well as new fields of work.[37] The prospects in Turkey were considered to be promising.[38] Under these circumstances, Mr. Bird was sent to Beirut to resume the mission and William Goodell was sent to Istanbul to open a new station.[39] As part of this new orientation, two new appointees, Dr. Eli Smith and Dr. H.G.O. Dwight, were commissioned to take a trip and explore Anatolia, Armenia and northwestern Iran.[40]

On May 21, 1830, Smith and Dwight left Istanbul.[41] The two undertook extensive research and made lengthy observations in Armenia and compiled a great deal of information on the peoples and the religions in the places they visited.[42] The journey lasted sixteen months and the missionaries wrote a book entitled *Missionary Researches in Armenia* to report their observations.[43] This book found an audience among the Americans as well as missionaries, and the American Board hastened to start work among the Armenians.[44]

On June 9, 1831, the Board's first missionary to Istanbul, the Rev. William Goodell, arrived in the city. A new gate was opened for the missionaries in Istanbul because the influential merchants and bankers of the Armenian community assumed that knowledge was power, and that the economic and military superiority of the European nations was due to their 'advanced' culture. As a result of this notion, they were searching for people to provide the community with Western style education since good schools were seen as the best channel to attain Western values and notions. The missionaries opened a school in Istanbul in 1834 which was transformed in-

---

37 Strong, *Story*, 88.

38 *ibid*. 88.

39 *ibid*. 88.

40 Julius Richter. *A History of the Protestant Missions in the Near East*. New York: Fleming H. Revell Company (1910): 106-107.

41 H. G. O. Dwight, Eli Smith. "Mediterranean: Letters from Messrs. Smith and Dwight." *Missionary Herald*, December (1830): 377.

42 Strong, *Story*, 89.

43 Richter, *History*, 106-107.

44 *ibid*. 106-107.

to a seminary in Bebek, a suburb of Istanbul, in 1844. The aim was to appeal to Armenian youth by offering Western style education.[45]

It was not long before the missionaries had their first results, because some Armenian students accepted the evangelical faith in 1833. Soon the activities spread from Istanbul to other places. New schools were established and with the arrival of new missionaries, new stations were opened. In 1834, a new station was opened in Bursa, missionaries were sent to Trabzon, and public interest was aroused in Izmit.[46] In 1835, the Board opened a station in Trabzon. As the policy was shifting towards undertaking extensive missionary work for the Armenians, Dr. Asahel Grant visited Diyarbakır, Van, Harput, Mardin, Mosul and other smaller towns in southeastern and eastern Turkey from 1839 to 1844. In 1839, a missionary station was opened in Erzurum, an eastern Anatolian city with a considerable Armenian population. The Bursa station was opened in 1848. The missionaries paid considerable attention to southeastern Turkey and as a result a station was opened in Antep in 1849, becoming the center for operations in the region. 1850s saw the opening of interior stations like Merzifon, Kayseri, Sivas, Harput and Bitlis. During this period the mission fields emerged as follows: Syrian field, center Beirut, language Arabic; Central Turkey region, center Antep, language Turkish; Eastern Turkey Mission, center Harput, language Armenian; Western Turkey (including Trabzon), languages Greek, Armenian, Turkish and Bulgarian. The missionary work was directed towards five groups, namely the Jews, Greeks, Turks, Syrians and Armenians, as of 1860.[47] The content of *The Missionary Herald* articles from the second half of the nineteenth century indicates that only missions for Armenians thrived.

---

45 *ibid.* 107; 110-11.

46 Strong, *Story*, 92-93.

47 James Levi Barton. *Daybreak in Turkey*. Boston: The Pilgrim Press (1908): 127; 139; 140; 144.

1.4 THE ARMENIAN REFORMATION

The years from 1840 to 1850 witnessed what the missionaries called the Armenian reformation.[48] In 1839, a station was opened in Erzurum to the east and other centers were founded in Izmit and Adapazarı, cities nearer to Istanbul. Moreover, a new mission was started in Anatolia, prayer meetings and preaching services for women were continued, and the missionaries kept traveling and preaching the Gospel. In this period, William Goodell's translation of the Old Testament into Armeno-Turkish was published and books and magazines in Armenian and Greek were used to propagate evangelical teaching.[49] Theological training began and the courses at the famous seminary at Bebek were broadened. As American missionaries became more influential among the Armenians, unrest arose in the Armenian Apostolic Church and persecution started in 1839 since the clergy feared that they would lose their power over the community and the Church might disintegrate.[50] Consequently, a new patriarch was elected and arrests were made. With the appointment of a new patriarch, Matteos, the persecution entered a new phase in 1844. In 1846, a bull of excommunication was issued against the Protestants. The result was the organization of the first Evangelical Armenian church in Istanbul on July 1, 1846. Bebek seminary was transformed into a theological school.[51] One thousand Armenians had joined the new church by 1848. The Board commenced missionary work in remote places such as Antep, Aleppo and Arapkir.[52]

The English ambassador interested himself in the activities of the Board and the related developments. Already in the first years of the mission, the help and protection offered by the English consuls and agents was undeniable. It can even be claimed that without English protection the mission could have failed from the very beginning or could have had serious problems. Even before they arrived at Smyrna, missionaries Parsons and Fisk were aware of the importance of British protection and help: "On the 9th inst. We set sail for Smyrna, having been previously furnished with a letter

---

48 Strong, *Story*, 102.
49 *ibid*. 103.
50 *ibid*. 104.
51 *ibid*. 106.
52 *ibid*. 106.

of introduction to the Rev. Mr. Williamson and to the British Consul at Aleppo."[53] In a letter written from Smyrna on 31 October, 1820, Parsons and Fisk gave the information that the English consul had written to Constantinople on their behalf to obtain a traveling *firman* (edict) from the Sultan.[54]

---

53 Levi Parsons, Pliny Fisk. "Palestine Mission: Letter from Messrs. Fisk and Parsons, to the Cor. Sec. of A.B.C.F.M." *The Missionary Herald*, April (1820): 173.

54 Pliny Fisk, Levi Parsons. "Letters from Messrs. Parsons and Fisk." *The Missionary Herald*, April (1821): 104. In another occurrence, Parsons arrived at Jaffa on 10 February, 1821, and the dragoman of the English Consul waited for him at the shore and ordered all his baggage to pass without the usual taxes at the customhouse, and from there he was taken to the house of the English Consul (Levi Parsons. "Journal of Mr. Parsons." *The Missionary Herald*, January (1822): 17). When Parsons returned from Jerusalem to Smyrna he moved to the island of Syra to spend the summer and he resided in the family of the English consul as instructor to his children (Levi Parsons. "Letter from Mr. Parsons to the Corresponding Secretary." *The Missionary Herald*, February (1822): 44). Before Parsons and Fisk set off for Egypt in 1822, they received introductory letters from Mr. Werry, the British consul in Smyrna, to Mr. Salt, the Consul General, at Cairo and "circulars addressed to all English consuls and agents, requesting them to afford us all the protection and assistance, which they would afford to English travelers, and guarantying the payment of any sums of money [...]" (Pliny Fisk, Levi Parsons. "Letter from Messrs. Fisk and Parsons to the Corresponding Secretary." *The Missionary Herald*, June (1822): 178). Pliny Fisk and Jonas King arrived at Jaffa on 22 April, 1823, having traveled Upper Egypt. They took lodgings in Mr. Damiani's house, who was the English consul there. They spent a couple of days in the house of the English agent in Saide (Sidon) in 1823 as well (Pliny Fisk, Jonas King. "Journal of Messrs. Fisk and King." *The Missionary Herald*, April (1824): 101). In their next stop, Beirut, they enjoyed the protection of the English consul which was to be a relief for the missionaries in the following years (*ibid.* 101). William Goodell and Isaac Bird were also quite fond of the British protection and the friendly approach of the consul in Beirut: "The English consul and his lady have treated us as if we had been their own children; and by taking us under the wing of their protection, and, as if it were, identifying our interests with their own, have given us an im-

More than 25 years later, Lord Stratford Canning de Redcliffe, the British ambassador at that time, consulted with his government and the missionaries in order to arrange a preliminary agreement with the Ottoman State regarding the status of Protestants.[55] On November 15, 1847, Reşid Pasha, the Grand Vizier, sent an order to local authorities stating that the Protestants were a separate body in the transaction and settlement of all their civil affairs.[56] This first agreement was followed by an imperial *firman* (edict) granting legal status to the Protestants by recognizing them as a new community in 1850.[57] The *firman* of 1850, obtained from Sultan Abdulmecid through the intervention of Lord Stratford de Redcliffe initiated a great advance in missionary work as the missionaries were confronted with the task of building up a separate Protestant church.[58] Finally, in April 1853, a special *firman* promising protection to all Protestant subjects,

---

portance and respectability in the view of the natives which we could not otherwise have enjoyed (Isaac Bird, William Goodell. "Journal of Messrs. Goodell and Bird." *The Missionary Herald*, August (1824): 242)." Fisk and King, too, enjoyed British protection when they encountered trouble from the Turkish authorities in Jerusalem as Mr. Abbott, the English consul at Beirut, procured a special document from the Pasha of Damascus (Pliny Fisk. "Journal of Mr. Fisk." *The Missionary Herald*, August (1824): 245). During the tumult following the attack of a Greek vessel to Beirut in 1826, British protection proved to be of utmost importance for the missionaries: "A French merchant, whose house was near mine, they sized by the throat, took a gold watch from his pocket, his money from his belt, and articles from his house to the value of five thousand Spanish dollars. My own house being about in the centre of their depredations, was much exposed. Many parties came at different times, and demanded entrance; but on my telling them that the house was English, and they must not presume to enter, they departed (William Goodell. "Letter from Mr. Goodell to the Corresponding Secretary." *The Missionary Herald*, November (1826): 355)."

55 Richter, *History*, 113.
56 Joseph K. Greene. *Leavening the Levant*. Boston: The Pilgrim Press (1916): 110.
57 Richter, *History*, 113.
58 *ibid.* 114; Greene, *Levant*, 110-111.

signed by the sultan himself, and accordingly called the Hatt-ı Şerif (lofty command), was given to the agent of the Protestants.[59]

The importance of this firmans can be better understood against the background of Ottoman *millet* system. Public law, especially all criminal law, was based on the secular decrees of the sultans. The Jewish and Christian groups had *dhimmi* (protected) status.[60] According to the *dhimmi* status, they were allowed to live in a Muslim state in exchange for the payment of a special tax and were protected against forced conversion, but they were regarded as second-class subjects.[61] The millet system is the key to understanding the social divisions in the empire. İlber Ortaylı explains it as follows:

It was a form of organization and legal status arising from the submission of monotheistic religions (*ehl-i zimmet*) to the authority of Islam after the annexation of a region to the Empire, under an *ahidname* or treaty granting protection. In addition to this definition, there are many different aspects to the legal principle of *millet*.[62]

An individual was not allowed to leave the millet system and the *milletbaşı* (patriarch and his representatives, chief rabbi and his representatives) was an administrator within the community who exercised the right to collect taxes, share them with the community, apply the laws, and inflict punishment.[63] The missionaries had to deal with this system, especially in the Holy Land and Mount Lebanon. Although some firmans were issued by the Sultan against the delivery of books, the main reason was the complaints lodged by the *milletbaşı*. The local authorities belonging to different millets did not hesitate to use the power invested in them by this system against the missionaries. Despite their complaints in subsequent years, the Board's policy was to gain the recognition of a Protestant community, which they achieved in 1850, eleven years after the Tanzimât Fermânı (Imperial Edict

---

59 *ibid.* 110-111.
60 Erik J. Zürcher. *Turkey a Modern History.* London: I.B. Tauris & Co Ltd (1993): 12.
61 *ibid.* 12.
62 İlber Ortaylı. *Ottoman Studies.* Istanbul : Bilgi Üniv. Yayinlari (2007): 19.
63 *ibid.* 18.

of Reorganization).[64] Accordingly, the Protestants were given the right to manage their affairs, to worship under imperial protection, and to choose their own political head to represent the new community at the Porte.[65]

1.5 AN ERA OF EXPANSION

By 1850, the Board had already established five missions, and eleven mission stations, occupied by sixty-four missionaries and more than thirty native helpers, were opened throughout the Ottoman lands. The schools on all levels were producing graduates and the mission press worked non-stop. By 1855, there were 141 members at the Protestant Church in Antep. Gradually the demand for indigenous help grew. In 1854, the missionaries reached Tokat and Kayseri and by 1860, there were houses of worship at Maraş, Kessab and Kilis. From 1850 to 1860 the region lying between the Tigris (Dicle) and Euphrates (Fırat) rivers was treated as a single mission field for the Assyrians. The mission stations in Mosul, Mardin and Diyarbakır were merged with the recently organized Eastern Turkey Mission in 1860. By 1861, the Board's activities reached their final boundaries in Anatolia.[66]

As of 1858, the Board started mission work in the Ottoman Balkans. The first missionaries were sent to Edirne, and Plovdiv became the second mission center. A school for girls was opened in Stara Zagora and in 1860 a school for young men called "The Collegiate and Theological Institute" was opened at Plovdiv. However, the school at Stara Zagora was attacked after the evangelical aims of the missionaries came to be understood by the locals.[67] Both the girls' and men's schools were temporarily closed and reopened at different times, until they were finally reestablished at Samokov in 1871. By the time the station in Samokov was opened in 1869, the Board had already established three stations in Bulgaria. These stations were managed as a part of the Western Turkey Mission until 1871, and on June 30, 1871 the missionary work conducted in Bulgaria was organized as the Eu-

---

64 Richter, *History* 113.
65 Strong, *Story*, 106.
66 *ibid.* 108; 197-200; 209; 211.
67 *ibid.* 211-213.

ropean Turkey Mission.[68] The first evangelical church in Macedonia was established in 1871 at Bansko and the Bulgarian Evangelical society was founded in 1875 in order to facilitate native agency. The Bulgarian uprising and the Russo-Turkish war of 1876-1878 brought turmoil to the land and interrupted missionary work. The missionaries were protected by Turkish officers and their neighbors, but they had to retreat to Istanbul.[69] The 1860s witnessed revivals among the Armenians, notably in Eastern and Central Turkey in the years 1861, 1866 and 1869.[70] During this period, the Board's main priority was organizing self-sustaining Protestant communities and churches. By 1866 the number of local helpers in the Western Turkey mission reached eighty-nine.[71] Eighteen young men who were trained as theological students in Harput started work there in 1864. In 1870, half of the churches had their own pastors. As the number of churches increased, the Board advanced its activities considerably. The historical Bithynia Union was established in the Western Turkey Mission in 1865, and the Evangelical Union was established in the Eastern Turkey Mission in 1866, so that the number of such unions reached four by 1870. These organizations acted as the missionary agencies of the churches.[72]

By 1880, the number of churches amounted to almost a hundred with a total of at least six thousand members. By this time, there were thirty-nine higher grade schools including the colleges, and together with the students at the missionary affiliated Robert College the total number of students was over a thousand.[73] An important conference was held in Istanbul in May 1883. The participants comprised the representatives of the four missions and the related churches, a deputation from the Prudential Committee of the Board, and a special committee appointed by the Board. Although it was concluded that the American Christians could not attend to all the necessities of the Armenian Protestants, it was seen that the new community could not become independent of foreign support soon.[74]

---

68 *ibid*. 213-214.
69 *ibid*. 214.
70 *ibid*. 218.
71 *ibid*. 218.
72 *ibid*. 211-214; 218-220.
73 *ibid*. 385.
74 *ibid*. 385-386.

The atmosphere grew tense in the 1880s.[75] In 1886, the Protestants were persecuted in Maraş.[76] Moreover, censorship of the mission press in Istanbul and the arrest and imprisonment of the teachers accused of disloyalty hindered missionary work.[77] The 1890s likewise proved to be hard times for the missionaries. In 1893, two Armenian teachers at Anatolia College, Merzifon, were arrested and imprisoned, and the missionary schools underwent close monitoring by the Ottoman State.[78] The unsuccessful rebellion of the Armenian town Sason in 1894 was harshly repressed by the Ottoman Military and the Hamidiye regiments, which led to great tension in the region.[79]

The culmination of the unrest was the Armenian massacres of 1894-96. On September 30, 1895, a group of Armenians who were proceeding to the Sublime Porte to hand over a petition were attacked in Istanbul, and within a week the events spread to Akhisar and Trabzon.[80] Five weeks later, violence broke out in Sivas and three days after the events in Sivas the Armenians in Merzifon were targeted.[81] The Armenians in Kayseri, Urfa and Maraş also suffered attacks and the wave of violence extended to Bitlis, the region of Harput, Mardin, Erzurum, Diyarbakır, Malatya and Amasya as well.[82] [83] After the incidents in Istanbul on August 26-28, 1896, the events abated.[84] During and after the wave of violence, the Missionaries provided the Armenians with relief and organized orphanages for the children.[85]

In 1895, there were 14 main stations, 268 out-stations, 46 missionaries, 42 missionary wives, 63 lady missionaries, 1 medical missionary, 90 Armenian pastors, 117 catechists, 529 teachers, 66 assistants, 112 churches with 11,835 full members and 20,000 adherents, and 32,092 adult and

---

75 *ibid.* 387.
76 *ibid.* 387.
77 *ibid.* 387.
78 *ibid.* 391.
79 *ibid.* 392.
80 *ibid.* 393.
81 *ibid.* 393.
82 *ibid.* 385-387; 391-393.
83 Richter, *History*, 140.
84 *ibid.* 140.
85 Strong, *Story*, 396-398.

24,132 child students in the Sunday schools.[86] As of 1908, there were 20 stations, 269 out-stations, 42 ordained missionaries, 12 medical missionaries, 68 lady missionaries, 92 ordained preachers, 102 lay preachers, 728 teachers, 130 fully organized congregations with 15,748 communicants and 41,802 adherents, 8 colleges, 41 boarding and high schools, and 312 elementary and village schools with 20,861 pupils.[87] To sum up, between the years 1859-1909 the number of evangelical churches increased from 40 to 140, the number of church members from 1,277 to 15,748, registered Protestants from 7,000 to 54,000, the native workers from 156 to 4082, the annual donations from $4000 to $128,273, the number of boarding and high schools from 2 to 52, and the number of pupils in common schools from 2,742 to 23,115.[88] Moreover, while there were no colleges in 1859 there were 10 by 1909, including the missionary affiliated Robert College and the Syrian Protestant College. 10 hospitals providing health services to more than 140,000 people had been established by 1909.[89] These numbers alone reveal the steadily increasing influence of the ABCFM mission in the Ottoman Empire.

---

86 Richter, *History*, 134.
87 *ibid*. 160.
88 Greene, *Levant*, 155.
89 *ibid*. 155.

1.6 EDUCATION, PRINTING PRESS, MEDICINE

Of all the different types of work, two methods proved to be the most influential in the mission field: literary and educational work.[90] After 1870, medical work also gained in importance.[91] One should bear in mind that all of these activities served one sole purpose: conversion of the local population and finally establishing self-sufficient Protestant communities comprising of natives. In this respect, missionary philanthropy was a practical tool rather than an end in itself.

1.6.1 The Mission Printing Press

Due to the Reformation tradition, printing was considered to be of crucial importance from the very beginning of the mission. Delivering pamphlets and books, including school books, proved to be an effective way of interacting with people and gaining friends. The missionaries created literature in the languages they encountered in the field. The Bible was translated into modern Armenian, Armeno-Turkish and Ottoman Turkish. Moreover, the New Testament and Psalms were published in ancient Armenian and Kurdish. In order to support their Bible work, they also published handbooks, concordances, commentaries and other related books. There were also handbooks on the subjects taught in the Board's schools and colleges.[92]

The first mission press was established in Malta in 1822 and remained there for eleven years. This press saw to the printing of 33 tracts in Italian, 90 tracts and books in modern Greek, and five tracts in Armeno-Turkish (Turkish in Armenian Alphabet).[93] In 1833, the press was moved to Izmir. Twenty million pages of books, mainly in Armenian, were printed here. In 1853, the press was moved to Istanbul, which became its final destination, and another press was set up in Beirut.[94] The mission's publication department prepared schoolbooks in the fields of arithmetic, geography, grammar, algebra, geometry, astronomy, physiology, intellectual philosophy, and the

---

90 Richter, *History*, 108.
91 *ibid.* 157.
92 *ibid.* 109.
93 Greene, *Levant*, 136.
94 *ibid.* 136.

natural sciences. In January 1855, the missionaries started to publish a newspaper called *Adavaper* ('bringer of good news' in Armenian). From 1860 on it was published in Armeno-Turkish for Turkish-speaking Armenians and from 1872 on in Turkish with Greek letters for Turkish speaking Greeks. A monthly magazine called the *Children's Adavaper* was published as well.[95]

1.6.2 Medicine

Medical work started relatively late for the Ottoman mission, but it gradually grew and gained immense importance for the Board. In the twenty-five years following the establishment of the Istanbul mission station in 1831, three medical doctors were sent to Turkey.[96] Dr. Asahel Grant was sent to the Nestorians inhabiting the mountains of Hakkari, Dr. Henry Lobdell to the Euphrates Valley, taking Mosul as its center, and Dr. Azariah Smith to Antep in Southeastern Turkey.[97] The idea behind starting medical work was to open opportunities and create contacts via medical help among the indigenous peoples of the region.[98] After the initial attempts, the first medical missionary, Dr. Henry S. West, an ordained minister who graduated from Yale College and Medical College in New York City, arrived in 1860 and was stationed at Sivas until his death in 1876.[99] Dr. West was extremely influential and during his stay in Turkey he educated nineteen young Armenians as physicians, performed over 1400 operations, served the poor without charge, and sufficing with his salary as a missionary turned over his fees to the Board.[100] The medical mission flourished in the 1870s and all of the main stations gradually had medical missionaries and hospitals.[101] The

---

95 *ibid.* 140.
96 *ibid.* 144-145.
97 *ibid.* 144.
98 *ibid.* 145.
99 *ibid.* 147.
100 *ibid.* 147.
101 Richter, *History*, 157.

first modern mission hospital was founded in Beirut in the 1870s.[102] It was followed by the first hospital in Anatolia, at Antep, in 1879.[103] As Dr. Henry S. West's students and other medical students in Antep and Beirut graduated, new medical missionaries joined the ranks of the Board and they in turn trained highly needed medical staff and health personnel.[104] Consequently, new hospitals were opened at Mardin in 1885, at Kayseri and Talas in 1887, at Merzifon in 1897, at Van in 1899, at Harput in 1903, at Sivas in 1903, at Adana in 1904, at Erzurum in 1904, and at Diyarbakır in 1908.[105] The medical missionaries formed the "Asia Minor Medical Missionary Association" and held their first conference in 1907.[106] By 1915, there were ten mission hospitals in Anatolia at Merzifon, Sivas, Harput, Erzurum, Van, Diyarbakır, Mardin, Antep, Adana and Talas, and two more hospitals operated by Americans in Beirut and Konya.[107] At its height, the missionary hospital and health network treated 50,000 patients annually in Asia Minor alone, and others were reached via medical tours and treatment at home, albeit off the records.[108] As one medical missionary stated, the medical work was an opportunity to "continually meet with friendly greetings and kind reception" and it was a "wide a door of usefulness among them." He added that he took great pleasure "in speaking to them concerning the truths of God's word" as the people gather around him at the shop, or assemble to see him in the surrounding villages to which he was called, or in their homes in the city.[109]

---

102 İdris Yücel. "An Overview of Religious Medicine in the Near East: Mission Hospitals of American Board in Asia Minor." *Journal for the Study of Religions and Ideologies*, Vol. 14, Issue 40 (Spring 2015): 52.

103 *ibid*. 52.

104 *ibid*. 52.

105 *ibid*. 52.

106 Richter, *History*, 158.

107 Greene, *Levant*, 148.

108 Yücel, "Mission Hospitals," 54.

109 Henry S. West. "Western Turkey: Letter from Dr. West." *The Missionary Herald*, April (1861): 100.

1.6.3 Education

The origins of American Board education can be found in its New England roots. The missionaries were mainly from the Connecticut Valley region and they had studied at frontier colleges such as Dartmouth, Williams, and Amherst.[110] The rural background enjoyed by the missionaries and their appreciation of the impact that a rustic environment had on the cultivation of the moral values they sought to inspire was best reflected in the establishment of mission stations and schools in remote parts of Anatolia. Yet the emphasis on vernacular studies, practical skills, and vocational training was also a direct result of developments in New England educational organizations.[111] In the same way, the establishment of institutes of higher education, academies or schools offering degree courses coincided with the rise of academies in the United States.[112] Even in centers such as Istanbul, the missionaries tried to open their schools away from the turmoil of mundane city life, as in the case of Robert College, which was opened in the remote suburban neighborhood of Bebek. The missionary contempt for city life was so great that even Bebek was considered to be in the immediate vicinity of detrimental influences to moral development, so the Board decided to move the theological seminary to Merzifon, a small rural town four hundred miles east of Istanbul, in 1864.[113] Merzifon was chosen because it was "less exposed to the allurements of the wide world."[114] It was not merely a matter of fashion or following the trends that had arisen in the country the missionaries had left behind. As Samir Khalaf puts it "[t]he evangelic imagination extended itself to embody more secular and civic-minded concerns for winning people to Christian truth [...]"[115] and it is "this infusion of the ethos of pietistic Evangelism into philanthropy and the moralistic tone of Christian benevolence and pragmatism which were nurtured in colleges and

---

110 Frank Andrews Stone. *Academies for Anatolia*. California: Caddo Gap Press (2005): 4.
111 *ibid*. 4-5.
112 *ibid*. 6.
113 *ibid*. 68.
114 *ibid*. 183.
115 Samir Khalaf. *Protestant Missionaries in the Levant: Ungodly Puritans, 1820-60*. London: Routledge (2012): 33.

universities."[116] All in all, "the public school movement in the nineteenth century was essentially the result of a desire to protect a Protestant orthodoxy,"[117] and "the common school movement was primarily designed to protect the ideology of an American Protestant culture."[118] The shift of American society from a pre-industrial to an industrial society, or from a rural to an urban one had an impact on missionary education as well.[119]

The report of the Prudential Committee on the mission to Palestine from 1820 gave a general outline of the planned educational investment in the Levant:

Two other important parts of missionary labor remain to be entered upon. The first is Education;- the other a translation, not of the Scriptures, for that is accomplished, but of all other good religious books and tracts. The printing of a religious monthly publication in Modern Greek, not offending the institutions of the country, is of primary importance, and would be, in the hands of prudent conductors, of incalculable service. The extensive fields of education are not, to foreign Protestant missionaries, so easily and completely accessible, as the rich and most abundant streams of a fount of types, which would ere long, silently water every portion of the field sowed with the word of God; and, with the divine blessing, would render luxuriant and plentiful the Christian harvest.[120]

After the initial tour and reports from the first missionaries, Pliny Fisk and Levi Parsons, the following evaluation was published in *The Missionary Herald* in 1821:

School books are constantly improving in all the most enlightened parts of the world. How pleasing must it be, to introduce at once all the advancement of centuries into the rising schools of the Russian and Turkish empires. What a delightful

---

116 *ibid*. 35.

117 Richter, *History*, 5.

118 *ibid*. 81.

119 Michael B. Katz. *Reconstructing American Education*. Cambridge (Mass.): Harvard University Press (1987): 13.

120 "Report of the Prudential Committee." *The Missionary Herald*, December (1820): 556.

and animating prospect is here opened for the operations of Christian benevolence.[121]

The first proper school was opened in 1825 in Beirut.[122] Soon others followed. The education of women and girls was likewise on their agenda.[123] The missionaries clearly detected an opening in this field. Over the following decades, missionary education was limited to simple schools of a mixed character.

The 1860s witnessed major changes in the educational activities of the American Board. One important event was the foundation of Robert College in 1863. Although legally the college was independent of the Board, the founders had close ties with the Board as former missionaries, and the college was defined as being a Christian institution. The college did not follow the Board's policy of teaching in vernacular and English became the language of instruction. Despite the fact that Robert College was promoted as a Christian institution, its educational policy relied heavily upon a scientific background and teaching the classics.[124]

Following Robert College, Syria Protestant College was founded in 1866. Although at the very beginning the education was in Arabic, SPC soon adopted English as the language of instruction as well. Several schools were opened by the American missionaries in the Ottoman Empire in the nineteenth century. This extensive network of missionary schools was very effective in creating a new generation with peculiar attitudes towards society and world affairs. The curricula of these schools were multi-faceted and the students were taught Western languages, liberal art subjects and natural sciences as a preparation for college entrance.[125] The colleges were provid-

---

121 "Thoughts Suggested by the Preceding Journal." *Missionary Herald*, April (1821): 101.

122 Isaac Bird, William Goodell. "Mission to Palestine: Beyroot." *The Missionary Herald*, September (1825): 271.

123 Pliny Fisk, Jonas King. "Palestine Mission: Journal of Messrs. Fisk and King, in Upper Egypt." *The Missionary Herald*, December (1823): 377.

124 Greene, *Levant*, 203-205.

125 Bayard Dodge. "American Educational and Missionary Efforts in the Nineteenth and Early Twentieth Centuries." *Annals of the American Academy of Po-*

ing society with professionals in business, teaching, theology and church service, and pharmacy and medicine, yet few graduates could actually find a position in governmental service.[126] Although it was called a college, Robert College actually formed a university center as a result of the excellent education it offered in the arts, sciences and engineering.[127] It should be noted that the first proper Turkish university (Darül Fünun) was founded in 1900.[128] The high schools for girls consisted of the Boarding School at Adapazarı and the Boarding School at Merzifon. There were two colleges for girls in Turkey, one being the Central Turkey College for Girls and the other the Constantinople College. Bithynia High School, Boys High School at Talas, and Sivas Normal School were the high schools for boys. Robert College at Constantinople, Central Turkey College at Antep, Anatolia College at Merzifon, Euphrates College at Harput, International College at Smyrna, St. Paul's Institute at Tarsus, and College at Van were the colleges for men. Apart from these high schools and colleges, there were theological schools at Merzifon, Harput, Maraş and Mardin. In the Balkans, which was partly Turkish territory, there were the Collegiate and Theological Institute at Samokov, the Agricultural and Industrial Institute at Thessaloniki, and the Girls Boarding School at Monastir.[129] The Syrian Protestant College was founded in Beirut and continued its education after Mount Lebanon was granted autonomy, preserving its ties with other missionary-affiliated educational institutions in the Ottoman Empire.

The case of Harput mission illustrates the general character and development of missionary education. The educational network that developed in Harput and its periphery started with modest means and investments, yet in less than fifteen years had grown into a school system that offered education from elementary levels to college degrees. At the beginning the students were offered a curriculum that took the Bible as its main text. The pupils and students were offered courses in Armenian language and gram-

---

litical and Social Science, Vol. 401, America and the Middle East, May (1972): 20.

126 ibid. 20.

127 ibid. 21.

128 Carter V. Findley. Bureaucratic Reform in the Ottoman Empire: The Sublime Porte, 1789-1922. New Jersey: Princeton University Press (1980): 276.

129 Greene, Levant, 161-254.

mar, geography, philosophy, chemistry, church history, mathematics and astronomy, theology and preaching. During the early years the Board educators opposed the idea of educating the youth "too much," for they were afraid of losing contact with target groups by creating a gap between the recently educated native clergy and the local population. Education in English became another problem because the Board's primary concern was creating a self-sustaining community and a clergy that adopted the notion of self-help. Yet after fierce discussions and objections from Armenians, new schools, including a teacher training school, a female seminary and a college, were founded and English was offered as a subject when higher education in vernacular proved increasingly difficult.[130]

The Sublime Porte took steps to curb the missionary activities in the empire because the effects of missionary education were detrimental not only to the native churches and non-Muslim communities, but also to the centralistic aims of the state.[131] There were several reasons for the precautions taken by the state, but the field of education was of utmost importance and "[i]n the second half of the nineteenth century the Ottoman Empire came into its own as an 'educator state' with a systematic programme of education/indoctrination for subjects intended to mould into citizens."[132] The 1869 Law on Education authorized the inspection of the curricula of non-Muslim schools, and in 1887, the inspectorate of non-Muslim and foreign schools was founded.[133] Any rival to the project of Ottoman education was seen as a threat to the existing order and to the state because the policy of that project was "to reinforce the ideological legitimacy of a social order which felt increasingly threatened by changing world conditions" and "[n]one of the challenges to the legitimacy of the Ottoman state, and all that

---

130 Barbara J. Merguerian. "'Missions in Eden': Shaping an Educational and Social Program for the Armenians in Eastern Turkey (1855-1895)." *New Faith in Ancient Lands : Western Missions in the Middle East in the Nineteenth and Early Twentieth Centuries.* Ed. Heleen Murre-van der Berg. Leiden: Brill (2006): 248-251.

131 *ibid.* 256.

132 Selim Deringil. *The Well Protected Domains: Ideology and the Legitimation of Power in the Ottoman Empire 1876-1909.* London: I.B. Tauris & Co Ltd. (1998): 93.

133 *ibid.* 105.

it stood for, was more dangerous in the long term than that posed by missionary activity."[134]

Through schooling the missionaries undermined Ottoman legitimacy.[135] Educational activities in general are closely related to the production of subjectivities since "[a] curriculum is a design for a future social subject, and via that envisioned subject a design for a future society."[136] Gunther Kress defines the curriculum and its associated pedagogy as "a set of cultural linguistic and social resources which students have available as resources for their own transformations, in relation to which [...] students constantly construct, reconstruct and transform their subjectivity."[137] From the second half of the nineteenth century onward, the types of schools in the Ottoman Empire can be grouped as follows: traditional Islamic schools, secular state schools, schools founded and funded by millets, and schools run by Catholic and Protestant missions and the Alliance Israélite Universelle.[138] This diversity was accompanied by a multiplicity of curricula and pedagogical approaches constructed according to various and competing visions of the future. This multiplicity and diversity created different views on the set distinctions between various reading and writing practices and the description of social values expressed in pedagogical sources used by various groups. To make things more complicated, during Sultan Abdulhamid's reign the missionary enterprise flourished as a result of the fact that "[t]he closing two decades of the nineteenth century witnessed the climactic phase of the foreign missions movement in American Protestantism."[139]

Akşin Somel points out that the missionary schools affected the target groups in a peculiar way and that "[t]hough the primary aim of these institutions was the diffusion of evangelical Christianity among the local communities, the pragmatic characteristics of the instruction adopted by evangelical Christians and their focus on the natural sciences unintentionally led

---

134 *ibid.* 107, 112.

135 *ibid.* 130.

136 Gunther Kress, Theo van Leeuwen. *Reading Images: The Grammar of Visual Design.* London: Routledge (1996): 15.

137 *ibid.* 16.

138 Zürcher, *Turkey*, 66.

139 Ahlstrom, *Religious History*, 864.

to the growing influence of secular notions of progress and individual-ism."[140] At these schools the students had the chance to receive education in vernacular and to learn a Western language (English at the ABCFM schools) and "[a]s a consequence, a young generation of non-Muslims emerged who were raised in a rather different educational environment from the cultural milieu of the traditional scholastic community schools."[141] The following example depicting the creative educational method of education championed by Cyrus Hamlin, the founder of Robert College, illustrates the sincere attempt to create a sense of solidarity and a basis for friendship among the students:

Once he had two quarreling young men named Silvio and Pierre sign a formal statement. "The two high contracting parties agree," the statement declared, "that in order to preserve peace... one shall not call the other an ass or a dog or a pig or a thief, robber, rowdy, pezevenk or other opprobius epithet in Italian, French, Turkish, Greek, English, Bulgarian, Armenian or any other language spoken at the tower at Babel or since that day. Silvio shall in no case strike Pierre nor Pierre Silvio."[142]

Promoting friendship among students was not as easy for the Ottoman government. The Tribal School (Mekteb-i Aşiret) opened its doors on October 3, 1892.[143] The idea was to train the children of leading Arab and Kurdish sheiks and some Albanians to be good Ottomans. In one instance, Arab and Kurdish students were involved in a fight "using stones, shoes and fists, resulting in light injuries to four Kurds and six Arabs."[144] Friendship and brotherhood were considered to be of political importance. It was assumed that through schooling they would learn to be brothers. It was state policy

---

140 Akşin Somel. "Christian Community Schools During the Ottoman Reform Period." *Late Ottoman Society: The Intellectual Legacy.* Ed. Elisabeth Özdalga. London: Routledge Press (2005): 255.

141 *ibid.* 256.

142 Grabill, *Protestant Diplomacy*, 23.

143 Deringil, *Well Protected Domains*, 101.

144 *ibid.* 103.

to promote friendship, but unlike missionary institutions the Tribal School failed to realize this aim.[145]

On the other hand, the missionary schools were offering education to a variety of nationalities, mainly non-Muslims. The cosmopolitan student profile offered an opportunity to research the conflicts and compromises among the students, and between the students and the instructors that either led to a sound personal understanding or to disagreements. The diverse cultural, economic, and political backgrounds of the students were important variables in the equation that was called the missionary enterprise. The students were expected to transform into independently-minded individuals and useful professionals by accepting the evangelical Protestant modernism that had its roots in New Divinity teachings. The data suggests that the missionaries were successful in creating a new generation of youths who profoundly differed from the closed religious communities they belonged to.

The multi-faceted nature of missionary activities in terms of friendship and patronage is striking. Acting as agents of education where the Ottoman 'Sublime Porte' failed to do so, the missionaries compensated for the lack of educational and medical services and with that claimed the position of patrons. At the same time, they needed, however, the protection of several Western states, mainly the United States and Great Britain. Although this need originated as a result of the political atmosphere, they maintained friendly relations with their protectors as well. Similarly, the missionaries had to be in close personal contact with the pupils and their families in order to spread the Word. The attempt to preach the gospel and the testament was not crude propaganda. Consequently, they were emotionally involved with their target groups. Moreover, the missionaries were dependent on donations. To give two illustrations: Robert College was named after its generous benefactor Christopher Robert.[146] Central Turkey College at Antep was founded as a result of the generous local support showed by Armenians (sixty thousand dollars), and a Muslim Turk helped pay for college property.[147] As can be seen in the latter example, the emerging *eşraf* (notables of a

---

145 See Chapter 5 for the transformation of Ottomanism from a Muslim identity to a Turkish identity.

146 Grabill, *Protestant Diplomacy*, 23.

147 *ibid*. 26.

town or village) and middle class facilitated the establishment of the college so that their children would have a proper education.

1.7 CONCLUSION

Despite its extensive efforts, the Board could not realize its aim to proselytize Jews, Muslims and Christians, and thus to facilitate the Millennium, before the demise of the Ottoman Empire. Since the majority of Protestant converts and native clergy consisted of Armenians, the Armenian Genocide and the subsequent 'cleansing' of Anatolia of its Christian population practically ended missionary activities in former missionary posts.

The social and political unrest that permeated the Ottoman Empire in the first two decades of the twentieth century and culminated in a world war was not what the missionaries expected. When the war was over, they found themselves in a new country with new demographics and a new political system. The small Protestant community was totally destroyed, and although the missionaries continued educational work within the confines of new secular educational reform in the new Republic, they never recovered from this blow.

In 1968, the institutions of the Near East Mission in Turkey were organized under the *Sağlık ve Eğitim Vakfı* (Health and Education Foundation) SEV.[148] As of today, the remaining remnants of ABCFM activities in Turkey consist of the Uskudar American Academy, Istanbul, the American Collegiate Institute, Izmir, the Tarsus American College, Tarsus, the Private SEV Primary Schools in Istanbul, İzmir and Tarsus, the SEV American Hospital, Gaziantep, the SEV Publishing House (publishing the prominent Redhouse Turkish-English dictionary among others), and the recently founded SEV American College, Istanbul.[149]

---

148 Stone, *Academies*, 327.
149 Sağlık ve Eğitim Vakfı, URL = http://www.sev.org.tr/kurumlarimiz [view date: 21 January 2017].

2 Research Questions, Theory and Methodology

2.1 RESEARCH QUESTIONS

Why look for concepts? A concept is a fundamental element for understanding the outer world because it enables abstraction. As in the case of missionary activities, the concepts are coherent and they survived generations as a guide to missionary work. In short, they formed a gateway to the missionary mind, and how the missionaries made sense of what they encountered, and expected to achieve.

How is one to approach the concepts? Human language is essentially metaphorical. The metaphorical expressions themselves are linguistic occurrences but for many metaphorical expressions, the background is the thought itself. Accordingly, the expressions are manifestations of a deeper order of thought, which is called conceptual metaphor. Put simply, a metaphor explains something in terms of another thing.[1] The underlying conceptual metaphors are used to explain one domain in terms of another domain by using certain mappings.[2] So the conceptual metaphor **TRYING TO ACHIEVE A PURPOSE IS AGRICULTURE** helps the reader of nineteenth century missionary texts to situate the metaphorical expressions of agriculture in a conceptual setting that is based on the Biblical parables as well as the approved means of economic production.[3] Furthermore, the same conceptual metaphor can be used for different events (e.g. religious-

---

1 George Lakoff, Mark Johnson. *Metaphors We Live by*. Chicago: University of Chicago Press (2003): 5.

2 *ibid*. 3-6.

3 This specific example will be thoroughly explained in the next chapter.

nonreligious), thus enabling us to detect the preferences of the missionaries. A quick example is the praise of American expansionism by the Congregationalists by employing old metaphorical expressions for this new era.[4] In short, conceptual metaphor is a unique tool for getting into the missionary mind and understanding how they created a sense of the real world.

Following on from the main question, several questions can be asked:

1. How did they see themselves?
2. How did they achieve sense-making and legitimacy?
3. How did they evaluate their target groups?
4. How did they explain the political, social and economic background?

The answers to these questions will be given in the framework of conceptual metaphors. Relying on the data derived from the research, this study locates the missionary way of looking at the world and conducting its activities to its historical background. Finally, how the notions from the nineteenth century are reflected through the missionary mind is exhibited.

Over and beyond this, the study shall look at the application (and if none, the absence) of these concepts and metaphors by the missionaries in the face of drastic or catastrophic events that would elicit a response. For this evaluation, among the series of such incidents that occurred in the second half of the nineteenth century it is decided to look at the failed attempt at starting a mission for the Muslims, 1856-1865, and their reaction to the Armenian massacres of 1894-96, mainly those that occurred towards the end of 1895, after an extensive examination of *The Missionary Herald* from different periods. In keeping with these expectations, the missionaries resorted to the well-established conceptual background presented in the next chapter, sometimes with modifications. It has been possible to establish that the main areas in which missionaries applied these conceptual metaphors were future plans, opportunities offered by the crisis, and the idea and propagation of the Kingdom of God; all of these were set against a millennialist-teleological backdrop, and all related directly to the subjects of relief work, notion of martyrdom, field work, such as education, health services etc., and work for Armenian orphans. The studies shall also present and ex-

---

4   See chapter 5 on how American nationalism influenced ABCFM.

amine the millennialist background of the missionary discourse in its intricate connections to the ideas of enlightenment and modernity.

What is the main theoretical issue this empirical study shall be addressing? The simplest question that initiated this project is: How did the missionaries interpret what they encountered in the Ottoman Empire and their own doings with their orientational concepts? The thesis is that the American Board of Commissioners for Foreign Missions as an institution with its many organizations has a specific type of discourse which can roughly be identified as an institutional discourse. This discourse has certain characteristics that make it peculiar and distinctive. Conceptual background is one of them, and perhaps the most important in terms of coherency. The conceptual background is best embodied in conceptual metaphors that the missionaries share in general, and this conceptual background finds its way into the missionary discourse via metaphorical expressions. The latter are so strong that they constitute an extensive web based on the conceptual background the missionary establishment preserves and passes on to new generations of missionaries. These metaphors are a key element in their understanding and depiction of the situations, people, and explanations of the past, their evaluations of the present, and their plans for the future. In short, they partly explain the missionaries' perception of reality via conceptual metaphors as well. It has been possible to identify the conceptual background and the metaphorical expressions that these rest upon. As anticipated, they have a pattern, and form an important part of the missionary discourse. By looking at how they are applied in certain situations;

1. it is possible to see how the missionaries made explanations to fit into the conceptual frame, but at the same time how this frame was used and modified to explain new experiences.
2. one can detect how the mission as an institution is also constructed discursively, and how discourse becomes an institution in itself.
3. as a consequence of this appropriation of a conceptual background, one can identify what may be termed a learning process at an institutional level. The analysis of the missionaries' interpretation of their circumstances was crucial in determining the key elements of this learning process against the historical backdrop.
4. from a broader perspective, examining well-established discourses in a hierarchical institution and its organizations operating in a transgenera-

tional, transnational manner might shed light on the nature of similar confrontations, and in the specific context of mission establishment in the Ottoman Empire may be illustrative of how 'unexpected consequences' occur. Intercultural relations, transfer of notions across borders, and traveling concepts are still important themes in the twenty-first century. The encounters that are examined in the dissertation are also important for understanding the historical dynamics of current encounters.

2.2 CONCEPTUAL METAPHOR

The type of discourse that will be scrutinized is underlined by its religious character. This aspect brings the advantage of a coherent imagery underlying the general arguments. As can be expected from a Christian discourse, the Congregationalist mode of written expression as it developed from Jonathan Edwards (1703-1758) to Edwards Park (1808-1900) and Horace Bushnell (1802-1876) relied on concepts and their metaphorical expressions from the Bible and other religious texts, as well as secular ones. Therefore, it is not surprising to see that Edwards discusses Isaac Newton by employing similar tropes and concepts to those used by his followers a century later, who invested them with new contents or rhetorical power in order to respond to the realities of their time.

The conceptual metaphor as understood by George Lakoff and Mark Johnson is an excellent tool with which to perform a sound analysis of Congregationalist discourse. The analysis of conceptual metaphor facilitates the process of relating the underlying and overlapping manifestations of concepts among diverse Congregationalist and missionary discourses, because traditionally accepted metaphors derived from Protestant theology and culture persist even though the meaning attributed to them changes. Although Lakoff and Johnson were primarily interested in how the cognitive nature of conceptual metaphors determines the way we think, what we experience and what we do every day, they also provided the humanities and social sciences with an invaluable tool for textual analysis with different perspectives.[5]

---

5   Lakoff/Johnson, *Metaphors*, 3.

What are the main tenets of Conceptual Metaphor Theory? The fore-most claim is that our ordinary conceptual system is fundamentally meta-phorical. Lakoff and Johnson abide by the traditional explanation of meta-phor as a starting point which states that the essence of metaphor is to un-derstand and experience one kind of thing in terms of another. Hence:

- Concept: metaphorically structured
- Activity: metaphorically structured
- Language: metaphorically structured.

Building on this notion of a metaphorically structured language, they come to the conclusion that we talk about certain things in particular ways be-cause we conceive of them that way and we act according to the way we conceive of things. Most of our conceptual system is metaphorically struc-tured.[6] That is, most concepts are partially understood in terms of other concepts. In this context, metaphor is understood as a metaphorical con-cept. Accordingly, metaphorical expressions in language are tied to meta-phorical concepts in a systematic way. Thus, we can use metaphorical lin-guistic expressions to study the nature of metaphorical concepts and to gain an understanding of the metaphorical nature of our activities.[7] The two au-thors also claim that systematicity, which allows us to comprehend one as-pect of a concept in terms of another, will necessarily hide other aspects of the concept.[8] This systematic functioning of metaphorical concepts rein-forces the idea that our values are not independent but must form a coherent system with the metaphorical concepts we live by.[9] Because things are usu-ally not equal, there are often conflicts among those values and hence con-flicts among the metaphors associated with them. To explain such conflicts between values (and their metaphors), we must find the different priorities that are given to these values and metaphors by the subculture that uses them. In general, which values are given priority is partly a matter of the

---

6   ibid. 5.
7   ibid. 3-6.
8   ibid. 6-13.
9   ibid. 22-24, 57.

subculture one lives in, and partly a matter of personal values.[10] Lakoff and Johnson also assert that the sentence in which the linguistic metaphor occurs does not possess a transcendent meaning. The meaning is dependent on the social and political attitudes of the speaker and the listener as well[11]:

Cultural assumptions, values and attitudes are not a conceptual overlay which we may or may not place upon experiences we choose. It would be more correct to say that all experience is cultural through and through, that we experience our "world" in such a way that our culture is already present in the very experience itself.[12]

Moreover, metaphors stress certain parts of narrated experience and bring coherence to it. Metaphor is capable of creating realities, especially social realities. Hence, they can be a guide for future action. This property contributes to the coherence of experience and may ultimately turn metaphor into a self-fulfilling prophecy.[13]

In short, in order to find the underlying ideological conceptualizations as conceptual metaphor, and its manifestations as linguistic metaphor, the sources and types of figurative language derived from the Bible and other sources will be detected, the mappings between source and target domains will be established, and the language used in the texts will be related to its social, cultural and political context. It is of crucial importance to find out how that figurative language was articulated in texts in relation to its historical context, such as Anglo-Saxon expansion in the nineteenth century, or practical applications of scientific advances, such as enhanced technologies for transport and communications. The way evangelizing, democracy, Western expansionism, education, history, democracy, women's rights, progress, civilization, being human etc. are conceptualized as metaphors, which are determined and in many occasions conditioned by the play between source domain, target domain and the root metaphor derived from tradition, underlies the missionary point of view. Since conceptual metaphors can be culture-specific, examining the discursive formations of the

---

10 Lakoff,/Johnson, *Metaphors*; Zoltán Kövecses. *Metaphor: A Practical Introduction*. Oxford: Oxford University Press, (2002).

11 Lakoff,/Johnson, *Metaphors*, 12.

12 *ibid.* 57.

13 *ibid. 156.*

Congregationalists also makes it easier to find the way of thinking that was supposed to be imposed upon the people that were expected to be converted all over the world. Consequently, the attribution of certain values to other peoples and cultures through metaphor can likewise be used to tease out the alienating element in those metaphors.

Only by understanding the conceptual metaphorical formulation of certain discourses it is meaningful that "the missionaries, following Jonathan Edwards' recast of Augustine's history of redemption, made the evangelization of the world the key to the coming Kingdom of God."[14] Without understanding the underlying tools for written expression, it is hard to examine how the ideas of F. P. G. Guizot, Herbert Spencer, and Albrecht Ritschl on the "coming of God's kingdom as progress in civilization through democracy, education, invention and altruism in society"[15] were echoed by American Congregationalism, how the Parable of the Leaven and many others were employed during this period of American history to legitimize the position of the Western world and the Congregationalist responses to it, and even how Schleiermacher and Coleridge found their way into American and consequently missionary discourse.

2.3 MISSIONARY TEXTS AS NARRATIVE

> [T]hese missionaries have been obliged to spend much of their time in acquiring various and difficult languages, and in travelling throughout the country, spying out the land, and becoming acquainted with its people. Travellers, indeed, there had been in Palestine before them. But none of these

---

14 John Edwin Smylie. "Protestant Clergymen and American Destiny: II: Prelude to Imperialism, 1865-1900." *The Harvard Theological Review*, Vol. 56, No. 4 (Oct. 1963): 300.

15 *ibid.* 301.

travellers explored the country with reference to missionary organizations.[16]

The missionary texts published in *The Missionary Herald* magazine display certain traits that underwent little or no modification over long periods of time. Some of these traits are related to the medium itself. For instance, a monthly periodical such as the missionary magazine has limited space for texts. Accordingly, a typical missionary letter published in *The Missionary Herald* rarely exceeds a few pages in length. The technology of the nineteenth century should also be taken into consideration. A letter sent from Beirut or Istanbul could not be delivered to the Boston offices that quickly. Moreover, the missionaries were active all of the time, traveling, preaching, teaching, dealing with bureaucratic obstacles, etc. Lack of space in the published media, long intervals in communications, and continuous activity resulted in episodic texts that refer to the same event or related set of events in more than one issue. Secondly, the printing technology and the choice of the Board dictated a particular layout that only evolved slowly.

The texts appear in this particular organization of the medium. However, they correspond to another level of existence that far exceeds the mechanical necessities dictated by the medium and the technological background. This is the content of the texts. The representations in the texts are articulated within the framework of the missionary establishment in general. The establishment covers the mission as an institution, and missionary work and infrastructure as an organization or a series of interrelated organizations.

In very general terms, the content of missionary writings from the Ottoman Empire published in *The Missionary Herald* can be elucidated as a series of narratives and a general narrative. The majority of the texts portray missionary travels, interpersonal communications, quasi-scientific data, and observations and reflections on new lands, people, and political and social systems. All these experiences and reflections on the missionaries' experiences are not enumerated in the form of a prescription or a list. Above all, the missionaries are selective. They do not convey all that they encounter. The criteria for selection seem to be the event's or reflection's

---

16 "State and Progress of Palestine Mission." *The Missionary Herald*, April (1827): 104.

compatibility with the missionary point of view, as well as with conversion and Protestantism.

Coming back to the context of the texts, the missionary texts and complimentary reports and comments are accepted as part of an institutional narrative. The term institution is applied because it is a broader term than organization.[17] Basically, it represents a social group that has a continued existence over time.[18] In an institutional setting, narrative enables the institution to continue and is used to reproduce the institution. It creates the identity of the institution and helps its members to adapt to change.[19] Thus, the institutional narrative depicts who the constituents of the institution are and what they do and should do.[20]

Another aspect of the institutional narrative is how it relates to power relations and structures both within and across institutional boundaries. The core power issue concerns what have been called 'storytelling rights.' Not everybody is allowed to tell every kind of story. Storytelling rights encompass the issues of who tells what and the type of stories to be told. In such a schema, some stories are promulgated and others repressed by people who have access to storytelling channels. Furthermore, institutions control official narratives.[21]

The term narrative has connotations of fictional texts and stories. To avoid confusion, a clear distinction must be made between fiction and non-fiction. The thesis is that missionary texts and the narratives recited in them are non-fictional and belong to the realm of real-world storytelling. According to David Gorman, fiction is "one kind of intendedly but non-deceptively untrue discourse" whereas "factual discourse is intended to be true."[22] In other words, factual narrative has a claim to be referential, namely to have a reference to 'our' world.[23]

---

17 *Routledge Encyclopedia of Narrative Theory.* Eds. David Herman, Manfred Jahn. London: Routledge (2005): 243.

18 *ibid.* 243.

19 *ibid.* 243.

20 *ibid.* 243.

21 *ibid.* 246.

22 *ibid.* 163.

23 Jean-Marie Schaeffer. "Fictional vs. Factual Narration." Paragraph 1. *the living handbook of narratology.* Eds: Peter Hühn et al. Hamburg: Hamburg University.

2.3.1 Travel Narrative

A considerable amount of missionary writing coincides with the field of travel writing and travel narratives. This is especially true for the first ten year period covered in the third chapter. The case studies also involve extensive amounts of travel writings. The difference between the founding years and later years is that there were already well-established mission stations and networks in Anatolia in the second half of the nineteenth century. In many instances, new missionaries visited already explored land or moved from occupied central stations and cities to the unexplored margins and periphery. The basic definition of travel writing as factual, first-person prose accounts of travels that have been undertaken by the author-narrator fits well to this portion of missionary writings.[24] Despite the fact that the generic definition entails a narrative structure, narrative writing also employs non-narrative modes of presentation, such as lengthy descriptions, expositions, prescriptions, suggestions and advice for traveling.[25] It should also be noted that travel narratives exhibit the culture-specific perceptions and knowledge brought by the travelers.[26] Thus, among other things, missionary writings were travel narratives. The texts functioned in what Marie Lousie Pratt has referred to as writings producing the rest of the world for a specific audience.[27] Pratt took the case of European travelers producing knowledge and the world for a European audience, but her ideas apply to the missionary travel accounts as well. Instead of the emergent bourgeoisie of Europe (and in some instances the Protestant networks of Europe that *The Missionary Herald* might have addressed and informed could be regarded as a category overlapping with that one), the immediate recipients of the missionary texts were predominantly American Protestant Congregationalists and Western evangelists sympathetic to the Board's cause, which

URL=http://www.lhn.uni-hamburg.de/article/fictional-vs-factual-narration [view date: 21 January 2017].

24 Tim Youngs. *The Cambridge Introduction to Travel Writing*. Cambridge: Cambridge University Press (2013): 3.

25 *Routledge Encyclopedia of Narrative Theory*, 620.

26 *ibid.* 619.

27 Marie Louise Pratt. *Imperial Eyes: Travel Writing and Transculturation*. London: Routledge (2003): 5.

is to say facilitating the coming of the Kingdom via missionary activities (the question of the readers of *The Missionary Herald* is discussed below in the section "Assumed Author and Assumed Reader").

Lastly, the classical story-discourse distinction in narrative theory comes in handy for evaluating the missionary texts. This distinction supposes two main parts in a narrative; story and discourse. Story includes the content or chain of events, i.e. actions and happenings, and existents, i.e. characters and items pertaining to the setting. Discourse, on the other hand, comprises the expressions and means by which the content is communicated. In short, story is what is depicted in a narrative and discourse is how it is depicted.[28] Metaphors are located on the discourse level of this distinction and can be evaluated as constituents of narrative discourse and the depiction of content present at the story level.

2.3.2 Implied Author and Implied Reader

The editorial interventions in *The Missionary Herald* articles refer to the readers in a variety of ways, such as "Christian friends"[29] (when asking for donations to the missions), "friends and patrons,"[30] "a millionaire or failing that a million poor men"[31] (when asking for financial aid and donations at the time of the Armenian Massacres), "friends of the Board,"[32] "brethren,"[33] and "our readers"[34] (a very common expression, used here to address the readers when explaining the relief work done for the Armenians). In some cases the magazine converses with the readers, as in the following

28 Seymour Chatman. *Story and Discourse: Narrative Structure in Fiction and Film*. Ithaca: Cornel University Press (1989): 19.

29 "To the Secretaries, Treasurers, and Collectors of Associations." *The Missionary Herald*, September (1825): 302.

30 Eli Smith. "Obstacles to the Growth of Evangelical Piety in Syria." *The Missionary Herald*, April (1828): 114.

31 "Western Turkey Mission." *The Missionary Herald*, January (1896): 23.

32 Wilson A. Farnsworth. "Some Results of Missionary Work in Turkey." *The Missionary Herald*, March (1896): 102.

33 *ibid.* 102.

34 Grace N. Kimball. "Relief Work at Van, Eastern Turkey." *The Missionary Herald*, June (1896): 231.

lines written during the massacres: "At just this time, when nearly every missionary station in Asia Minor has been baptized in blood, the question is asked, What are the results of sixty years of missionary work in that land?"[35]

The Missionary Herald mainly referred to itself in the first person plural as "we."[36] That "we," being the editorial Board and decision-makers, also interfered with the flow of writing and made the intervention clear by stating "we do not think it necessary to copy them all," or "we omit the paragraph," to inform the reader about the missing parts.[37] The distinction should be clear to the editors as well, because in one instance the editorial intervention follows a "[h]ere again we use the language of our author."[38] Later on, editorial intervention became more institutionalized and had its proper place in the magazine under the title "Editorial Paragraphs."[39] The authors of articles and journal entries were referred to by their proper names, though.

Implied author is a useful term that enables the interpreter to evaluate the ideological and moral positions of a narrative without any reference to the biographical author.[40] Implied author is the result of the investigation of the meaning of a text, not the source of its meaning. Thus, it can be talked about after interpreting the text. Another advantage of the term is that the notion of an implied author is not restricted to narrative texts.[41] Since he or she is bound to textual interpretation, the implied author can be regarded as representing the elements of the narrative discourse the reader is aware of.[42]

---

35 "Some Results of Missionary Work in Turkey." *The Missionary Herald*, March (1896): 99.

36 "Thoughts Suggested by the Preceding Journal." *The Missionary Herald*, April (1821): 101-102.

37 Pliny Fisk, Levi Parsons. "Palestine Mission: Journal of Messrs. Fisk and Parsons." *The Missionary Herald*, September (1821): 276-277.

38 "Religious Denominations in Syria." *The Missionary Herald*, April (1826): 126.

39 "Editorial Paragraphs." *The Missionary Herald*, May (1896): 179.

40 Mieke Bal. *Narrratology: Introduction to the Theory of Narrative*. Toronto: University of Toronto Press (1997): 119.

41 *ibid.* 120.

42 H. Porter Abbott. *The Cambridge Introduction to Narrative*. Cambridge: Cambridge University Press (2003): 77.

In this sense, the implied author is a construct for anchoring the narrative.[43] S/he is, or they are in the case of *The Missionary Herald* magazine, an inference from the text made by the reader who is attempting to glean the intended meaning of a narrative.[44] Despite certain attacks on the concept of the implied author, the term has proved extremely useful and well-suited in the context of intentional reading.[45] The creator of the term, Wayne C. Booth, further defends his position in his article "Resurrection of the Implied Author," in which he repeatedly states that the FBP (flesh and blood person) who writes the text makes constant revisions and omissions, resorts to certain degrees of masking, thus contributing to the emergence of an implied author who or which is independent of the real person, and is in line with the opinions and events represented in the narrative.[46] The single person as the creator can be extended in our case to the multiplicity of missionary writers or authors and magazine editors. In short, implied author is the source of values and norms in a text.[47]

At this point, another distinction between the actual reader and the implied reader is indispensable. The text produced by the Board and the missionaries presumed a given reader typology that would understand the message related by the magazine. In this regard the implied reader assumed by the missionaries fitted the category of a presumed addressee as the receiver of the text whose language compatibility, ideological stance and cultural background is of crucial importance for a better understanding of the texts.[48] Likewise, the texts were very likely produced by taking this presumed addressee into account. The authors and editors who wrote the arti-

---

43 *ibid.* 77.

44 *ibid.* 78.

45 *ibid.* 78-79.

46 Wayne C. Booth. "Resurrection of the Implied Author: Why Bother?" *A Companion to Narrative Theory.* Eds. James Phelan, Peter J. Rabinowitz. Malden: Blackwell (2005): 75-78.

47 Luc Herman, Bart Vervaeck. "Ideology." *The Cambridge Companion to Narrative.* Ed. David Herman. Cambridge: Cambridge University Press (2007): 226.

48 Wolf Schmid. "Implied Reader." Paragraph 5. *the living handbook of narratology.* Eds: Peter Hühn et al. Hamburg: Hamburg University. URL = http://www.lhn.uni-hamburg.de/article/implied-reader [view date: 21 January 2017].

cles constantly addressed such readers. The addressee definitely had real world equivalents (New England Congregationalists, Western Christians, millionaires from New York, American Board members, workers, associates etc.). Yet the general category was a supposed group of people who could not be specifically named in person, who were evangelists and could understand and decode the meaning of texts and associate themselves with the cause of the Board.

2.3.3 Coherence

Coherence is the meeting point of implied author and implied reader; it is not an ontological trait of the texts under discussion. The idea might have been appealing to the missionaries, but textual coherence as represented in missionary writings from *The Missionary Herald* and their assumed reception by a specific audience is contextual. Coherence as a quality depends on the sense made of the text in its cultural context.[49] Beaugrande's and Dressler's explanation of the notion as ways in which the components of the text, such as the concepts and relations underlying the surface text, are mutually accessible and relevant sheds light on the missionary texts as well.[50] As will be shown in the following chapters, one aspect of the conceptual background, the metaphors, acts as the main contributor to the textual and hence discursive coherence of the missionary writings. The Kingdom of God is regarded as a contextual, commonly accessible and relevant underlying element of coherence.

2.4 BLENDING OF CONCEPTUAL DOMAINS AND THE NARRATIVE ELEMENT

Conceptual Metaphor Theory (CMT) presupposes two domains of interaction: the source and the target. The linguistic metaphor we see in everyday

---

49 Michael Toolan. "Coherence." Paragraph 1. *the living handbook of narratology*. Eds: Peter Hühn et al. Hamburg: Hamburg University. URL = http://www.lhn.uni-hamburg.de/article/coherence [view date: 21 January 2017].

50 Robert-Alain de Beaugrande, Wolfgang Ulrich Dressler. *Introduction to Text Linguistics*. London: Longman (1981): 4.

language or a specific discourse in any medium is a result of this interaction. This notion entails a hierarchy of conceptual domains governing the occurrence of a metaphor. Certain metaphorical concepts are supposed to precede others as their conceptual basis. This fact will be displayed in the next chapter when conceptual metaphors and their linguistic manifestations will be analyzed. There seems, however, to be a limit to the application of conceptual metaphor analysis as far as a fully established written discourse, in this case the missionary discourse from *The Missionary Herald*, is concerned. It is true that detection and analysis of an existing metaphor and concept network is impossible without revealing underlying metaphorical concepts and their apparent incidences as linguistic metaphors. By doing so, one reaches a level of abstraction and generalization that enables us to comprehend and exhibit the systematic conceptual substrata as a central element of missionary discourse. Because then the general concepts and the systematic application of these general concepts can be detected and documented. Moreover, Conceptual Metaphor Theory provides tools for discerning the interconnectedness of conceptual domains, metaphorical concepts, and consequently metaphorical expressions.

Yet conceptual metaphor analysis has a limited ability to depict the whole conceptual background. It works extremely well within the general domains and their specific applications. It also has the capacity to connect seemingly separate discursive elements by detecting the conceptual interconnections among a variety of metaphorical concepts. CMT can tease out a general picture of conceptual domains and also display the interrelated categorization and usage of those domains. In short, CMT enables us to delve into the very fabric of missionary discourse, to start examining the conceptual background, to detect the metaphorical and thus conceptual networks and ultimately the systematicity of those networks as one of the main contributions to the missionary discourse. CMT is crucial for the first and most important phase of conceptual analysis.

The study of the narrative aspect of the missionary texts has already been proposed as a complementary theoretical stance to conceptual metaphor analysis, in order not to remain on a general level of approach to the conceptual background. The dichotomy of story and discourse in a narrative creates space for the conceptual formations to fit into one aspect of the narrative, namely the discourse. The content is what is being told and the discourse is how it is being told. Narrative, however, is a unified formation consisting of both parts. There seems to be no binary opposition between the story and discourse components. On the contrary, both parts are interrelated and affect each other to varying degrees.

Conceptual metaphor analysis sheds light on the interaction between two aspects in a general and limited fashion. Conceptual domains can be detected by spotting linguistic metaphors in the written story and those linguistic metaphors are transformed in turn into agents of an underlying discursive formation, namely conceptual metaphors, not perceived at first glance.

If one wants to delve into the analysis of specifics of missionary discourse as well as in general terms an overarching theory that builds on the general framework established by conceptual metaphor, an analysis and examination of the narrative character of missionary texts in question is needed. As a consequence, the evaluation of the general conceptual framework can be extended to include the whole narrative articulated by the missionaries.

The missionary discourse was a narrative that created the Ottoman Empire it encountered as a narrative mental space by relying on a multiplicity of texts that are underlined by conceptual metaphor networks. The majority of the networks inspected in this research are religious in essence and, apart from Calvinist, New Divinity postmillennialist and modernity based sources, the very origin of the conceptual formations is Biblical. And the core of these Biblical sources is the parable. Thus, the narrative of the missionaries is already preceded by a pre-established narrative-story vein that has an immediate impact on the general conceptual background of the ABCFM discourse pertaining to the Ottoman mission. The parabolic nature of an underlying narrative source has an impact on the missionary narratives both at story and discourse level. The conceptual basis of both originates from and has an impact on the parabolic Biblical background as well.

To sum up, the interaction of Biblical background with the missionary texts not only influences the use of general conceptual domains but also the story part of the narrative. In turn, the missionary narrative also manipulates the Biblical input in a manifold way, according to its needs. Therefore, as one conceptual domain is projected on another in order to create a metaphoric concept, the stories, parabolic in nature, are projected onto the missionary narrative in accordance with the more general conceptual projections. The case of second projection exceeds the general-generic domain of conceptual metaphor. The study of this narrative projection involves a theory that does not reject the general conceptual basis but is complementary to it. It should be a tool that places the generic conceptual domains into the narrative context and that explains the interaction of a multiplicity of narrative sources such as Biblical parables as well as missionary texts.

For this purpose a special approach to story, metaphor and parable will be used that has been developed by Mark Turner. Mark Turner, one of the two original developers of Blending Theory (the other is Gilles Fauconnier), has extensively discussed the notion of story, narrative imagining and projection of one story onto another, namely the parable, in his ground-breaking book *The Literary Mind*.[51] For Turner, narrative imagining is creating a story, and it is the main tool we use for evaluating the future, prediction, plans, and explanations in general. He then discusses the notion of parable. Parable starts from narrative imagining. Narrative imagining enables us understand the components of a story: objects, events, and actors. Parable combines story with projection, as when Turner says "one story is projected onto another." In short, parable is the combination of story and projection. According to Turner, "parable is the projection of story," and literary parables and proverbs as condensed stories are the results of the mental process of parable.[52]

The mental patterns of parable as understood by Turner consist of prediction, evaluation, planning, explanation, objects and events, actors, stories, projection, metonymy, emblem, image schemas, counterparts in imaginative domains, and conceptual blending, with language as its medium.[53] Where does this understanding of narrative imagining and parable stand in relation to the proposed analysis of missionary narrative? It covers the basic narrative elements such as objects, events, and actors, which are also represented conceptually in terms of metaphorical expressions. It also denotes the notion of purposeful activity inherent to the missionary discourse by dwelling on prediction, planning, evaluation, and explanation. Conceptual metaphors are also applied to these narrative components. Image schemas, projection, conceptual blending, counterparts in imaginative domains can likewise be detected in conceptual metaphor formations. Furthermore,

---

51 Mark Turner. *The Literary Mind.* Oxford: Oxford University Press (1996).
52 *ibid.* 3-7.
53 *ibid.* 9-11.

Turner's evaluation of narrative imagining covers areas of metonymic and emblematic elements in a discourse. Metonymy and emblem are not instances of metaphoric occurrences. Thus, when necessary, non-metaphorical conceptual structures that emerge in missionary narratives next to analogous metaphoric concepts can also be analyzed.

The underlying conceptual metaphors are instances of the projection of one conceptual domain onto another. The target domain is understood in terms of the source domain. These core conceptual structures contribute to the organization of a story-narrative. Yet the choice of a particular core conceptual domain rather than another is not haphazard. These domains originate from Christian sources. Therefore, single conceptual metaphors and their sub-categories constitute the skeleton of an already related story or narrative, Biblical parables being the main source. As such, there is also another set of stories that is being projected onto a recently formed narrative in a special setting. Since metaphors are projections of one domain onto another, the missionary narrative is a set of stories projected onto other nonfictional stories at a conceptual level, and more. However, we should not assume that Biblical parables are the only instances of parables. Turner's theory embraces any instance of a story projected onto another story, be it the parable proper from literature or the Bible, proverbs, or indeed "from telling [the] time to Proust."[54]

One of the central fields where metaphors and parable meet is that of image schemas. According to Turner, image schemas are "skeletal patterns that recur in our sensory and motor experience," and "*Motion along a path, bounded interior, balance*, and *symmetry* are typical image schemas."[55] Image schemas correspond to the conceptual substrata of the conceptual metaphors and are central to conceptual metaphor formation as well.

Turner's idea of 'blending' is the crucial notion that explains how conceptual metaphor and parable can be understood and evaluated in the same context. Unlike CMT, which has two main domains and posits a straightforward positive and unidirectional interaction between those domains, blending presupposes at least four domains which Turner denotes as input spaces: source input space, target input space, a generic space, and blended

---

54 *ibid.* 7.
55 *ibid.* 16.

space. Not all blending is metaphorical, but metaphorical blends are common:

Sometimes those input spaces will be related as source and target, in just the way we have seen so often. Crucially, blended spaces can develop emergent structure of their own and can project structure back to their input spaces. Input spaces can be not only providers of projections to the blend, but also receivers of projections back from the developed blend.[56]

The unidirectional two-domain understanding of conceptual metaphor is extended by the multidirectional four space theory of narrative-parable. Blending works via three basic mechanisms. These are *composition, completion*, and *elaboration*. In blending, "we project partial structure from input stories and *compose* that structure in a blended story, "[c]*ompletion* provides additional structure not provided by composition," and "[e]*laboration* develops the blend through imaginative mental simulation according to the principles and internal logic of the blend."[57]

Yet how can these two systems be compatible as means of scrutinization? Grady, Oakly, and Coulson claims that these systems are compatible and complement each other:

If conceptual metaphor theory is primarily concerned with well-established metaphoric associations between concepts, and blending theory focuses on the ability to combine elements from familiar conceptualizations into new and meaningful ones, then conceptual metaphors are among the stable structures available for exploitation by the blending process. As we have just seen [...] conventional metaphors feed the blending process by establishing links between elements in distinct domains and spaces.[58]

Their conclusion is that "conventional metaphoric relationships may be the starting points for the process of creating complex conceptual blends" and

---

56 *ibid*. 60.

57 *ibid*. 83-84.

58 J. E. Grady, T. Oakley, S. Coulson. "Blending and Metaphor." *Metaphor in Cognitive Linguistics*. Eds. R. W. Gibbs, G. J. Steen. Amsterdam/Philadelphia: John Benjamins (1999): 110.

"identifying a metaphoric relationship holding between source and target elements is sometimes only the starting point for analyzing a blend."[59] Conceptual Metaphor Theory and Blending Theory are considered to provide complementary formalisms and deal with different aspects of the same data.[60]

As far as metaphorical blends are considered, Turner's analysis of parable focuses on the projection of source and target stories and blended spaces regarding source and target, as inputs to the blend, and on the capacity of blend to project back onto the source and target input spaces.[61]

To sum up, Turner's analysis of parable and Blending Theory deals with the same conceptual formations that are the focus of conceptual metaphor analysis. While Conceptual Metaphor Theory provides us with the general underlying conceptual formations, such as master metaphors and their subcategories, the study of metaphorical narratives uses this underlying conceptual framework as a starting point and elaborates on the narrative part and the contribution of the metaphorical concepts to the narrative-story-parable. As such, both approaches are necessary and complement each other.

---

59 *ibid.* 113.

60 *ibid.* 121.

61 Turner, *Literary Mind*, 67.

3 Metaphors of the Founding Years, 1820-1830

> You see that window. There are glasses in it of different colors. One is blue, one red, another white, another green. The sun shines on them; they cast shadows of different hues; the light is all one – from the same sun. So with man. Here are the Mussulmans, Druses, Christians, – different shades – the same sun – the same light. (The answer of a dervish to missionary Jonas King at Deir el Qamar, Lebanon, in 1824)[1]

In this chapter, the infrastructure of the conceptual background, its metaphorical expressions, and the narrative(s) interacting with the conceptual background will be discussed. To this end, the first ten years of the Ottoman mission as presented in *The Missionary Herald* magazine has been chosen. During this period, the missionaries laid the foundations for the missionary discourse surrounding their activities in the Ottoman Empire. Hence, the founding years are representative of the missionary point of view, the missionary narrative, and its relevant conceptual background.

Metaphors are used with high frequency in these texts. But at this point a distinction must be made. It would be impossible and irrelevant to list all

---

1   Jonas King. "Palestine Mission: Journal of Mr. King." *The Missionary Herald*, November (1825): 341.

of the conceptual metaphors and their textual occurrences in the missionary texts. Some of them are ordinary daily usages that have little connection with the general missionary discourse. They are instances rather of general linguistic competency. A few metaphors are used idiosyncratically without a proper general background, and add nothing to the wide-ranging conceptual background that is under scrutiny in this work. The set of metaphors this chapter focuses on has above all one common characteristic: they appear in the missionary texts throughout the entire time span covered by this work, namely from 1820 to 1898. It is not only their long enduring persistence that makes them worthy of examination. Ordinary daily metaphorical usages can display the same trait. These metaphors, as it turned out, constitute a core discursive formation in the missionary writings, which embrace a core conceptual and narrative vein. As such, they are persistent metaphorical formations that form a pattern. The conceptual formations in turn constitute a part of the missionary narrative. As a consequence of the relation between narrative and conceptual background, the missionary narrative was also scrutinized to detect and underline the narrative elements that are conceptually presented, and to show how multi-layered parabolic structures are formed against this conceptual backdrop.

The textual material used in this chapter is taken from *The Missionary Herald* issues from 1820 to 1831. The texts cover the first ten years of the establishment of the mission in the Ottoman Empire. In order to detect metaphorical expressions, all of the textual data related to the missions in the Ottoman Empire was investigated. This time period was not taken at random. The textual data on the founding years of the Ottoman mission is representative of missionary discourse. For the Board, this time period was a decade of research, exploration and constant learning. The pioneer missionaries were confronted with a new environment of which they had nothing more than second-hand knowledge and predetermined ideas. What they actually found was a multiplicity of cultures, an indeterminate and hard to grasp political environment, and obstacles that hindered mission work. As a result, they had to employ almost everything in their conceptual toolbox to reflect on and make sense of this totally new world. The texts published during this period in *The Missionary Herald* exhibit the power and versatility of a well-established institutional discourse in its immediate relation to a fresh setting. The usages and conceptual methods established during this era continued to dominate missionary writings for almost a century.

Moreover, ten years is more than enough for the explication of the underlying metaphorical data and patterns. Doing so facilitates the examination of later metaphorical occurrences for specific case studies in Chapter 4, by presenting them against the background developed in this chapter. Before dealing with the period, some general information on the intellectual roots of the Board is indispensable for a thorough grasp of the material discussed here.

3.1 THE KINGDOM OF GOD

One thing that the initial reading suggests is that metaphors do not arise in a vacuum. The very first context that comes to mind is the social and cultural influences from the historical background of ABCFM, as shown in Chapter 2. But a general knowledge of the social background only helps create a shared understanding. In the light of this knowledge, it can be stated that the New Divinity roots of American Congregationalism determined the recurring use of metaphorical expressions and the conceptual world that forms their backdrop. There seems, however, to be a more specific thematic source behind the use of certain metaphors as far as the missionary establishment is concerned. The missionaries' aim to convert the world was not for philanthropic reasons. Their main idea was to pave the way for the Second Coming and with that the Millennium. Their main motivation was the eschatological beliefs they had inherited from Calvinism. The way they displayed their activities and ideological stance(s) was teleological, as can be expected from any organization based predominantly on activities aimed purposefully at influencing the future. The eschatological dogmas of the missionaries might be intricate and sophisticated on a scholarly level. But it seems that for practical purposes, such as smooth inter-group communication or, more importantly, getting their meaning across clearly, precisely and briefly to their lay supporters who read *The Missionary Herald* and to their target groups in the field, they used their ultimate aim as the conceptual substratum for the texts they produced for *The Missionary Herald*. That ultimate aim was establishing the Kingdom of God.

What is the Kingdom of God? The Kingdom, as referred to by Jesus, is an allusion to God's reign that would save and transform, as proclaimed in the Old Testament, but which at the same time is actualized in himself and his ministry.[2] In the Old Testament, God has sovereignty over all the nations, and this gives the theme a missiological and universal setting. Jesus transformed the term and, despite preserving the apocalyptic, prophetic and knowledge aspects, linked the term to himself and his mission.[3] Accordingly, the Kingdom would be realized in a new age, the end of history, when the people would start living under the reign of God.[4] Hence, the Kingdom of God can be considered as "a hope for the future" by being "the *eschaton*, or ultimate, with which 'eschatology' is concerned."[5]

There are various views regarding the Kingdom as a personal spiritual experience, as a future hope, as a new social order, or as a manifestation of power.[6] The inflection of the idea entertained by the missionaries covers all of these ideas, future hope being the foremost. Although all of the missionaries' conceptual metaphors are linked to the notion of Kingdom of God, their connection varies by degree. Some of them are a result of direct Biblical allusion or have open connections with the notion, while others are not directly linked but can be explained through their interconnectedness to the notion of Kingdom and the mission's eschatological aims. Metaphors of cultivation and growth, and metaphors of war, metaphors of light, of way-path-road, and of an opening or open door may be regarded as conceptual domains that are associated with the Kingdom to varying degrees.

The missionaries understood the Kingdom in postmillennialist terms. Jonathan Edwards was their theological and intellectual source in this regard. The rise of New Divinity was clearly a reaction to the strict doctrines of Calvinism on predestination and the bestowal of divine grace, and the liberal ideas of Arminianism defending rational conviction and free will for salvation.[7] While trying to resist the ideas originating from liberal thought, Edwards' efforts focused on attaining a balance between seemingly contra-

---

2 *Dictionary of Mission Theology: Evangelical Foundations.* Ed. John Corrie. Nottingham: Inter-Varsity Press (2007): 195.

3 *ibid.* 195.

4 *ibid.* 196.

5 Charles Harold Dodd. *The Parables of the Kingdom.* New York: Scribner (1961): 23.

6 *Dictionary of Mission* Theology, 196-198.

7 Samir Khalaf. *Protestant Missionaries in the Levant: Ungodly Puritans, 1820-60.* London: Routledge (2012): 5.

dicting opinions.[8] Samuel Hopkins, another influential New Divinity figure, related Edwards' ideas to the millennialism adopted by the Board. The gist of his ideas can be found in his influential and important work *Treatise on the Millennium,* which became the standard text for the New Divinity School.[9] According to Hopkins, human agency was important to hasten the Millennium. By human action, he meant evangelical religious activities, such as prayer, the spreading of the Word, and the continuation of the church, since he did not believe in the role of other activities in accelerating its advent.[10] His emphasis on evangelical activity provided the later missionary establishment with a firm theoretical background. Yet, notwithstanding his focus on human agency, he believed that the Millennium would be brought about by supernatural means. For him, in the Millennium, "[t]he world would abound with bountiful crops, and very little labor would be required to produce the necessities of life," with a vast increase in population, harmony among humans and, the most vital point that he stressed, humanity would reach the pinnacle of learning.[11] What he indicated was a point that would be reached after a leap in scientific knowledge and enormous advances in industry.[12] In short, he argued "that the great learning and peace found during the Millennium will result in dramatic improvements in agriculture and industry, which will allow the earth to support a great population of true Christians."[13]

Beginning in the 1790s, postmillennialism started to dominate American liberal theology. As stated by Ruth Bloch, "[p]ostmillennialism came to signify an optimistic belief in progressive human action towards the millennium, according to which God's providential plan would be carried out by human means and the world would enjoy a period of social perfection before the supernatural intervention at the end of time."[14] This notion was

---

8   *ibid.* 6.

9   Ruth H. Bloch. *Visionary Republic: Millennial Themes in American Thought, 1756-1800.* Cambridge: Cambridge University Press (1985): 124.

10 *ibid.* 125.

11 *ibid.* 128.

12 *ibid.* 128.

13 Frederic J. Baumgartner. *Longing for the End: A History of Millennialism in Western Civilization.* London: Macmillan (1999): 130.

14 Bloch, *Visionary Republic,* 131.

adopted by most of the Calvinist congregational clerics and New Divinity was no exception. Postmillennialist ideas were firmly established before the Second Great Awakening.

Millennialist ideas before and during the American Revolution were essentially politicized by the social and political atmosphere in America, and Edwards' original idea that the number of saints would be small was challenged by Joseph Bellamy, who predicted that the vast majority of people will be accepted to the Kingdom.[15] Similar to Hopkins, Bellamy was of the opinion that enhancements in industry, agriculture, and social organization would support larger numbers, and right before the Millennium there would be a considerable number of conversions. Bellamy's claim for larger numbers coincided with a tense political atmosphere, and his efforts can be seen as a democratization of the Millennium as opposed to the oligarchic thesis of a limited number of saints.[16] Ernest Lee Tuveson satirically states that "[i]t is a sign of the times that the politics of God has expanded to include demography," while noting the worldly spirit of the Millennium because, according to Bellamy's writings, "the millennium itself will have a strong this-worldly character."[17] These notions are clearly discernible in many of the letters and journals written by missionaries at the Ottoman mission.

Figures like Edwards, Hopkins, Bellamy, and Dwight transformed traditional Calvinist theology into a new school of thought that promoted the idea of conversion on a global scale, thus making these theologians the "architects of evangelical imagination."[18] In this context, millennial visions underpinned the formation of a new generation of Protestants which saw the commencement of missionary work as an urgent prerequisite for the coming of the Millennium.[19] Those people "[n]otwithstanding their differences [...] all shared the belief that history, under some divine guidance, would bring about the triumph of Christian principles and [...] that the

---

15 *ibid.* 130.
16 *ibid.* 130.
17 Ernest Lee Tuveson. *Redeemer Nation: The Idea of America's Millennial Role.* Chicago: University of Chicago Press (1968): 58.
18 Khalaf, *Missionaries*, 10.
19 *ibid.* 21.

years were hastening on towards the Millennium and that something must be done to prepare the heathen world for such an imminent eventuality."[20]

3.2 METAPHORS OF CULTIVATION, PARABLES OF GROWTH

The missionaries frequently alluded to Biblical parables when writing about the Kingdom of God. A group of parables that can be distinguished by their common theme of growth constitute recurring reference points here. These parables are the Parables of the Sower, the Tares, the Growing Seed and the Mustard Seed.[21] The Parables are as follows:

The Parable of the Sower:

Hearken; Behold, there went out a sower to sow: And it came to pass, as he sowed, some fell by the way side, and the birds of the air came and devoured it up. And some fell on stony ground, where it had not much earth; and immediately it sprang up, because it had no depth of earth: But when the sun was up, it was scorched; and because it had no root, it withered away. And some fell among thorns, the thorns grew up, and choked it, and it yielded no fruit. And other fell on good ground, did yield fruit that sprang up and increased; and brought forth, some thirty, and some sixty, some an hundred. He said unto them, He that has ears to hear, let him hear.

—Mark 4:3-9, Holy Bible: King James Version

The Parable of the Tares:

Another parable put he forth unto them, saying, The kingdom of heaven is likened unto a man which sowed good seed in his field: But while men slept, his enemy came and sowed tares among the wheat, and went his way. But when the blade was sprung up, and brought forth fruit, then appeared the tares also. So the servants of the householder came and said unto him, Sir, didst not thou sow good seed in thy field? From whence then hath it tares? He said unto them, An enemy hath done this. The servants said unto him, Wilt thou then that we go and gather them up? But he said, Nay; lest while ye gather up the tares, ye root up also the wheat with them. Let

---

20 *ibid.* 23-24.
21 Charles Harold Dodd. *The Parables of the Kingdom.* New York: Scribner (1961): 140.

both grow together until the harvest: and in the time of harvest I will say to the reapers, Gather ye together first the tares, and bind them in bundles to burn them: but gather the wheat into my barn.
—Matthew 13:24-30, Holy Bible: King James Version

Parable of the Growing Seed:
And he said, So is the kingdom of God, as if a man should cast seed into the ground; And should sleep, and rise night and day, and the seed should spring and grow up, he knoweth not how. For the earth bringeth forth fruit of herself; first the blade, then the ear, after that the full corn in the ear. But when the fruit is brought forth, immediately he putteth in the sickle, because the harvest is come.
—Mark 4:26-29, Holy Bible: King James Version

The Parable of the Mustard Seed:
Another parable put he forth unto them, saying, The kingdom of heaven is like to a grain of mustard seed, which a man took, and sowed in his field: Which is indeed the least of all seeds: but when it is grown, it is the greatest among herbs, and becometh a tree, so that the birds come and lodge in the branches thereof.
—Matthew 13: 31-32, Holy Bible: King James Version

With the elucidation of the metaphors of cultivation and growth in the missionary texts, the relationship between the missionary discourse and the parables can be comprehended in large measure. The relation of Biblical allusions and direct references will be dealt with more thoroughly after the conceptual background has been revealed.

Right from the beginning of the Ottoman mission, missionary texts were crammed with concepts of cultivation. The first missionaries of the Board to the Ottoman Empire, Pliny Fisk and Levi Parsons, lost no time in embarking on their mission work, and in an early letter from the field, they explained the usefulness of distributing tracts and scriptures and of conversing with individuals. They were of the opinion that "[b]y these methods perhaps a little seed" might "be sown" which might "grow, and bring forth fruit."[22] Thus, the distribution of tracts at a Greek school at Chios in the

---

22 Pliny Fisk, Levi Parsons. "Palestine Mission: Letter from Messrs. Fisk and Parsons." *The Missionary Herald*, January (1821): 20.

summer of 1820 was represented as sowing "precious seed."[23] A couple of days later they visited a college and they believed that their visit and the distribution of scriptures would "bring forth fruit to eternal life."[24] The missionaries were convinced that they needed a printing facility "for the people on the shores of the Mediterranean" for "the dissemination of Christian" truth.[25] The idea of distribution is articulated in a different way by applying the word 'dissemination.' One sees here the application of an archaic metaphorical expression to a new setting in these lines.

These lines also indicate that the need for a printing establishment was deemed crucial at the very beginning of the mission. The missionaries were using the power of oral interaction but they were aware of the power of the written word. As early as 1821, a special fund was set up for a mission press for 'Western Asia' which was to be established at Izmir or Jerusalem.[26] Daniel Temple arrived in Malta in 1822 and printing in Greek and Italian began that year.[27] Temple was not a professional printer and demanded that someone else be sent, since he wanted to work in the field as a missionary.[28] Human Hallock arrived in December 1826 to replace him.[29] Under his supervision, the amount of printing rose steadily: 2.9 million pages in 1830 and 4.8 million in 1831.[30]

The missionaries had supplied themselves with Bibles from Izmir, Malta, or the British and Foreign Bible Society.[31] However, for both financial and practical reasons they preferred to have their own press. Consequently, the establishment of the printing press became a major issue for the

---

23 *ibid.* 79.
24 *ibid.* 80.
25 "Printing Establishment for Western Asia." *The Missionary Herald*, March (1821): 81.
26 J. F. Coakley. "Printing Offices of the American Board of Commissioners for Foreign Missions, 1812-1900: A Synopsis." *Harvard Library Bulletin*, Volume 9, Number 1 (Spring 1998): 11.
27 *ibid.* 13.
28 *ibid.* 13.
29 *ibid.* 13.
30 *ibid.* 13.
31 Pliny Fisk, Levi Parsons. "Letters of Messrs. Parsons and Fisk to the Corresponding Secretary." *The Missionary Herald*, March (1821): 78.

Board.[32] The report of the Prudential Committee on the mission to Palestine stressed the importance of printing and the establishment of a printing press. The comments related to the suggestions of a Mr. Williamson.[33] Another report by the Prudential Committee dwelled on the necessity of a printing facility for the Palestine mission.[34] Meanwhile Fisk and Parsons made an agreement to have a tract printed at the college press on the Island of Chios in 1820.[35] Their achievements on the Greek islands were deeply appreciated.[36]

However, because of the tumult in Western Anatolia, the missionaries started to search for another location, since Izmir was no longer an option. Daniel Temple, a young missionary, sailed from Boston on January 2, 1822 for Malta. He was bringing a printing press with him.[37] The Board gave detailed instructions to Temple:

Who does not know that the art of printing is the greatest of human inventions? If regarded merely as an instrument of refinement and civilization- of intellectual improvement,- and of securing and preserving liberty, the highest strains of eloquence would be poured forth in its praise. But it is destined to a nobler use, than any which is confined in its operation to this world. Next to the living voice of the earnest and affectionate preacher, it is to become the most powerful mean of diffusing the knowledge of the Gospel, of awakening a dead world to spiritual life [...].[38]

---

32 "Printing Establishment for Western Asia." *The Missionary Herald*, March (1821): 81.

33 "Report of the Prudential Committee." *The Missionary Herald*, December (1820): 556.

34 "Report of the Prudential Committee." *The Missionary Herald*, January (1821): 10.

35 Pliny Fisk, Levi Parsons. "Palestine Mission: Journal of the Missionaries." *The Missionary Herald*, July (1821): 201.

36 "Report of the Prudential Committee." *The Missionary Herald*, March (1821): 68.

37 Daniel Temple. "Extract of a Letter from Mr. Temple to a Gentleman in Boston." *The Missionary Herald*, June (1822): 179.

38 "Instructions to Mr. Temple." *The Missionary Herald*, October (1822): 335.

The qualities of the press as a means of diffusing the light of civilization and intellectual refinement and securing liberty were taken for granted by the Board. They wanted to employ the transformative effects of the press for their own purposes. It should be remembered that the question of 'civilization' was central to missionary discourse. Thus, their aims were founded on the basic precepts of the utilization of the printing press. The Rev. John Hartley from the Church Missionary Society remarked in a letter to Jonas King that "Malta may become a second Wittenberg."[39] Considering that printing was meant to alter the minds of the people and consequently the cultural and political fabric of the society, the association of metaphors of cultivation and growth makes sense.

The missionaries were well equipped with metaphors of cultivation. For them, distributing tracts at a nunnery was "to sow a little precious seed"[40] and "to see fruits of their labors."[41] The seed might "lie buried long in the earth; but the crop [...] is insured"[42] and Levi Parsons cited the line "Mount Zion shall be plowed like a field" when he visited Mount Zion in February 1821.[43]

By 1824, the missionaries had already built up an audience in Syria. Although "[t]he harvest" was plenteous, the laborers were few and they wished that "the Lord of the harvest" send forth more laborers.[44] Missionary activity in Syria was portrayed as "heavenly dews [...] dropping down upon the wilderness, and converting the desert into a fruitful field."[45] As a

39 "Mediterranean: Operations of the Church Missionary Societies Press at Malta." *The Missionary Herald*, November (1826): 360.

40 Pliny Fisk, Levi Parsons. "Palestine Mission: Journal of Messrs. Fisk and Parsons at Scio." *The Missionary Herald*, April (1821): 97.

41 *ibid.* 104.

42 Pliny Fisk, Levi Parsons. "Palestine Mission: Journal of Messrs. Fisk and Parsons, During Their Tour in Asia Minor." *The Missionary Herald*, August (1821): 256.

43 Levi Parsons. "Palestine Mission: Journal of Mr. Parsons, While at Jerusalem." *The Missionary Herald*, February (1822): 35.

44 Pliny Fisk. "Palestine Mission: Journal of Mr. Fisk." *The Missionary Herald*, September (1824): 273.

45 William Goodell. "Letter from Mr. Goodell to the Corresponding Secretary." *The Missionary Herald*, January (1826): 11.

result, "some of the good seed" was "springing up."[46] Yet, within a short time, the missionaries gained adversaries and they realized that although "[w]ith a fertile soil, and a propitious sky" they might expect "an abundant crop," they were on "strong, and thorny ground."[47] These metaphorical expressions denote affirmative missionary endeavors and the hardships they encountered while conducting their work. When we look at the invectives they employed for the indigenous people, expressions such as 'desert' or 'thorny' ground are all-encompassing means of expressing negative experiences, occasions or entities. The missionaries were constantly traveling and making observations. The nature of their observations can be seen in the light of evangelical notions of progress, civilization, and the Kingdom. For instance, the early missionaries described the state of the infrastructure extensively. One explanation is that they were introducing new places to a curious American audience. Yet, the way they picked and represented certain themes can also be related to the postmillennialist notion of progress and this-worldly development. Thus, it is possible that city infrastructure was evaluated as part of the conditions that would make the Kingdom come true. The missionaries needed a fertile soil, namely favorable conditions to achieve success. However, they also needed fertile soil for a greater harvest of agricultural produce, for the Kingdom was supposed to accommodate huge masses with food for both soul and body in this world, as Hopkins stated. The affirmative quality attributed to cultivation and the negative quality to adverse conditions detrimental to growth clearly had its roots in Biblical parables. As such, the metaphorical value is undeniable. In the missionary writings, the metaphorical domains were transferred into a new era with novel developments in science and agriculture. The intellectual roots of New England Protestantism – Edwards, Hopkins and Bellamy, to mention just the most influential figures – evaluated new times from a new perspective. It is highly probable that the missionaries were thinking of the contemporary postmillennialist notions of progress in agriculture when they applied the Biblical metaphors of cultivation and growth. They hoped for increase in the number of people to accept 'truth,' along with an increase in

---

46 William Goodell. "Mediterranean:- Letter from Mr. Goodell." *The Missionary Herald*, November (1826): 358.

47 Eli Smith. "Obstacles to the Growth of Evangelical Piety in Syria." *The Missionary Herald*, April (1828): 113-114.

the amount of crops to be harvested for the realization of the Millennium. As such, conceptual metaphors of cultivation and growth were a peculiar combination of core Christian concepts and their contemporary interpretations, arising from ideas connected to enlightenment and modernity as technical progress.

It can also be claimed that the missionaries felt at home when they used a language full of agricultural references. The missionaries' rural roots and the rustic character of American Congregationalism in that era may likewise have had an impact on their choice of conceptual references. Yet the main criterion for such a choice seems in the first place to be religious.

The metaphors, however, remained as allusions to propagation, and allusions to conditions, human interactions and political bodies in the context of propagation. What is central to the notion of growth in the missionary texts is the spread of Protestantism and evangelist belief among the target groups. The Kingdom would come by converting people, and conversion is possible only if they choose to believe what the missionaries preached. In this respect it can be said that the use of metaphors of cultivation is an instance of the metaphors **Encouraging Beliefs is Cultivating a Plant**, because what the missionaries did was foster their belief system, and **Development of a Belief is Growth of a Plant**, because the missionaries sow the seed of belief in their targets' minds. These metaphors are special sub-cases of **BELIEFS ARE PLANTS**, and this metaphor is a special case of the metaphor **BELIEFS ARE BEINGS WITH A LIFE CYCLE**. Moreover, one can detect the metaphor **Necessary Prerequisites are Necessary Prerequisites for Plant Life**. This conceptual metaphor is behind expressions like "fertile ground," "fertile soil," "propitious sky," and "heavenly dews." The use of these expressions refers to favorable conditions for the commencement and final success of the missionary work.

The application of metaphors of growth links the missionary discourse with its Biblical background. The metaphors allude to propagation, albeit not to the whole phase of propagation as a complete process. Firstly, sowing seeds is an allusion to the very beginning of missionary interaction. It illustrates missionary teachings taking root in the target groups' world view. Nevertheless, inception by itself is not sufficient for ultimate success. The ideas need to be internalized and broadly accepted by their target groups. Therefore the next domain of conceptualization refers to the middle phase; the gradual prevalence of missionary ideas. Lastly, concepts such as harvest, fruit and crop illustrate the supposed final success, namely the conversion of individuals and target groups.

The conceptual setting creates a dichotomy that also helped the missionaries to refer to and depict the political and cultural atmosphere of the lands they visited. For them, propagation, the acceptance of Congregationalist ideals by people, and the prevalence of these ideals are all affirmative and productive. The opposite is negative, empty or counterproductive. They imagined green, fruitful fields and plentiful yields as opposed to desert landscapes and thorny ground.

3.3 METAPHORS OF WAR

The Kingdom of God can also be regarded as a manifestation of power.[48] According to this view, the Kingdom is God's way of confronting and destroying the powers of evil and Jesus' ministry is a manifestation of this confrontation.[49] As a result, the world is seen as a battleground between the Kingdom of God and the kingdom of Satan.[50] This conflict is regarded as spiritual warfare.[51] Spiritual warfare can be summarized as the conflict between humanity and Satan in relation to the Kingdom of God.[52]

From the very beginning, the missionary enterprise tried to convince its audience in the US of the feasibility of missionary work among its target groups. In a short article titled "Present Encouraging Aspect of the Unevangelized Parts of the World" published in the February 1820 issue of *The Missionary Herald*, the anonymous writer discusses the prospects for missionary work among the Jews, Muslims and 'pagans.' Her/his aim is to answer the questions put by the 'Christian of the present day' as to why these groups should yield to the influence of evangelical Christianity and why they present a better prospect for mission work. The article proceeds by showing how these peoples were increasingly enjoying "the blessings of science and civilization," what had been done to bring the Word to the

---

48 *Dictionary of Mission Theology*, 198.
49 *ibid*. 198.
50 *ibid*. 198.
51 *ibid*. 198.
52 *ibid*. 367.

"barbarous nations," the importance of Sabbath Schools for missionary work, and God's favor for their future plans. It ends by pointing out that "Surely the time to favor Zion [...] is come – when the heathen shall fear the name of the Lord and all the kings of earth his glory."[53] One might assume that the Board had already defined its enemies even before setting foot in the Ottoman Empire.

In the light of this, Levi Parson's letter to the treasurer of the Board is not surprising when it ends with the sentence "[f]orget not to pray for us, that we may be permitted to see and to take possession of the land of promise."[54] Parsons wrote the letter from the Greek Island (then Ottoman territory) of Chios in June 1820. He and Pliny Fisk were still to go and start a mission in Jerusalem and the surrounding area. His expression 'land of promise' is another way of expressing the Biblical Promised Land. Even at this early stage of the mission, the missionaries were applying Biblical imagery that alludes to acts of war. In a decade of turmoil and warfare, their stance was about to prove perilous to the mission and their own well-being. The conceptual category of an enemy and the metaphorical allusions to war clearly affected the way they conducted their activities, and although it is not stated in their own writings, it may be assumed that hostilities incurred by their presence were partly aroused by the way their conceptual understanding of certain groups and beliefs influenced how they behaved.

Parsons and Fisk continued distributing tracts and Bibles around the region of Izmir before they took off for Jerusalem. The printing press, which is also conceptualized via metaphors of cultivation, found another domain of expression: "The press is a species of artillery, which, if well and perseveringly served, on the side of justice, benevolence, and truth, is perfectly invincible."[55] The paradoxical use of military language and positive concepts is striking. It is as if the missionaries justified their attack on other belief systems and people by alluding to the higher moral ground they

---

53 "Present Encouraging Aspect of the Unevangelized Parts of the World." *The Missionary Herald*, February (1820): 55-56.

54 Levi Parsons. "Palestine Mission: Extract of a Letter from the Rev. Levi Parsons to the Treasurer of the A.B.C.F.M." *The Missionary Herald*, December (1820): 288.

55 "Thoughts upon the Printing Establishment in Malta." *The Missionary Herald*, July (1826): 211.

claimed to occupy. Once again, certain conflicts caused by distributing tracts and books might have been the reason why the target groups sensed the aggressiveness that missionaries attached to these activities and felt threatened.

Upon visiting the relics of the ancient city of Sardes, the missionaries experienced a feeling of discontent at the city's desolate state. For them "[e]very thing seems, as if God had cursed the place, and left it to the dominion of Satan." The missionary mind regarded the concept of a city or landscape as a 'dominion' that belonged either to them or to their adversaries. On occasions like this, the boundary between a mental space and mundane place is blurred. The missionary language employs the conceptual domain of war in seemingly abstract ways. The idea of a dominion in this sentence, however, is not only of an imagined place, a mental construct which Protestants and their rivals compete over. The dominion is real. It is a geographical location and a political and religious power that literally controlled the place.

On a similar occasion, Parsons' and Fisk's visit to the seven churches was described by the Prudential Committee with the comment that "[t]he marks of degradation and misery are visible in every place, where the dominion of the false prophet is felt."[56] Similar to the criticism about the city of Sardes, the region is depicted as backwards because it belonged to Muslim rule. The criticism of Islamic rule and the prevalence of Islam in general was not only a matter of abstract ideas for the missionaries. It was also a matter of infrastructure and economic degradation.

Readers of *The Missionary Herald* and associates of the missionaries were also considered to be participants in spiritual warfare. The mission enterprise depended heavily on individual donations. It was not uncommon for the Board to call for donations in *The Missionary Herald*. In the September issue of 1825, a call was made to the secretaries, treasurers and collectors of the various associations. They were addressed on the importance of collecting money from the public and were given hints on how to deal with subscribers. They were reminded that if these were followed, "wider

---

56 "Report of the Prudential Committee." *The Missionary Herald*, March (1821): 68.

invasions" would be made "into the empire of darkness."[57] As in any war, financial means were of crucial importance.

Daniel Temple, a missionary stationed at Malta for the mission press, summarized the background notion of considering places as dominions when he stated that "the few Christian missionaries stationed in the Mediterranean are increasing in zeal, and extending their plans and labors for the enlargement of our adorable Redeemer's kingdom." The mission enterprise was involved in creating a new political entity on a global scale. They were ready for opposition and Temple anticipated that "the enemies of this sacred cause" might start a corresponding activity against the mission.[58] Their trust in the power of the printing press and their aggressive strategy can be seen in the following lines: "American press at Malta [...] have a free and constant operation, for an age to come, and the foundations of Papacy will be undermined, and Islamism will tremble to its centre."[59]

Soon after they had settled, the missionaries started to meet with opposition after they commenced mission work in Palestine and Greater Syria. Most importantly, there was growing discontent among the Catholics. Roman Catholics saw them as a threat to their influence in the region and to the social order established by the *millet* system of the Ottoman Empire. As a result, in 1824 they obtained an edict from the Sultan prohibiting the distribution of Bibles by American missionaries. To the missionaries "the Beast and the False Prophet" were "uniting their armies" but "the Lamb shall overcome them."[60] This is one of the pitfalls the missionaries could not foresee, although they had already defined the mission press as an artillery and their activities as an invasion. Their attack was repelled by a counterattack.

---

57 "To the Secretaries, Treasurers, and Collectors of Associates." *The Missionary Herald*, September (1825): 302.
58 Daniel Temple. "Mission to Palestine: Malta." *The Missionary Herald*, September (1825): 273.
59 "Thoughts upon the Printing Establishment at Malta." *The Missionary Herald*, July (1826): 212.
60 Jonas King. "Palestine Mission: Journal of Mr. King." *The Missionary Herald*, December (1825): 373.

Having encountered growing opposition from various opponents, Mr. King cited the following poem from James Montgomery reflecting on what might await him before he arrived at Jerusalem:

The lowering battle forms
Its terrible array,
Like clashing clouds in mountain storms,
That thunder on their way.[61]

For him, "[f]lesh and blood, principalities and powers, rulers of the darkness of this world and spiritual wickedness in high places" were united to oppose them.[62] Yet God, "under whose banner" the missionaries were enlisted, was "sure to conquer." He believed that "the God of armies" called them to the contest and they hoped for "victory." His aim was to "fight the good fight."[63] Their rivals, mainly Roman Catholics and Greek Orthodox Christians, "seized upon the artillery of heaven" and "god of this world" turned it to the defense of his own kingdom.[64] The Board expected them to make their "firmest, most deadly stand" which would result in "the most painful struggles, and the fiercest conflict."[65] The mission work in Palestine was considered to be "a long and arduous, but glorious struggle" and "the fierce and long-contested battle" which would result in "ultimate and triumphant success."[66] To sum up, from the missionary perspective the missionary operations were "destined to hasten the battle of the great day, when the Beast and the False Prophet, united in counsel and interest and hostile effort" would be "overthrown, and their kingdom subverted."[67]

The Board was aware that without appropriate preparation and foreknowledge, the mission did not have the chance to become influential and successful. The missionaries of the Palestine mission were supposed to be

---

61 *ibid.* 377.
62 *ibid.* 377.
63 *ibid.* 377.
64 "Reasonable Expectations in Relation to the Palestine Mission." *The Missionary Herald*, July (1826): 213.
65 *ibid.* 213.
66 *ibid.* 213.
67 *ibid.* 214.

acquainted "with every strong hold, and assailable point, in the ancient and mighty kingdom, which Satan has established in those parts" and "with the most effectual modes of assault."[68] The missionary excursions and explorations are conceptualized in these lines as a military expedition. For the missionaries, travel meant an opportunity for propagation and an opportunity to scrutinize the weak points of the adversaries to the missionary cause. They had a keen eye for detecting a weak point, a crevice in the texture of metaphorical fortifications, and they developed new modes of assault to overcome and subdue their enemies. It is a peculiar way to represent travel experiences and impressions. On one level, there were real castles, strongholds, military powers and formations. They are aptly portrayed in the missionary texts. After all, one of the main reasons for publishing field reports and letters was to inform the American public of the conditions in new lands, the peoples and their mindsets. On another level, one comprised of abstractions, there were missionary conceptualizations of dominance, resistance, repression, opposition, anti-propaganda and persecution. Via metaphors of war, missionaries constructed imaginary armies, abstract castles, and spiritual wars that overlapped with their mundane counterparts. In that respect, the resemblance between postmillennialist eschatology and the way missionaries reflected a totally new world is striking. They portrayed a land that belongs to this world and yet was a gateway to another realm. The mundane was closely knit with the spiritual, albeit in this case undesirably. They considered scientific progress and improvement in living conditions as a step towards the coming of the Kingdom. Lack of progress or the existence of counter-functioning mechanisms were considered to be hindrances. After all, the missionaries were there to fix such problems so that they could facilitate the coming of the Kingdom.

What kind of a war did the missionaries imagine? As already shown, on certain occasions real warfare and tumult was genuinely celebrated by the missionaries as long as it served their purposes and long term aims. Yet, when they expected that Palestine was to be shaken with political revolutions, their reaction was to keep restrained. The chosen course that was to be followed was "to pour the influence of Christianity into the warring ele-

---

68 *ibid*. 212.

ments, and thus to moderate the direful tempest."[69] For the Board the real opponents were "the enemies of truth and piety."[70] In the context of the Palestine mission, this corresponds to the ancient Christian Churches and the Muslim authorities. Mundane political struggles seem to have been supported or opposed in direct relation to the mission's cause. Hence, despite the fact that the missionaries opposed the Greek Orthodox Church, they might support the Greek rebellions against the Muslim rule with the expectation that the missionaries could conduct their work with more freedom under Christian rule. Moreover, and perhaps more importantly, the missionaries cherished the destruction of the Ottoman fleet at Navarino in the belief that the Orthodox Church might be less cooperative with the Catholic Church, unlike the Ottoman State.[71] Despite this practical stance, they hoped that God intended "to employ the sword in preparing the way for the Gospel in those countries, from whence the Gospel was by the sword driven into banishment."[72] These lines can hardly be taken as allusions to spiritual warfare, unlike other occurrences of the metaphor. Yet the missionaries seem to have aimed at "destroying the influence of the Pope, and blunting the sword of Mahommed, in Mount Lebanon"[73] by mainly resorting to "spiritual warfare."[74] In order to understand the tactics and methods of this warfare, one can take the example of Tanoos El Haddad, the former teacher of the Arab School in Beirut and a former Greek Catholic, who engaged in a series of discussions on religious affairs with a Greek Catholic priest. Tanoos was depicted in an editorial note as "a firm adherent of the prevalent superstition, now coming forward as a bold and zealous champion of the truth, skillfully wielding the sword of the spirit; and con-

---

69 "Reasonable Expectations in Relation to the Palestine Mission." *The Missionary Herald*, July (1826): 214.

70 Eli Smith. "Western Asia: Extracts from a Letter of Mr. Smith to the Corresponding Secretary." *The Missionary Herald*, October (1827): 306.

71 "Destruction of the Turkish and Egyptian Fleets at Navarino." *The Missionary Herald*, January (1828): 19-20.

72 *ibid*. 20.

73 "Obstacles to the Growth of Evangelical Piety in Syria." *The Missionary Herald*, April (1828): 114.

74 "Suggestions with Regard to Future Measures." *The Missionary Herald*, November (1828): 352.

founding, if not convincing, the enemies of evangelical religion" in his defense of evangelical Christianity against the priest.[75] Spreading the Word through the distribution of the Bible, religious tracts and pamphlets, and through educational establishments, preaching and conversation, was the ammunition of missionary warfare. Nevertheless, the missionary imagery of warfare occasionally oscillated between the spiritual and the mundane.

The reader can see that there was a rivalry between the missionaries and other religious creeds. This is understandable because every party had a claim to be propagating the truth, and to appeal to the people. In many cases, the Roman Catholic missionary establishment was irritated by the existence of Protestants and saw them as opponents. Hence the metaphor **COMPETITION IS WAR**. Despite supporting certain military interventions and operations, the missionaries themselves assumed a position in a spiritual war as shown above. They mainly used the power of one-to-one conversation, printing presses, school education and preaching in the field. But the propagation of ideas was their main weapon. Consequently, the conceptual metaphor **ARGUMENT IS WAR** can be detected in the background. This conceptual metaphor entails the notion that theories, in this case Protestant ideas, are defensible positions. A special sub-species is **Theories are Fortifications**, which covers the metaphor **Attacking a Theory is Attacking a Fortification**. All these metaphors are enlisted under **THEORETICAL DEBATE IS COMPETITION**.

The missionaries were quick to gain adversaries and enemies, possibly not only because their teachings were unwelcome by other creeds, but also because they had a well-entrenched outlook to oppose anything that did not fit their worldview. By viewing themselves as fighting a spiritual war, they defined themselves as soldiers of a spiritual war. Their writings bear testimony to the unyielding, self-assured and seemingly unchanging missionary point of view.

---

75 Eli Smith. "Syria: Communications from Mr. Smith." *The Missionary Herald*, August (1829): 244.

3.4 LIGHT AND DARKNESS[76]

In February 1824, William Goodell wrote an informative letter from Beirut which was published in *The Missionary Herald*. The letter contained extensive information on roads, cultivation, mountain churches and convents, climate, impressions from a funeral, the scenery around Beirut, and the importance of religious instruction for the locals. While handling the last topic, Goodell mentioned that the service of the Catholic churches was in Latin, "that of the Greek church, in ancient Greek; that of the Syrian and Maronite churches, in Syriac; that of the Jews, in Hebrew; that of the Turks, in Arabic," and added that the common people belonging to these religious groups knew as much of these languages as the people of America knew old Saxon.[77] Goodell described the situation with a direct reference to the Bible: "They grope for the wall like the blind, and they grope as if they had no eyes; they stumble at noon-day as in the night [...]" and "they know not

---

76 One of the first works that comes to mind regarding metaphors of light is Hans Blumenberg's article "Light as a Metaphor for Truth" (Hans Blumenberg. "Light as a Metaphor for Truth." *Modernity and the Hegemony of Vision*. Ed. David Michael Levin. Berkeley: The University of California Press (1993): 30-67). This article, first published in 1957, deals with the historical aspect of metaphors of light from a philosophical perspective. Blumenberg aims at laying the foundations of a search for the history of concepts, to be more precise, philosophical concepts, which would consequently create what he calls a philosophical metaphorology. His stress on changes in self-understanding and world-understanding "via detecting transformations of a basic metaphor" is likewise a central tenet of this work. Yet, Blumenberg's views are deeply philosophical and as a consequence of the date the article was written, do not address issues and specific aspects of conceptual metaphor theory that were to emerge in the following decades. In one of the endnotes to his article, Blumenberg states, having enumerated works dealing with metaphors of light from specific historical periods, "[w]ith regard to the modern age, it evidently needs to be proven that the history of metaphors of light continues at all" (p.55). It is hoped that this small section and the related parts of the case studies in the following chapter will serve as a brief and humble contribution to that proof.

77 William Goodell. "Palestine Mission: Journal of Mr. Goodell." *The Missionary Herald*, November (1824): 342.

at what they stumble." The first quotation is from Isaiah 59:10 and in the King James Bible it reads "We grope for the wall like the blind, and we grope as if we had no eyes; we stumble at noonday as in the night; we are in desolate places as dead men." The second one is from Proverbs 4:19: "The way of the wicked is as darkness; they know not at what they stumble."[78] Goodell's allusions were windows opening to the very core of a series of metaphors employed extensively by the missionaries, namely the metaphors of light and darkness.

The passage is important regarding two aspects. Firstly, the apparent trope is a simile not a metaphor. As will be seen later, this does not hinder the employment of metaphors arising from the conceptual metaphors originating from the Bible. Since conceptual domains can constitute important elements of a parabolic expression, a parabolic expression can in turn lend those domains to any discourse. The concepts are derived to be used metaphorically, rather than in the exact form. Secondly, and more importantly, a direct connection is established between the conceptual domains of DARKNESS (and therefore LIGHT) and DEATH (and therefore LIFE). This characteristic might help clarify similar connections. It is not possible for us to determine how exactly the missionaries interpreted these passages. From the way they employed the metaphors, however, it seems that they were quite aware of their abstract and conceptual value. Actually, their awareness is sufficiently strong for them to intentionally use this conceptual background as a substrate on which to build their discourse and their organizational coherence. Similarly, when Goodell cites the lines from Isaiah 59:10, blindness is related to a lack of a clear view of the truth. Since being unable to find one's way is related to being dead, a lack of orientation and correct view is blended with the concept of death. In short, lack of knowledge is being spiritually dead, or alternatively, not knowing the truth is being spiritually dead.

These abstractions seem to be the essence of responding flexibly to the changing times, without losing organizational sense-making abilities. The domains as categories undergo little or no change (LIGHT, DEATH, PATH etc. in relation to morality, spirituality, politics etc.). The content of the conceptual framework and the categories is constantly redefined, both in-

---

78 "Isaiah 59:10, Proverbs 4:19." *The Bible: Authorized King James Version.* Oxford: Oxford University Press (1997): 819, 726.

tentionally, by means of intellectual contributions, and unintentionally, by not being exempted from exposure to external conditions. Thus, the very idea of spiritual death, which in its source is articulated in the context of ancient Israel, can well be presented against an American Middle Class Congregationalist background, and brought to the nineteenth century Ottoman Empire.

The application of an old trope for a new setting can also be witnessed when Goodell mentions the beggars of Beirut, who come to his house twice a week to receive bread, as being literally "the poor, the lame, the halt, and the blind," then adding that their external appearance was "but a faint image of their moral wretchedness."[79] The lines are taken from Luke 14:21: "So that the servant came, and showed his lord these things. Then the master of the house being angry said to his servant, Go out quickly into the streets and lanes of the city, and bring in hither the poor, and the maimed, and the halt, and the blind."

The passage itself is from the Parable of the Dinner. As the context is the missionaries' need of a medical doctor in the field in the Ottoman Empire, the metaphorical expressions have clear double meanings. But since they refer to the spiritual rather than the biological (medical) field, it can be argued that the notion of physical healing is implicitly transferred into the field of spiritual healing, i.e. the missionary activity of bringing the 'Word' to heal the souls of people. By doing so, the missionary establishment not only highlights the practical importance of a medical doctor in the field for reaching the people, but also, and more importantly, displays how the secular is subordinate to the religious, and how neither is exempt from the other.

The relationships of the metaphorical concept of LIGHT will be discussed when the metaphors in the field are analyzed. It is sufficient to mention that LIGHT is associated with human understanding through its connection to sight. In this passage from the Bible, the image of someone lacking certain knowledge as being blind is in perfect accord with this idea. As in the related Biblical quotation from Isaiah, transfer of the field of seeing to the field of understanding is achieved by projecting the field of physical healing onto spiritual healing. Therefore, a blind person is someone who has no knowledge and who is spiritually sick. This combination suggests

---

79 Isaac Bird, William Goodell. "Mission to Palestine: Beyroot." *The Missionary Herald*, September (1825): 272-273.

the idea, through a new level of conceptual blending, that lack of knowledge is tantamount to being spiritually sick, which in turn is being blind and which in turn is being in a state of darkness. According to the missionaries, a sickness should be healed.

The missionaries made much use of metaphors of light in their correspondence, and they are also to be found in editorial notes and evaluations. In an article explaining the 'present encouraging aspects of the unevangelized [sic] parts of the world,' the mixture of missionary action and divine intervention was reflected as "a far brighter day."[80] The same expression can be seen in the "Journal of Missionary Bird" as he wrote "[...] a brighter day is coming"[81] when commenting on the desolate state of this ruined city of Baalbek during a visit. A brighter day is an element of hope for the missionaries. They associate the situation in the areas where they conduct their missionary work with darkness. The idea of a brighter day, on the other hand, has a positive connotation and is a reason to celebrate. This notion is based on the conceptual metaphor of **HOPE IS LIGHT**. In line with this metaphor and the affirmative value of brightness/light are **GOODNESS IS LIGHT / BADNESS IS DARKNESS**.

Messrs. Fisk and Parsons, the two pioneer missionaries, gave an account of what they had thus far experienced and stated optimistically in one of their very first letters from the field in Smyrna that "[a] ray of light already dawns upon" their path.[82] The light is depicted as a ray. This metaphorical expression is related to the conceptual metaphor **LIGHT IS A LINE**. The missionaries cleverly conveyed the message to their audience that they knew which direction to follow. This allusion to a clear and direct light indicates that they were far from being confused and were able to figure out some future plans of action. By doing so, they assured their superiors, audiences and lay supporters that the mission had good prospects and was worthy of being supported. The metaphorical expression is a compact

---

80 "Present Encouraging Aspects of the Unevangelized Parts of the World." *The Missionary Herald*, February (1820): 56.

81 Isaac Bird. "Extracts from the Journal of Mr. Bird." *The Missionary Herald*, February (1829): 48.

82 Pliny Fisk, Levi Parsons. "Palestine Mission: Letter from Messrs. Fisk and Parsons, to the Cor. Sec. of A. B. C. F. M." *The Missionary Herald*, April (1820): 174.

discursive element for addressing the readers. It reinforces the detailed accounts given by the missionaries and places those accounts on a conceptual level shared mutually by the producers and consumers of missionary texts. As a result, intergroup communication is maintained.

For instance, one of the things the missionaries understood pretty early on was the need for a printing press and during this early phase of the mission, the missionaries were preoccupied with the idea of setting up a press for 'Western Asia.' The aim, in their words, was "to diffuse religious knowledge."[83] Referring to books, Bibles and pamphlets, and their reception by the Greek Orthodox priests, the same missionaries mention their wish to "enlighten" those priests in the fashion of the Reformation.[84] Mr. Parsons' ideas on reading the scriptures with inquirers is along the same lines. For him, reading the scriptures is one of the most effective methods "to diffuse the spirit of piety."[85] The Prudential Committee defined Fisk's and Parson's activities as "spread[ing] [...] divine truth."[86] In short, the way seems prepared for enlightening that part of the world very extensively by means of the press.[87] They could have expressed their intention of setting up a mission press and the importance of this without using any specific conceptual language. But such a narrative would seriously lack religious foundations. In the previous sections, it has been shown that a printing press is defined conceptually by metaphors of cultivation and metaphors of war. In this case, the conceptual backdrop is the domain of light. In all categories, they speak of the same notion with a slightly different emphasis. Subtle changes like this were achieved by changing the conceptual reference points. Moreover, all the conceptual metaphoric allusions are interrelated because they originate from a strictly Christian discourse. In short, the

---

83 "Printing Establishment for Western Asia." *The Missionary Herald*, March (1821): 81.

84 "Thoughts Suggested by the Preceding Journal." *The Missionary Herald*, April (1821): 101.

85 Levi Parsons. "Journal of Mr. Parsons, While at Jerusalem." *The Missionary Herald*, February (1822): 37.

86 "Report of the Prudential Committee." *The Missionary Herald*, March (1822): 67.

87 "Report of the Prudential Committee." *The Missionary Herald*, March (1821): 68.

missionary discourse is equipped with interrelated conceptual tools that can be used to refer to the same phenomena or events while at the same time maintaining the coherence of the discourse.

During their tour of Egypt in 1823, the missionaries used every opportunity to get acquainted with local people in order to propagate the 'Christian faith.' Their main activity was to deliver tracts, Bibles and pamphlets, as well as to have a chat on a personal basis. For them, "[b]y enlightening and reforming nominal Christians in Turkey" they were "preparing the way" for "convincing the followers of the false prophet of their errors, and teaching them the truth."[88] The concluding reflections in the editorial to the report by missionary Mr. Goodell on the great meeting of Armenians at Istanbul also touched upon the issue of printing presses: "[…] by the side of the presses already in operation, they might erect one for Armenia, and the pious priest and archbishop might assist in diffusing the light of life among their intelligent countrymen […]."[89] In the extracts to the missionaries Bird and Whiting, the distribution of scriptures was considered to be part of the systematic running of an evangelical mission in Lebanon and Palestine. According to the instructions given to the missionaries by the Prudential Committee of the ABCFM in 1830, "[a]s might be expected, this diffusion of light awakened much attention."[90] The source of illumination was the "light of the gospel."[91] The missionaries were sowing the good seed, cannon-balling enemy fortifications, and bringing light to people by conducting missionary work.

In order to be diffused, light needs to emanate from a source. Consequently, one can detect the conceptual metaphor **LIGHT MOVES FROM A LIGHT SOURCE**. The notions that are diffused and associated with the concept of light are knowledge, and missionary discourse. By bringing them to light, by bringing light or by bringing and diffusing them like light, the missionaries helped their targets to gain awareness. This is a typical ap-

---

88 Pliny Fisk, Jonas King. "Palestine Mission: Journal of Messrs. Fisk and King, in Upper Egypt." *The Missionary Herald*, December (1823): 376.

89 William Goodell. "Great Meeting of Armenians at Constantinople." *The Missionary Herald*, April (1827): 115.

90 "Mediterranean: Views and Proceedings in Reference to this Mission." *The Missionary Herald*, March (1830): 77.

91 *ibid*. 77.

plication of the conceptual metaphor **Aids to Gaining Awareness are Aids to Vision**, which is under the metaphor **Understanding is Seeing** and both are covered by **IDEAS ARE PERCEPTIONS**. Following the association of light with the concept of an idea, we encounter the underlying metaphor **IDEAS ARE LIGHT SOURCES** and, by expanding the notion of idea into a broader concept, namely a discourse, this conceptual background can be linked to **DISCOURSE IS A LIGHT MEDIUM**. Therefore, we can see that the missionaries were actually using a mutually understandable set of concepts displayed by metaphorical expressions that enabled them to get their meaning across clearly and precisely. By this means, the missionaries were avoiding long and arduous ways of explaining the relation of printing and distributing text materials in order to make their work flourish.

Likewise, Mr. Bird's conversation with a Maronite in Palestine about the Maronite patriarch's order that the Maronite Christians of Mount Lebanon should burn, or destroy all the books distributed by the missionaries in the year 1824 is of importance. The missionary tells the Maronite "[w]e see you in ignorance and we hope to enlighten you. We see you without the word of God, and we come to give it to you."[92] The source in the first instance is the missionaries, because they are the bearers of light. But the real source is the evangelical teaching. This case is representative of the importance of human agency and the missionary belief in divine providence. The missionaries are sources or at least carriers of light as well, and the line in this context is based on the conceptual metaphor **LIGHT MOVES FROM A LIGHT SOURCE**. Bringing light helps people see the spiritual 'truth.' By enlightening their targets, they cure their spiritual 'blindness' and help them understand the 'truth.' This brings us to the metaphor **Aids to Gaining Awareness are Aids to Vision** and its related **Understanding is Seeing**. This concept is covered by the more general concept that **IDEAS ARE PERCEPTIONS**. As the light is emanating from the teachings of the missionaries, we can also assume that this passage relies on the metaphor of **IDEAS ARE LIGHT SOURCES**. The teaching of the Gospel, the ideas in it bring light (by the help of human agency, hence missionary work to diffuse evangelical Christianity). More specifically, the organized discourse of the missionaries transports the teaching. Among other media (the Bible as

---

92 Jonas King. "Palestine Mission: Journal of Mr. King." *The Missionary Herald*, October (1825): 316.

the light giver and the missionaries as the enlighteners and light bringers), discourse is a medium that conveys the message and helps the missionaries 'enlighten.' Therefore, the line also relies upon the conceptual metaphor **DISCOURSE IS A LIGHT MEDIUM.**

The sources of light diffused as a result of missionary activities are cited in Mr. Bird's letter to the assistant secretary. He asked for the prayers of the American Christians so that the city Jerusalem might change from its desolate state because "[t]he new light, which would beam from the divine word, the pure worship and effectual prayers that would be offered, and the inquiries that would be likely to be excited among the Mussulmans, would all furnish a subject of sublime and delightful contemplation."[93]

The light is a beam, so it is consistent with the metaphor **LIGHT IS A LINE.** The light does not emanate from a vacuum, it has a source. The source mentioned in this quotation is the divine word, the Bible and other congregational texts reinforcing it. As religious knowledge is related to understanding, which is related to seeing, which is related to light, the divine word can be understood as a legitimate light source in the missionary discourse. Hence the underlying general metaphor **LIGHT MOVES FROM A LIGHT SOURCE.** It may sound like a truism that the missionaries hold the 'divine word' in high esteem and regarded it as the sole origin of what they called the 'truth.' They attach a positive value to it. The association of the divine with light/light source is a classical metaphor. When they apply this metaphor the metaphor functions through the conceptual metaphor **GOODNESS IS LIGHT / BADNESS IS DARKNESS.** The divine word includes ideas if it does not indeed consist of them. Regarded in this way, **IDEAS ARE LIGHT SOURCES** can be seen as contributing to the quotation. As the divine word is articulated in the framework of a discourse for the humans to understand, we can detect the conceptual metaphor **DISCOURSE IS A LIGHT MEDIUM** behind the linguistic metaphor.

We can also see that the missionaries used this conceptual background in daily conversation as well. In his discussion with the principal priest of the village of Deir el Qamar during his summer stay in 1823 about whether the mother of Jesus had any children subsequently to his birth, Mr. King replied to the priest, after some speculation about the possibility of this

---

93   Isaac Bird. "Letter from Mr. Bird to the Assistant Secretary." *The Missionary Herald*, November (1824): 344.

claim, that "[i]f I am in the dark, I wish to be enlightened; I do not wish to remain in the dark and go to destruction."[94]

Here the missionary is attributing the quality of a container to darkness as he depicts himself to be 'in' darkness or 'in' the dark. Therefore, the metaphorical background is **DARKNESS IS A CONTAINER**. The missionary wishes to be enlightened. The assumption is that he receives 'consciousness' with the help of God, but according to the Congregationalist teaching also through conscious efforts to attain certain knowledge. In both cases the 'light' has a source; either (or both) God or (and) the scriptures and education. This notion results from the conceptual metaphor **LIGHT MOVES FROM A LIGHT SOURCE**. In this quotation, both domains, LIGHT and DARKNESS, are articulated together with their basic connotations of being positive and negative. Apart from this normative evaluation of the concepts, the missionary subjectively states that one is his choice the other not. Hence, **GOODNESS IS LIGHT / BADNESS IS DARKNESS**. The missionary does not want to remain in the dark, because it is a metaphorical way of saying that one does not have the necessary knowledge and spiritual awareness to attain a level which will help her/him to get to the 'Kingdom of God.' Lack of understanding due to 'darkness' is a common theme. So darkness here can be seen in the light of **Impediments to Awareness are Impediments to Seeing**. In such a position one cannot 'see' (understand) the alleged 'truth.' We can assume that the missionary is also referring to an obstacle to vision by using the concept of darkness, and this brings the reader to the conceptual metaphor **Not being Aware of Reality is not Seeing Reality**. As he wants to be enlightened he wants to have a state of 'consciousness' so as to be a 'good' Christian, which is possible only through a certain kind of awareness. The light he expects to make him a good Christian is a help, an aid. Unlike the way darkness and blindness associated blindness with darkness, light will help him 'see' (understand) things. We can discern the conceptual background as **Aids to Gaining Awareness are Aids to Vision**. All these assumptions rely upon the more general conceptual metaphor **Understanding is Seeing**, which in turn is covered by **IDEAS ARE PERCEPTIONS**. Since this awareness partly results from an understanding of ideas, which is to say the missionary is also

---

94 Jonas King. "Palestine Mission: Journal of Mr. King at Dar el Kamer." *The Missionary Herald*, July (1824): 213.

enlightened by understanding certain notions, we can claim that this line is related to **IDEAS ARE LIGHT SOURCES**. In addition, since the ideas constituting the missionary and Congregationalist discourse are coherent and organized, they constitute a general discourse (which the missionaries tried to spread throughout the Ottoman Empire). This discourse is a main contributor to the 'enlightenment' process, which means one can assert that the passage contains a linguistic metaphorical use of the conceptual metaphor **DISCOURSE IS A LIGHT MEDIUM.**

We also find mixed metaphorical expressions that display two or more domains in one sentence. The sentence "[...] the way seems prepared for enlightening that part of the world very extensively [...]" is a good illustration.[95] The use of the conceptual domains 'way' and 'light' takes place in an interrelational setting. The way is prepared so as to bring evangelical teaching and increase awareness among the people. This is in accord with the missionary aim. They regard achieving this aim as reaching a point at the end of a way: hence, **Purposes are Destinations**. This concept is covered by **STATES ARE LOCATIONS.** Since the change in a person's awareness is 'reaching a point,' it can also be asserted that the missionaries employ the conceptual metaphor **CHANGE IS MOTION (Location).** In this instance, the purpose of enlightening is facilitated by the preparation of the right way. This metaphorical statement that a way to move along is prepared is a means of saying that missionary activity is made possible. This situation is reflected conceptually as **Aids to Action are Aids to Motion.** Since entering the 'way' is a requisite for 'enlightening' people, this concept is covered by **Starting a Purposeful Action is Starting Out for a Destination.** These two metaphors are parts of the general conceptual metaphor **Purposeful Action is Directed Motion to a Destination.** Similarly, whatever conditions these metaphors refer to by the concept of way, it includes certain means to enhance the process of enlightenment, and this notion can be stated as **The Means for Achieving Purposes are Routes.** This concept connects with the concept **Long Term Purposes are Destinations** because the route has the goal of enlightening people. Both metaphors are covered by the general conceptual metaphor **Life is a Journey**, which in turn is subsumed under the conceptual metaphor **LONG TERM**

---

95 "Report of the Prudential Committee." *The Missionary Herald*, March (1822): 68.

PURPOSEFUL ACTIVITY IS A JOURNEY. As the concept of enlightening is part of the quotation, we can assume that it relies on the concept that **LIGHT MOVES FROM A LIGHT SOURCE** and that the source is giving out a beneficial message, thus **GOODNESS IS LIGHT / BADNESS IS DARKNESS.** Enlightening is making the evangelical teaching available to the target groups. The idea behind bringing light to scatter an assumed darkness, as will be seen later, is helping people to see things. This spiritual awareness facilitated by human agency that brings certain teachings can be called **Aids to Gaining Awareness are Aids to Vision.** This is a sub-domain of the metaphor **Understanding is Seeing.** From here, the reader can see the umbrella metaphor **IDEAS ARE PERCEPTIONS.** The evangelical teaching and the scriptures are the main sources of enlightenment and this situation can be summarized in the metaphor **IDEAS ARE LIGHT SOURCES.** Therefore, the general discourse the missionaries derive from the scriptures and Christian teaching is the main means of enlightenment, and it can be said that this line is also a linguistic expression of the conceptual metaphor **DISCOURSE IS A LIGHT MEDIUM.**

Metaphors of light had a wide-ranging field of application. The political and social scene was no exception. Mr. Fisk and Mr. King call Egypt a "land of darkness" in their journal they kept on their travels to Upper Egypt in 1823.[96] Prior to his journey to Jerusalem from Beirut in 1825, Mr. King remarked on the hostile mood in the Holy City against the missionaries and considered the 'earthly' powers to be the "rulers of the darkness of this world."[97] Mr. Goodell provides a thorough analysis of the political and social state of the Ottoman Empire when he describes a meeting of Armenians that took place in the city. He starts his reflections by introducing the country as the "oldest and darkest part of the globe."[98] In a letter from Mr. Goodell to Mr. King dated 2 November 1826, that is published in extracts in *The Missionary Herald*, one can see that Mr. Goodell employs the metaphor of darkness while addressing his friend. He describes the opposition

---

96 Pliny Fisk, Jonas King. "Palestine Mission: Journal of Messrs. Fisk and King, in Upper Egypt." *The Missionary Herald*, December (1823): 375.

97 Jonas King. "Palestine Mission: Journal of Mr. King." *The Missionary Herald*, December (1825): 377.

98 William Goodell. "Great Meeting of Armenians at Constantinople." *The Missionary Herald*, April (1827): 114.

against the missionary activities in greater Syria as "the powers of dark-ness."[99] We see a similar expression in the journal of Mr. Smith from 1828. While conducting missionary work in Mount Lebanon at Mar Chaaya, a Greek Catholic convent, he refers to this country as a "land of darkness."[100]

The assumption here is that certain geographical locations are covered in darkness. This usage is a standard case of the metaphor **DARKNESS IS A COVER**. The association of the Ottoman Empire or its vassal states, lo-cal authorities and leaders with darkness is in line with the discontent among the missionaries with the then prevalent political and cultural envi-ronment in those locations. The attribution of the quality of darkness points to the metaphor **GOODNESS IS LIGHT / BADNESS IS DARKNESS**. Here we see that darkness, in contrast to light, is a case of either not being aware of the evangelical teachings or of intentionally rejecting them. As far as the indigenous people are concerned, the missionary position is that the people are not aware (hence missionary work among them). This unaware-ness is a major contributor to the 'darkness' in those locations. The under-lying concept is that **Not being Aware of Reality is not Seeing Reality**. This negative connotation is a different and non-affirmative articulation of its root metaphor **Understanding is Seeing** which, in turn, is related to the more general conceptual metaphor of **IDEAS ARE PERCEPTIONS**. The use of these conceptual metaphors is yet another way of writing about the place the missionaries arrived at. In the previous cases, the Ottoman Empire is defined as enemy territory (dominion of Satan, stronghold etc.) and a spiritually and politically barren land (desert, stony ground).

Mr. Smith shared his opinions on the religious prospects of Egypt after his residence in Cairo with the Corresponding Secretary of the Board in a letter dated March 1, 1827, as follows: "Egypt is at present a land of dark-ness and of the shadow of death, a land where ignorance, indifference, and wildness produce a moral darkness which may be felt."[101] The passage re-fers to darkness as an entity that can be felt. It is not clear to which sense

---

99 William Goodell: "Palestine Mission: Communications from Mr. Goodell." *The Missionary Herald*, June (1827): 178.

100 Eli Smith. "Extracts from the Journal of Mr. Smith." *The Missionary Herald*, June (1829): 178.

101 Eli Smith. "Western Asia: Letter from Mr. Smith to the Corresponding Secre-tary." *The Missionary Herald*, November (1827): 337.

the verb feel refers to, but there is a probability that this metaphor originates from the conceptual metaphor **DARKNESS IS A SOLID**. By enumerating indifference, ignorance and wildness as the origins of moral darkness, the missionaries underline that one of the fundamental conceptual metaphors is **GOODNESS IS LIGHT / BADNESS IS DARKNESS**.

Mr. Smith was uncertain about the future prospects, as can be seen in his own words: "Whether the long oppressed and suffering church of Egypt will greet with joy the light which is about to dawn upon her, or cling to the darkness in which she is enveloped as a covering to her errors, God only knows."[102] In this instance, darkness is depicted as an entity one can cling to. This tangible quality attributed to darkness originates from the conceptual metaphor **DARKNESS IS A SOLID**. The church of Egypt is depicted as enveloped in the cover of darkness. Without much effort, the conceptual metaphor **DARKNESS IS A COVER** can be detected as the source. Although the **DARKNESS IS A COVER** metaphor does not always entail it, the use of the proposition 'in' and the idea of an envelope relate it to **DARKNESS IS A CONTAINER**. Once again, the light emanates from a source because it is portrayed as dawning upon the church of Egypt. For that reason, it can be taken as being based on the metaphor **LIGHT MOVES FROM A LIGHT SOURCE**. Light is represented as a giver of joy and darkness is portrayed as a cover for errors. These notions originate from the metaphor **GOODNESS IS LIGHT / BADNESS IS DARKNESS**. Darkness is the envelope covering the errors of Egypt. The indication is that the church will receive and see the 'truth' that the missionaries propagate through light. Since the darkness hinders this process, it can be asserted that one of the functional background conceptual metaphors is **Impediments to Awareness are Impediments to Seeing** as **Seeing is Understanding**. Another assumption that can be derived from the passage is that the church of Egypt needs to be enlightened. This is the reason for conducting missionary work. If the church needs to be reminded of the teaching of the missionaries we can conclude that they lack a degree of awareness. Darkness hinders their perception and understanding. This metaphorical expression is based on the conceptual metaphor **Not being Aware of Reality is not Seeing Reality**. The missionary's suggestion for

---

102 Eli Smith. "Western Asia: Letter from Mr. Smith to the Corresponding Secretary." *The Missionary Herald*, November (1827): 337.

overcoming this problem of awareness and perception is to accept the 'light,' hence the metaphor **Aids to Gaining Awareness are Aids to Vision**. All of these metaphors originate from the metaphor **Understanding is Seeing** which is based in turn on the conceptual metaphor **IDEAS ARE PERCEPTIONS**. This passage might also be related to the conceptual metaphor **IDEAS ARE LIGHT SOURCES** because the light dawning on the church partly comes from the teachings of the missionaries. If this position is accepted, missionary discourse is also a contributor to the emanating light and this notion is related to the metaphor **DISCOURSE IS A LIGHT MEDIUM**.

Mr. Goodell's optimistic remarks following on from his account of the hardships the missionaries encountered in Syria in 1828 employs the metaphor of light as well: "But we see much evidence, that light is gradually increasing, and the knowledge of divine truth, by various ways and means, extending."[103] By these lines, missionaries are referring, among other things, to the diffusion of missionary evangelical teachings and the increase in the awareness of the target groups. Light, as associated with truth, denotes many of the qualities of what the missionaries accept as truth, but it also is the main means of converting people. The 'truth,' depicted as light, facilitates the process of conversion by changing the perceptions of the people. From a missionary point of view, it helps both the people and as a result the missionaries by enabling the targets to understand missionary ideas. **Understanding is Seeing**, for which people need light. Hence, **Aids to Gaining Awareness are Aids to Vision**. These metaphors originate from the general metaphor **IDEAS ARE PERCEPTIONS**.

The missionaries had already encountered many difficulties by 1826. As already shown, they employed metaphors of cultivation and metaphors of war in their writings in reference to the opposition and trials caused by their adversaries. These domains, however, were not the sole conceptual domains applied in missionary discourse in times of distress and tribulation. In an editorial reflection, the impediments and the missionary stance were referred to with the words "[...] amid the blackness and thundering of the

---

103 William Goodell. "Extracts from Mr. Goodell's Correspondence." *The Missionary Herald*, June (1828): 173.

impeding storm, we discern the bow of promise [...]."[104] These lines are in harmony with Mr. Goodell's reports on the state and progress of the Palestine mission from 1826. His reaction to the persecution of Protestant converts and missionaries reads as "[t]he heavens do indeed sometimes gather threatening blackness over our heads; but if we look up, we are always able to discern a 'bow in the cloud'."[105]

In these passages the darkness is over their heads and covering the sky. This is an instance of the metaphor **DARKNESS IS A COVER**. The two are also special cases of the conceptual metaphor **GOODNESS IS LIGHT / BADNESS IS DARKNESS**. Here the reference to darkness is also reinforced by the use of 'blackness.' Hence, it has the conceptual background **GOODNESS IS WHITE/ BADNESS IS BLACK**. The missionaries refer to a bow, a colorful occurrence of light as an escape from darkness and blackness. In this way, they do not lose their motivation and keep their spirits up. The bow metaphor is related to the metaphor **HOPE IS LIGHT**. The most original conceptual background is the application of weather conditions to depict their situation. The blackness, which is most likely due to the clouds and the storm, is definitely an indication of adverse situations and problems. This metaphorical expression is based on the metaphor **Adversity is Adversity due to Bad Weather**. This one is based on the conceptual metaphor **EXTERNAL CONDITIONS ARE CLIMATE**.

Lastly, the conceptual domain of light appears in connection to weather conditions. In the communications of Mr. Brewer, stationed in Istanbul, from 1827, these lines regarding the issue of converting the Jews and the prospects awaiting the missionaries are worth of notice: "The clouds, which momentarily darken its morning horizon, cannot long delay the approach of the millennial day."[106] The missionaries employ weather conditions when referring to unwanted events and obstacles to their missionary activities. This metaphorical expression results from the conceptual metaphor **Adver-**

---

104 William Goodell. "Great Meeting of Armenians at Constantinople." *The Missionary Herald*, April (1827): 115.

105 William Goodell. "State and Progress of the Palestine Mission." *The Missionary Herald*, April (1827): 110.

106 Josiah Brewer. "Mission to Western Asia: Communications of Mr. Brewer." *The Missionary Herald*, March (1828): 73.

sity is Adversity due to Bad Weather and the encompassing metaphor for it is **EXTERNAL CONDITIONS ARE CLIMATE.**

All in all, the missionaries' discourse attains a high level of effective language by projecting their activities and impressions through the filter of metaphors of light, and with that spares them the need for additional elucidation. What is more, in conjunction with its accompanying or implied metaphors of darkness, the conceptual background poses dichotomies that are central to missionary thinking. The basic distinction is made between good and bad. By relying on the assumption derived from conceptual metaphors that imply the superiority of the missionaries, they have a constant claim to be on the right side. Namely, through the association of missionary activities and discourse with 'goodness" in the context of light, they can venerate their position and undermine that of their opponents on a discursive level.

If we further pursue this basic dichotomy, we see that the missionaries represent what they narrate by automatically assuming the moral and ideological upper hand. Once the basic assumptions of the conceptual metaphors are accepted and internalized, both by the missionaries and the readers, their claims were most likely presented as the truth or the way things really were. The consequence of such a process of naturalization is the missionary claim to ultimate truth. Any idea, person, political entity, geographical region or activity that does not belong to the realm of light belongs to the realm of darkness. As such, they are by default false. As displayed, other conceptual metaphors derived from this background define the nature of knowledge and the state of knowing. Accordingly, the missionary narrative applies the motif of missionary discourse as untainted truth confronted with obstacles that are in the realm of darkness. It is a highly efficient means for maintaining a monopoly on knowledge.

3.5 WAY / PATH / ROAD

This line of conceptual metaphors and their metaphorical expressions in the texts are important as far as the missionary idea of conducting purposeful activity is concerned. The metaphors not only shed light on the mechanisms of conceptualization in the notions of purpose and aim in the missionary context, but also on the underlying teleological web of ideas that enables them to reproduce the missionary discourse at an institutional level that transcends generations. The idea of the Millennium is all over the texts, wherever these metaphors occur.

Regarding the motion and the mobility of the missionaries during this period of extensive exploration, it is quite probable that they also employed these metaphors as a reference to the physical ways-roads-paths they traveled along. Yet, the main meaning seems to lie in the domain of abstraction and conceptual metaphors, and as tools of interpretation for their experiences and situations. The notion of a way is a substratum on which the missionaries can make their discourse in reference to a spiritual journey and the whole missionary endeavor conducted on that way.

The very first use of this conceptual domain is in the letter of Fisk and Parsons to the Corresponding Secretary of the Board written in 1820. The lines read "the way is preparing for the diffusion of the blessings of salvation."[107] The diffusion of the blessings of salvation will be achieved by using a 'way' according to the missionary discourse. This way is a metaphorical way 'on' which the missionaries conduct their activities and encounter opportunities. The concept of way entails the idea of a journey and an end. It is not hard to guess what the missionaries regarded as the end of the way: conversion of their target groups and the coming of the Millennium. The implied end is the achievement of the purpose and this idea comes from the conceptual metaphor **Purposes are Destinations**. It is subsumed under the more general metaphor **STATES ARE LOCATIONS**. The missionaries were of the opinion that their efforts would change the state of mission work and the people they propagate it to. The metaphor of the way requires the concept of motion (journey, travel) and the attempted change is conceptualized as motion, hence, **CHANGE IS MOTION**. The preparation of the way helps the activity of the missionaries. Conducting activity is conceptualized as a journey by the use of the metaphor 'way.' A journey indicates motion. The metaphor behind this understanding is **Aids to Action are Aids to Motion**. The missionaries are willing to 'walk' the 'way' that is prepared. They will walk and reach their destination, the Millennium. This understanding is the result of the metaphor **Starting a Purposeful Action**

---

107 Pliny Fisk, Levi Parsons. "Palestine Mission: Letter from Messrs. Fisk and Parsons, to the Cor. Sec. of A. B. C. F. M." *The Missionary Herald*, April (1820): 173.

is Starting Out for a Destination. Both metaphors are based upon **Purposeful Action is Directed Motion to a Destination**. As already stated, the way as a metaphor is related to how the missionary activities are conducted. Missionary activities are purposeful actions. The idea that those activities are conducted on and through a way is connected to the metaphor **The Means For Achieving Purposes are Routes**. It is also stated that the notion of way is connected to the notion of a destination (the Millennium). Implicitly we encounter here the conceptual metaphor **Longterm Purposes are Journey Destinations**. Both of them originate from the commonly applied metaphor **Life is a Journey** and it occurs under **LONGTERM PURPOSEFUL ACTIVITY IS A JOURNEY**.

Conceptualizing mission work in terms of a way also appears in an editorial note accompanying letters from Parsons and Fisk from 1820. The people who facilitated mission work were depicted as "employed as agents and pioneers, in preparing the way for the gospel."[108] The following phrase appeared in the report of the Prudential Committee of the Board from 1821 is another instance of the application of the metaphor of way in the missionary texts: "[…] the way seems prepared for enlightening that part of the world very extensively [...]."[109] Still at the very early stage of mission work, the missionaries denote future activity and success by this conceptual domain, as can be seen in the sentence: "[…] by enlightening and reforming nominal Christians in Turkey, we are preparing the way."[110] A similar example can be found in the following lines from the journal of Mr. Goodell, written on March 20, 1824, in which he displays his concern for the success of the Palestine mission: "The way may be prepared for preaching the Gospel [...] to these men of cruelty and blood, and for directing unto Him, who is 'the way, the truth, and the life,' these wanderers from happiness and heaven."[111] These examples are instances of **Purposes are Des-**

---

108 Pliny Fisk, Levi Parsons. "Letters of Messrs. Parsons and Fisk to the Corresponding Secretary." *Missionary Herald*, March (1821): 77.

109 "Report of the Prudential Committee." *The Missionary Herald*, March (1822): 68.

110 Pliny Fisk, Jonas King. "Palestine Mission: Journal of Messrs. Fisk and King, in Upper Egypt." *The Missionary Herald*, December (1823): 376.

111 William Goodell. "Palestine Mission: Journal of Mr. Goodell." *The Missionary Herald*, November (1824): 343.

tinations, which is a subcase of **STATES ARE LOCATIONS, Progress is Forward Motion** which is a subcase of **CHANGE IS MOTION, Progress is Forward Movement** and **Starting a Purposeful Action is Starting Out for a Destination,** which are subcases of **Purposeful Action is Directed Motion to a Destination,** and **The Means For Achieving Purposes are Routes** and **Progress is the Distance Traveled,** which are subcases of **LONG TERM PURPOSEFUL ACTIVITY IS A JOURNEY.**

At least on one occasion the concept aids personal self-reflection and orientation. Levi Parsons wrote in his journal from 1821 that he was reminded by a crowing of a cock of Peter on his first Sabbath in Jerusalem. His reaction was to utter the following words, and to write them down in his journal: "Cause me to know the way wherein I should walk; for I lift up my soul unto thee."[112]

These quotations are instances of the conceptual metaphor **Purposes are Destinations** which comes under **STATES ARE LOCATIONS.** The notions of walking on a way and being guided entail the notion of motion. Hence, **Guided Action is Guided Motion.** The guidance is the incentive to start 'walking' on the right path, which actually is achieving a purpose, and the conceptual metaphor here is **Starting a Purposeful Action is Starting Out for a Destination.** These metaphors are covered by **Purposeful Action is Directed Motion to a Destination.** Guidance is reminiscent of the notion of a right path and having a proper destination to reach. Lifting the soul up to God or achieving eternal life is a purpose that can be achieved over a very long time. The concept behind the metaphorical expressions is **Longterm Purposes are Journey Destinations.** It comes from **Life is a Journey,** which is a subordinate case of **LONGTERM PURPOSEFUL ACTIVITY IS A JOURNEY.**

It is no surprise to find metaphors that denote long-term purposeful activities in missionary discourse. The Congregationalist presupposition that history has an end is treated thoroughly by conceptually integrating it into missionary writings. Metaphors of way/path/road lie at the center of this conceptualization (another set of metaphors that stem from the conceptual metaphors of door and opening is discussed in the following section). The purpose is to facilitate the coming of the Kingdom by converting the peo-

---

112 Levi Parsons. "Journal of Mr. Parsons, While at Jerusalem." *The Missionary Herald*, February (1822): 33.

ples of the world. The end point to which missionary activities should bring humanity is the Millennium. The missionary narrative functions in the confines of a conceptualization of time which progresses in a linear direction towards the future. In this linear progression, the sum of events and everything related to them inevitably goes in one direction which will end up with the coming of the Millennium. The missionary narrative takes missionary activity to be at the core of a linear historical time flow as it is one of the, if not the most influential, elements in defining the path for the Second Coming. As such, the missionary activity in particular and the Congregationalist endeavor more generally are separate from the overall flow. They are limited, narrow, and have the aim of funneling all human activity into its clear cut and well defined borders: a way.

3.6 DOOR / OPENING

The conceptualization of the teleological ideas of the missionaries and the propagation of the Millennium by the metaphors of way/path/road is not enough for an organization whose first priority is to start a well-functioning mission. The missionary spirit entails a keen eye for opportunities, and the missionaries of the Board were well aware of this. While relating their observations and experiences, the missionaries employed an interesting set of conceptual metaphors to refer to the opportunities they encountered. Like the rest, these metaphors also constitute a coherent web interacting with other networks of metaphors, especially with that of way/path/road. In a way, this set of metaphors is complementary to the metaphors of road. While the road defines or shows 'the path to be walked upon,' the metaphors for referring to opportunities indicate the entrance points to this road.

Fisk and Parsons wrote to the Corresponding Secretary of the Board from Malta, on December 23, 1819, to express their excitement at their journey from Malta to Izmir which is to take place in a couple of days. They were "anxious to be there" and "see what prospects open before" them.[113] Having arrived at Izmir, Fisk and Parsons realized that the mission

---

113 Pliny Fisk, Levi Parsons. "Letter from the Rev. Messrs. Fisk and Parsons, to the Corresponding Secretary of the A.B.C.F.M." *The Missionary Herald*, May (1820): 232.

field is a rough one. In another letter to the Corresponding Secretary from Izmir, dated February 8, 1820, they made it clear that there were "many adversaries," yet they "trust a great and effectual door is opening."[114] Fisk and Parson's journal from the summer of 1820 that tells of their work on the island of Chios is followed by an editorial commentary titled "Thoughts Suggested by the Preceding Journal." Considering various opportunities for the mission work, the commentary expressed the opinion that "a delightful and animating prospect is here opened for the operations of Christian benevolence."[115] In another letter from Izmir, dated December 4, 1820, Fisk and Parsons wrote that the distribution of Bibles and religious tracts was the most effective method at the time and "[i]n this respect a wide and effectual door of usefulness is opened."[116] In his journal from the end of 1820 and beginning of 1821, Parsons related his observations during his journey from Izmir to Jerusalem and reflected on his three month stay in the Holy City. For him "[t]he station must not be relinquished" because "the door" was "already open."[117] On November 22 1821, Pliny Fisk wrote to the Corresponding Secretary on the tumultuous situation in the Ottoman Empire, and reflected on the Greek uprisings. He was not concerned and he believed that the turmoil was not detrimental to the missionary cause. On the contrary, Fisk believed that "[i]t may open a wide door, for the circulation of the scriptures, the establishment of schools, and the diffusion of evangelical truth."[118] In February and March 1823, missionaries Fisk and King visited Upper Egypt. They received a letter written by one Mr. Salt on behalf of the pasha, requesting them in a kind manner to forbear discussing religious subjects with the Muslims. The missionaries interpreted this warning as "a wide and promising field actually laid open before" them "for labors among

---

114 *ibid.* 265.

115 "Thoughts Suggested by the Preceding Journal." *The Missionary Herald*, April (1821): 101.

116 Pliny Fisk, Levi Parsons. "Letter of Messrs. Parsons and Fisk to the Corresponding Secretary." *The Missionary Herald*, July (1821): 206.

117 Levi Parsons. "Palestine Mission: Journal of Mr. Parsons." *The Missionary Herald*, January (1822): 19.

118 Pliny Fisk. "Palestine Mission: Extracts of a Letter from Mr. Fisk to the Corresponding Secretary." *The Missionary Herald*, April (1822): 111.

nominal Christians and Jews."[119] They were cautious though not to disobey the pasha's warning: "It seems improper to cause it to be shut against us, by attempting to force open a door, which Providence seems to have closed against us."[120] This was a tactical retreat as the following sentence reads "[s]till opportunities may occasionally occur of giving the Scriptures to Mussulmen, and of speaking to them about Christianity."[121]

At the early stages of the mission, the missionaries were still preoccupied with the issue of converting the Muslim population of the Empire. Pliny Fisk's letter from Syria dated October 1823 includes a section headed "On the Conversion of the Mussulmen." The missionary believed "[p]ossibly some great political evolution" was "to open the door for preaching of the Gospel to the followers of the false prophet."[122] Missionary Bird's letter from March 1824 dwells on the same issue. To him their chances of converting the Muslim population of Jerusalem could be easily judged before they have the opportunity of conversing with the people. In this respect "the door" seemed "quite open for effort among them [...]."[123]

One of the topics in the April 1827 issue of *The Missionary Herald* is the state and progress of the Palestine mission. The information was compiled from the intelligence reports given by Goodell from January 3 to October 18, 1826. He gave an overall encouraging and positive account. For the conversion of the Maronite Christians around Mount Lebanon, which had become an important topic due to the severe persecution conducted by the Maronite patriarchate, Goodell likewise espied an open door: "A wide and effectual door does [...] seem to be opening for us, and work, more than we can do, to be ready prepared for our hands."[124] In a letter from October 1826, missionary Bird wrote that he and Goodell held reading sessions with the locals in their houses in Beirut. Although he was content that

---

119 Pliny Fisk, Jonas King. "Palestine Mission: Journal of Messrs. Fisk and King, in Upper Egypt." *The Missionary Herald*, December (1823): 376.

120 *ibid*. 376.

121 *ibid*. 376.

122 Pliny Fisk. "Journal of Mr. Fisk." *The Missionary Herald*, October (1824): 306.

123 Isaac Bird. "Letter from Mr. Bird to the Assistant Secretary." *The Missionary Herald*, November (1824): 344.

124 "State and Progress of the Palestine Mission." *The Missionary Herald*, April (1827): 110.

they had an audience, he was looking forward to preaching in the field; an activity which later extended the reach of the missionaries enormously: "When the time will come that we can venture to appear abroad as field preachers, we know not, but when the door shall be open for this sort of labor, I hope we shall have grace to enter it without delay."[125]

In another instance, the missionaries appealed to war and disorder as an opportunity that emerged on the scene in 1827. On October 20, the joint English, French and Russian forces destroyed the Ottoman fleet at Navarino, Greece. The missionaries could not find a proper mission field in Greece during the founding years and they celebrated this occasion by stating that "[...] it must open Greece to the influence of the Gospel, hasten the decline and fall of the bloody crescent of Mahommed, and ultimately exert no small influence on all the missionary operations in the east."[126] The missionaries did not stop there. Their hope was that "[...] the Greek Empire may rise again from the dust, and take possession of her own capital" and "Asia Minor may be opened to the researches of the scholar, and to the labors of the missionary."[127] These exemplary lines are a great demonstration of the missionaries' character as pragmatic opportunity-seekers. One can see here a 'the enemy of my enemy is my friend' mentality, even though the missionaries presented themselves as peaceful men of religion to the Ottoman State and hid their real aims.

But not every case of war was a welcome opportunity. The possibility of war in Syria in 1829 worried the missionaries. They prayed to God "[...] to open a wide and effectual door to the blessed Gospel in these dominions of the prince of darkness."[128] Their appeal is understandable in the light of the fact that the Syrian field including Mount Lebanon had proven to be promising, as expressed in a letter from Goodell in which he compares Malta and Syria. The missionaries chose Malta as the location of the to-be-

---

125 Isaac Bird. "Palestine Mission: Journal of Mr. Bird." *The Missionary Herald*, October (1827): 305.

126 "Western Asia: Proceedings of Messrs. Brewer and Gridley." *The Missionary Herald*, January (1828): 19.

127 "Destruction of the Turkish and Egyptian Fleets at Navarino." *The Missionary Herald*, January (1828): 20.

128 Isaac Bird. "Syria: Journal of Mr. Bird." *The Missionary Herald*, April (1829): 112.

established mission press because of the favorable atmosphere created by the umbrella of British protection. Despite this choice, Goodell cannot help expressing his opinion that "[...] though a great and effectual door cannot be said to be open in Syria, so long as the civil power [...] lends its aid to" the adversaries of the missionaries, Syria appears to be a far more promising field for missionary labor, than Malta.[129]

An opening implies entrance. In order to go through an open door, one should move forward. To the missionaries these openings are opportunities and a crucial element of success. That is why they were eager to seek and take advantage of 'openings.' By going through, they would move forward and gain ground, in other words they would progress. Accordingly, these passages can be evaluated as verbal expressions of the conceptual metaphor **Progress is Forward Motion**. It is covered by **CHANGE IS MOTION**. As they saw opportunities these lines are also instances of **Available Opportunities are Objects within Reach, Opportunities are Open Paths** and consequently **OPPORTUNITIES ARE OBJECTS**.

An Armenian convert and missionary associate, Dionysius Carabet, traveled with Armenian pilgrims from Jerusalem to Beirut in 1827. He celebrated the opportunity to converse with the pilgrims and concluded that a "[...] great and effectual road was opened to" him.[130] In this passage, the opening is to a road. The missionary uses the opportunity. Hence, **Opportunities are Open Paths**. This is an instance of the application of the metaphor **Purposes are Destinations** and it comes under the general conceptual metaphor **STATES ARE LOCATIONS**. The missionary enters from an opening to a road, according to his own expression. He advances in his endeavor to propagate the Gospel on this road. In other words, he moves forward and gets closer to his aim. This is a case of the application of **Progress is Forward Motion**, which is based on **CHANGE IS MOTION**. As the missionaries were not fond of the way mission work was conducted as a result of the restrictions imposed on them associating with the local people, this opening was the cause of positive change in missionary activity. Hence, **Means of Change of Action is Path**. This metaphor is related to a

---

129 William Goodell. "Mediterranean: Letter from Mr. Goodell." *The Missionary Herald*, December (1830): 375.

130 Eli Smith. "Western Asia: Letter from Mr. Smith to the Corresponding Secretary." *The Missionary Herald*, November (1827): 343.

more general metaphor: **MEANS OF CHANGE IS PATH OVER WHICH MOTION OCCURS**. The opening is an opportunity, thus an aid to missionary activity. By means of this aid, the missionary can enter the open road and continue his way. The underlying conceptual metaphor is **Aids to Action are Aids to Motion**. Since missionary work is highly structured and serves a higher purpose, entrance to a road is based on the conceptual metaphor of **Starting a Purposeful Action is Starting Out for a Destination**. Both are covered by **Purposeful Action is Directed Motion to a Destination**.

New missionaries in the field were likewise adept in using missionary discourse. Missionary Eli Smith wrote a report headed "Hints Respecting the Political State of the Countries Near Mount Lebanon" published in *The Missionary Herald* in September 1829. The short article, which handled the matter precisely and presented the situation in a nutshell, starts with the sentence "[t]here are various ways, in which Providence can open this interesting land to the power of the Gospel."[131]

This quotation is based on the metaphor **MEANS OF CHANGE IS PATH OVER WHICH MOTION OCCURS**. This motion can be regarded as forward movement occurring on the metaphorical road, and the conceptual background for this notion is **Progress is Forward Movement**. Since this journey is aimed at reaching a certain destination (missionary aims), the metaphor is covered by **Purposeful Action is Directed Motion to a Destination**.

These examples make the connection between metaphors of opening to metaphors of road more comprehensible. The two sets of metaphors seem to be functioning in the same conceptual domain. Yet the relation is not an equal one. Road metaphors determine the central domain and are more general. This is not to say that road metaphors encompass opening metaphors, though. Rather, conceptualization of road in the missionary metaphors is a requirement for metaphors of opening. The reason is that metaphors of opening refer to the entrance of a road and these metaphorical expressions of entrance express the concept of opportunity.

Missionary activity depends on opportunities. Without favorable or advantageous circumstances or suitable occasions, the mission is destined to

---

131 Eli Smith. "Syria: Hints Respecting its Political State." *The Missionary Herald*, September (1829): 279.

abort itself. Thus, the first action the missionaries took was to consider their opportunities. For instance, there were no favorable 'openings' regarding Muslims and Jews. But the missionaries kept looking and found a suitable 'door' among the Armenians of the empire and followed that 'path.' It is displayed in the fourth chapter that they did not abandon all hope of starting a mission among the Muslims, and metaphors of opening were still at use as a handy conceptual tool. Another example is the application of metaphors of opening in the aftermath of the Armenian massacres of 1894-96. As shown in the second part of chapter four, these metaphors still highlighted the opportunity-seeking nature of missionary activities on top of being discursive tools of empowerment and motivation. In short, one aspect of these metaphors is that they depict and indicate opportunities. Another aspect is that they reinforce patterns of opportunity-seeking at a discursive level and make this quality a central part of missionary narrative.

3.7 INVECTIVES

The missionaries were representing the outer world by their own means. Invectives are a part of that representation. Metaphors are a more organized means of presentation (in themselves and for others). Invectives are related to their intellectual background as well, but they do not immediately relate to higher abstractions such as Christian theology or ideology. As exploratory tools they have limited use in this discourse because they lack deeper conceptualizations. Metaphors have that value and do display a pattern. Actually, all of the metaphorical domains discussed in this chapter are interrelated in the missionary discourse as a web of meanings, just as they are in the Bible. As such, it may be claimed that the metaphorical network is a mega- or meta-topographical trope used to depict an era of exploration and travel. No other element in their discourse constitutes such a powerful tool as the metaphors. An underlying network of conceptual metaphor web constantly defines and redefines external situations and depicts them to the American audience (which also changes constantly) while the missionaries are forever exploring and learning about a land, a country, namely the provinces of the Ottoman Empire, they have already explored in the past.

The form of language discussed in this section is comprised by insults and hasty generalizations, either uttered with preconceived ideas or drawn from the missionaries' personal encounters with the local people during their trips to the Eastern Mediterranean. In imagological terms, the Ottoman Empire, which reached its zenith in the seventeenth century, was the strongest 'other' of European Christendom with the attributed qualities of alienness, cruelty and tyranny underlined by an Islamic character.[132] The image was so strong that the Ottoman Empire also became exemplary of the image of 'oriental despotism.'[133] It is also very likely that the missionary discourse was aware of these stereotyped images. But biased opinions only partially explain the process of resorting to invective. Its use might be a result of frustration, lack of knowledge, limited experience, anger, fundamentalist views, or a combination of some or all of these.

The organizational standpoint of the Board regarding their target groups is summarized by the Prudential Committee as a one-way influence from "the Christian world for the benefit of the heathen."[134] The dichotomy of Christian people versus "the heathen" seems to be a deeply-rooted motif with descriptive and operative value. Consequently, the affirmative value attributed to being a Christian is defined in contrast to a negation. A less subtle way of putting the matter into words was calling foreign people "barbarous nations."[135] The official aim was summarized as "work of evangelizing and civilizing pagan and uncultured people."[136]

Emerging from such a substrate are the missionary observations conveyed to the American public via *The Missionary Herald*. Hence, one of the first published comments of Fisk and Parsons reads "Mahomedans are fatalists in theory, and probably are influenced more in practice by their theory, than any other class of men who ever lived."[137] The observation can be

---

132 Nedret Kuran-Burçoğlu. "Turkey." *Imagology*. Eds. Manfred Beller; Joep Leerssen. Amsterdam: Rodopi (2007): 255.

133 *ibid.* 255.

134 "Address of the Prudential Committee." *The Missionary Herald*, March (1820): 137.

135 "Present Encouraging Aspect of the Unevangelized Parts of the World." *The Missionary Herald*, February (1820): 55.

136 "Report of the Prudential Committee." *The Missionary Herald*, January (1821): 3.

137 Pliny Fisk, Levi Parsons. "Letter from the Rev. Messrs. Fisk and Parsons." *The Missionary Herald*, June (1820): 266.

regarded as a generalization inferred from limited factual evidence or experience. One year later, the two pioneer missionaries fall into the pit of generalization again, this time reducing their sample group. Having visited an inn, they concluded that "[t]he Turk seemed to live principally by his pipe and his coffee."[138] It should be noted that throughout the history of the mission, the missionaries struggled to get in touch with the Muslims and the Turks. One of the main drawbacks, among many others, was the lack of access to what the missionaries called the "Turkish mind."[139] [140] The Ottoman government's harsh policy of confining the missionaries to a restricted audience and practically shunning them from conducting mission work among Muslims, and therefore Turks, was one of the reasons for their limited success in figuring out how the 'Turkish mind' worked. Yet, the biased opinions and self-centered exclusive standpoint of the missionaries were other elements in the failure to convert Turks. Since they were not hesitant in drawing conclusions from anecdotal evidence, they hastily resorted to insult and humiliation as well. For Parsons and Fisk, prophet Mohammad was "the false prophet."[141] The expression can also be found as a stock phrase in later missionary writings.

One of the main reasons that triggered abusive language in the early missionary discourse was the missionaries' ideas of civilization and progress. Being part of an inherently reactionary institution alluding to a past golden age that was to be revived in future times, millennialist missionaries had a keen interest in ancient Biblical history and archeology. Yet what they found did not match their ideas and expectations. When Fisk and Parsons visited the relics of the ancient city of Sardes near Manisa, they could not bear the contrast between an idealized past and the reality. The Turkish

---

138 Pliny Fisk, Levi Parsons. "Palestine Mission: Journal of Messrs. Fisk and Parsons, During Their Tour in Asia Minor." *The Missionary Herald*, August (1821): 252.

139 George F. Herrick. "Western Turkey: Letter from Mr. Herrick." *The Missionary Herald*, April (1862): 120.

140 For further information see Chapter 4.

141 "Report of the Prudential Committee." *The Missionary Herald*, March (1821): 68; Pliny Fisk, Levi Parsons. "Palestine Mission: Letter from Messrs. Parsons and Fisk to the Corresponding Secretary." *The Missionary Herald*, July (1821): 206.

village next to the ruins lacked a proper infrastructure and it was economically hindered as well. Moved by the desolate state of a city named in the Bible and that housed one of the Seven Churches of Asia, Fisk and Parsons blamed the "ignorant, stupid, filthy Turks."[142] The disappointment grew even larger when they entered the 'Holy Land.' Describing the surroundings of the Pool of Siloam in Jerusalem, Fisk and King attributed the place's safety problems to "wild Arabs and infatuated Turks."[143] For the missionaries, everybody else was wrong and they were right. Whatever other people believed was flawed and only the missionaries preached the truth. Their first impressions from Jerusalem were as follows:

The Jews hate the name of Christ, and when you mention it, some of them will almost gnash on you with their teeth. The Turks exalt the name of their false prophet above his most glorious name, and are pre-eminently distinguished for their hypocrisy, tyranny and lying. The Greeks and Armenians profane the temple of the Lord, and seem to know very little of the true nature of Christianity.[144]

The writers of this passage, Pliny Fisk and Jonas King, had already displayed their aptitude in stereotyping and degrading other people on their way to Jerusalem. In one instance, as they visited the ruins of Karnack, Egypt, they ascribed the apparent poverty to "ignorant and miserable Arabs, and Mussulmans."[145] Likewise, William Goodell and Isaac Bird resorted to their repertoire of stereotypes and clichés and pointed to the "desolation of Turkish despotism" as the main reason for the silent atmosphere in Larnaca, Cyprus.[146] The idea of oriental despotism was a recurring theme in mission-

---

142 Pliny Fisk, Levi Parsons. "Palestine Mission: Journal of Messrs. Fisk and Parsons, During Their Tour in Asia Minor." *The Missionary Herald*, August (1821): 252-253.

143 Pliny Fisk, Jonas King. "Palestine Mission: Journal of Messrs. Fisk and King." *The Missionary Herald*, March (1824): 66.

144 "Palestine Mission: Journal of Messrs. Fisk and King." *The Missionary Herald*, March (1824): 68.

145 Pliny Fisk, Jonas King. "Palestine Mission: Journal of Messrs. Fisk and King in Upper Egypt." *The Missionary Herald*, November (1823): 348.

146 William Goodell, Isaac Bird. "Palestine Mission: Journal of Messrs. Goodell and Bird." *The Missionary Herald*, August (1824): 240.

ary writings. Expressions such as "land of oppression and sin"[147] and "Turkish barbarity"[148] were common. Pliny Fisk reported from Beirut that they were "in a land of Turks, tyranny, superstition, and intolerance."[149] Beirut was chosen by the missionaries for their mission headquarters and as a consequence, their reflections on the locals were widely published. One of the first encounters and the way the missionaries conveyed it is exemplary of the missionaries' position. On the first day William Goodell and Isaac Bird arrived in Beirut, their ship dropped anchor 4 miles off shore at Beirut in order to wait for boats that would convey the cargo and passengers to harbor. The missionaries did not like the turmoil that ensued on the arrival of the boats and called the porters "half naked and barbarous Arabs."[150] Their discontent was not to abate. In one of his letters, William Goodell complained about the "wretchedness of the present inhabitants of this country"[151] while Jonas King referred to the Alawite population of Lebanon as "impure" and "barbarous."[152] Their first years in Beirut were a time of trial and tribulation, and the inexperienced missionaries had difficulty coping with the misfortunes their new settings brought them. This fact might have added to the bitter tone stirred up by their deeply rooted prejudices. Discouraged and demoralized, Goodell started one of his reports with his records of the weather in Beirut, continued with the shortage of bread and goods, and finally complained about "the stupidity, ignorance, superstitions, bondage, and wickedness, in almost every form, of the people."[153] The reflections on a German colony and a church service the missionaries

---

147 Jonas King. "Palestine Mission: Journal of Mr. King." *The Missionary Herald*, October (1824): 312.

148 William Goodell. "Mediterranean: Letter from Mr. Goodell." *The Missionary Herald*, November (1826): 358.

149 Pliny Fisk. "Palestine Mission: Letter from Mr. Fisk." *The Missionary Herald*, March (1825): 68.

150 William Goodell, Isaac Bird. "Extract from the Journal of Messrs. Goodell and Bird." *The Missionary Herald*, July (1824): 214.

151 William Goodell. "Palestine Mission: Journal of Mr. Goodell." *The Missionary Herald*, September (1824): 275.

152 *ibid.* 275.

153 William Goodell. "Palestine Mission: Climate of Syria." *The Missionary Herald*, November (1825): 347.

attended at that colony near Tbilisi by H. G. O. Dwight and Eli Smith can likewise be read as an allusion to the missionary aims, experiences and ideology regarding the 'other' in a nutshell:

It cannot but be regarded as a peculiar providence, that these people were induced to leave their native land, and come to this distance, and settle down among nations in many respects uncivilized and barbarous; and their influence cannot fail to be salutary, bringing with them, as they do, the arts of civilization and the privileges of religion."[154]

All these generalizations, stereotypes and ethnic slurs can be termed invectives. Invective is censure of a person by means of pejorative epithets.[155] The missionary language of prejudice, name-calling and humiliation functions through these invectives on the surface of the missionary discourse. The people of the 'Orient' were thus represented in plain words to the American public. Sharp dichotomies such as civilization versus barbarity, progress versus backwardness, intelligence versus stupidity, cleanliness versus filthiness portrayed the new mission as legitimate and necessary, both to the Board itself and to the supporters of the missionary cause.[156]

---

154 Eli Smith, H. G. O. Dwight. "Mediterranean: Extracts from Letters of Messrs. Smith and Dwight." *The Missionary Herald*, January (1831): 18.

155 M.H. Abrams; Geoffrey Galt Harpham. *A Glossary of Literary Terms*. Boston: Wadsworth (2009): 164.

156 The missionary writings are reminiscent of Edward Said's definition of Orientalism as "the corporate institution for dealing with the Orient – dealing with it by making statements about it, authorizing views of it, describing it, by teaching it, settling it, ruling over it: in short, Orientalism as a Western style for dominating, restructuring, and having authority over the Orient." (Edward W. Said. *Orientalism*. New York: Pantheon Books (1978): 3). Yet Said's dichotomy of an ontological and epistemological distinction between the 'Orient' and the 'Occident,' together with his methodic exclusion of the United States from his analysis, makes it hard to incorporate his notion into this work, which deals mainly with conceptual metaphorical formations originating from the United States.

Invective, unlike irony, is direct.[157]

The clarity of plain invectives, however, should not be confused with simplicity. The missionaries assumed that their audience was quite capable of decoding and perceiving the intellectual background behind their words. All the allusions to civilization, progress, the people's level of intelligence, moral issues, infrastructure and moral decay was articulated through a Congregationalist Calvinist intellectual and religious heritage. Therefore, any idea of civilization was strictly connected to Christianity and it was a specific form of Christianity. The readers of *The Missionary Herald* were probably well informed about Protestant notions on such matters. Postmillennialism's dependence on human agency in preparing the Kingdom was the key to the missionary stance.[158] The belief in the realization of the Golden Age or Millennium before the Second Coming was the greatest reason and justification for the commencement of the American overseas missions. Given these postmillennialist religious roots, secular advancements in agriculture, infrastructure, education, sciences and government were cherished.[159] The missionaries were well equipped with religious ideas pertaining to secular issues, as were their readers. As propagators of 'truth,' they had no doubt in their minds of the superiority of 'Christian civilization.' As a consequence, a simple word like 'stupid' was laden with a set of meanings derived from the Calvinist roots of New England Protestantism. While events unfolded, millennialist thought exhibited its ability to conform to political and social changes in the appropriate manner. The French and Indian War was seen as a millennial event and the French and the Indians were associated with the Antichrist, while British victory was cheered by the millennialists as a sign that the colonists were the chosen people who would build the New Kingdom.[160] As the threat of French dominion dwindled and the colonists gained considerable economic success, the issue of

---

157 M.H. Abrams, Geoffrey Galt Harpham. *A Glossary of Literary Terms*. Boston: Wadsworth (2009): 165.

158 For 'human agency' see Chapter 4.

159 For a more detailed discussion of antinomies arising from acceptance of secular progress and Christian eschatology at the same time see section "4.3.3.1. Teleology and the Millennium" in Chapter 4.

160 Robert Fuller. *Naming the Antichrist: The History of an American Obsession*. Oxford: Oxford University Press (1995): 68-70.

taxes imposed by the British government grew to be a new problem. The outbreak of violence brought about by the American Revolution compelled the millennialist rhetoric to consider King George III as the Antichrist.[161] As a reaction to this politicization, New Divinity thought turned to the meaning of the scriptural word. According to Ruth Bloch, it was "[...] a theological backlash against the earlier politicization of prophecy and a revitalization of the more universalistic, cosmic, and utopian elements in millennial symbolism."[162] The violent character of the French Revolution accompanied by religious decline caused great distress among American Protestant circles and this revolution was associated with the imminent Millennium.[163] After the revolution, the ties between Republicanism and postmillennialist thought were loosened and millennialists focused on spreading their belief.[164] Under these circumstances, the identification of the Antichrist and millennial actors shifted again. After a brief interval, the Roman Catholic Church, Muslims (as the Turkish Antichrist), and Jews regained their importance as millennial actors. Turks and Muslims as an antichristian power became one of the main subjects in the postmillennial theory once again. Ruth H. Bloch analyses the situation as follows:

This renewed eschatological interest in the downfall of the Pope often came along with similar predictions about the destruction of the Turkish Empire. Although the Islamic Turks had long been regarded as an antichristian power throughout the European world, and had been viewed as such in earlier English and American works of prophetic interpretation, it was only late in the eighteenth century that this became a major theme in American millennial literature. In the late 1780s both Charles Crawford and Benjamin Gale described the future demise of the Turks as an event almost equivalent to the collapse of the Papacy [...] Samuel Osgood in 1794 insisted that one of the Beasts in Revelation represented the Turks alone, not a combination of Turkish and papal power. He expected the final defeat of the Turkish Empire to occur in 1890, after which would proceed the Second Advent and, finally, the beginning of the millennium in 1960 [...].[165]

---

161 ibid. 71-73.
162 Bloch, *Visionary Republic*, 122.
163 ibid. 214-215.
164 ibid. 215.
165 ibid. 145.

In 1805, Nathan Strong, the Hartford evangelical leader, asserted that Christianity would progress throughout the globe by winning over Turks, Heathens, and Jews.[166] The conversion of Jews was another question. For Edwards "[i]n the fullness of time, the beast of Rome will be destroyed; all Christians will accept the true church; the Jews and the heathen will be converted to Christianity."[167] In addition, it was assumed the Jewish people must return to the Holy Land so that the Millennium could come into its own.[168] Millennialism turned its face to the global scene and it was considered that the Millennium was close at hand. In all these events, the source of explanation and assessment is religion. William Goodell, one of the first missionaries to Palestine, underlined this fact when he disapprovingly commented on how various groups and religions of the region hold their services in archaic languages that could not be understood by the congregations, and mentioned that the sixth chapter of Jeremiah and the Book of Prophets had already represented the "character and wretchedness of the present inhabitants of this country."[169]

The use of invective was justified by referencing the Bible and had its roots in Biblical allusions. Yet unlike conceptual metaphors, which likewise originated from the Bible, they were easy to articulate and understand. Being so, they provided the missionaries with a blunt but effective tool when introducing their target groups and the state of the lands where these people dwelled. In short, abusive language was employed to refer to people, geographical places and abstract entities such as state organs, political regimes and religious formations. Despite the mutually understood intellectual background, these invectives lacked conceptual depth. They consisted of condensed value judgments entailing prior knowledge of context. Yet, the invectives seem to have functioned well even when in all likelihood the readers did not fully grasp the context. After all, one did not have to read

---

166 *ibid.* 229.

167 Nathan O. Hatch. *The Democratization of American Christianity.* New Haven: Yale University Press (1989): 129.

168 Ernest Lee Tuveson. *Redeemer Nation: The Idea of America's Millennial Role.* Chicago: University of Chicago Press (1968): 138.

169 William Goodell. "Palestine Mission: Journal of Mr. Goodell." *The Missionary Herald*, November (1824): 342.

the corpus of Edwards and Hopkins' writings to figure out what 'stupid' and 'filthy' meant. Knowledge of the basic premises of Congregationalist postmillennialism might have helped the readers to discern the binary oppositions, and a better and deeper knowledge improved their perception.

One explanation might lie in the process of alienation and strangeness as a learning process. Ralph Buchenhorst explains strangeness as a mental state that is produced when actors, narratives and artifacts meet.[170] Such interactions might facilitate the detection of blind spots for a possible attempt at 'translation' and a possibility for learning.[171] Werner Nell, in his discussion of alienation as a learning process, points to the possibility that being acquainted with the 'other' bears the risk of developing misunderstandings and resorting to prejudices.[172] The missionaries' metaphorical-parabolic conceptual narratives were extremely successful. However, fixed networks of tropes, metaphors and parables might have placed limitations on making sense of the outer reality in complex situations. Consequently, it is quite likely that at times, as in the examples above, the author might have found that metaphors of darkness or a parable of growth failed to convey the real meaning of a situation and as a result might have applied a straightforward explanation digging into another toolbox of fixed images of narrative, namely invectives.

3.8 CONCLUSION

In this chapter, the way in which missionary narrative created meaning through the interaction of its components has been examined. As shown above, the non-fictional narrative of the missionaries consists of an intricate web of conceptual metaphors and story elements. The interrelations between these elements have been expressed. Nevertheless, an all-

---

170 Ralph Buchenhorst. "Einleitung: Das Fremde im Übergang." *Von Fremdheit lernen*. Ed. Ralph Buchenhorst. Bielefeld: Transcript (2015): 11.

171 *ibid.* 17.

172 Werner Nell. "Innenansichten von der Außenseite: Befremdung und Marginalität als Erkenntnis-Chancen in einigen autobiographischen Texten aus dem 18. Jahrhundert." *Von Fremdheit lernen*. Ed. Ralph Buchenhorst. Bielefeld: Transcript (2015): 147.

encompassing examination is possible at this stage because the conceptual background has been thoroughly explained.

To start with, one needs to have a general outlook on missionary travels. The storyline for the first ten years of mission activity in terms of mobility, as gleaned from the missionary writings published in *The Missionary Herald,* is as follows:

Table 1: Mission and mobility, 1820-1830

17 January 1820	Levi Parsons and Pliny Fisk landed in Smyrna.[173]
Spring and Summer of 1820	They spent five months at Chios in order to learn Greek and get acquainted with the archipelago.[174]
1 November 1820	They left Izmir to visit the countryside and do research.[175] During that journey they traveled over 300 miles, visited Ayvalık, Pergamos, Thyatira, Sardis, and Philadelphia among other places, giving away 21 Bibles and Testaments and distributing 1,300 religious tracts.[176]
21 December 1820	Parsons sailed to Jerusalem.[177]
17 February 1821	Parsons arrived at the city after a long journey.[178]
8 May 1821	Due to the unrest and tumult in Jerusalem,

173 Pliny Fisk, Levi Parsons. "Palestine Mission: Letter from Messrs. Fisk and Parsons, to the Cor. Sec. of A. B. C. F. M." *The Missionary Herald,* April (1820): 173.

174 Pliny Fisk, Levi Parsons. "Letters of Messrs. Parsons and Fisk to the Corresponding Secretary." *The Missionary Herald,* March (1821): 78.

175 Pliny Fisk, Levi Parsons. "Letters from Messrs. Parsons and Fisk." *The Missionary Herald,* April (1821): 105.

176 *ibid.* 105.

177 Pliny Fisk, Levi Parsons. "Letter from Messrs. Parsons and Fisk to the Corresponding Secretary." *The Missionary Herald,* July (1821): 207.

178 Levi Parsons. "Palestine Mission: Journal of Mr. Parsons." *The Missionary Herald,* January (1822): 18-19.

	Parsons left the city and returned to Syra.[179]
24 February 1822	Daniel Temple arrived at Malta.[180]
Winter of 1821	Parsons and Fisk traveled to Alexandria.[181]
January 1822	Jonas King arrived at Alexandria, having proposed to continue in the mission for three years.[182]
10 February 1822	Parsons died in Alexandria.[183]
13 April 1822	Hearing of Temple's arrival in Malta, Fisk decided to visit the island and set sail from Alexandria.[184]
10 January 1823	Fisk and King returned back to Egypt in order to travel in Upper Egypt.[185]
7 January 1823	William Goodell and Isaac Bird arrived at Malta.[186]
7 April 1823	Jonas King and Pliny Fisk started their Journey from Cairo to Jerusalem through the desert.[187]
25 April 1823	They entered the holy city of Karnack[188].
16 November 1823	William Goodell and Isaac Bird arrived at Beirut.[189]

179 Levi Parsons. "Letter from Mr. Parsons to the Corresponding Secretary." *The Missionary Herald*, February (1822): 44.

180 Daniel Temple. "Extract of a Letter from Mr. Temple to a Gentleman in Boston." *The Missionary Herald*, June (1822): 179.

181 "Mission to Palestine." *The Missionary Herald*, January (1823): 4.

182 *ibid*. 4.

183 *ibid*. 4.

184 "Report of the Prudential Committee." *The Missionary Herald*, July (1823): 206.

185 "Palestine Mission." *The Missionary Herald*, April (1823): 213.

186 *ibid*. 213.

187 Pliny Fisk, Jonas King. "Journey of Messrs. Fisk and King from Cairo to Jerusalem, through the Desert." *The Missionary Herald*, February (1824): 33.

188 *ibid*. 39.

189 William Goodell. "Letter from Mr. Goodell." *The Missionary Herald*, July (1824): 214.

2 January 1824	Bird left Beirut with Jonas King for Jerusalem.[190]
22 October 1825	Pliny Fisk died in Beirut.[191]
Summer of 1826	Eli Smith arrived at Malta.[192]
1826	Elnathan Gridley and Josiah Brewer arrived at Izmir.[193]
2 February 1827	Brewer left for Istanbul.[194]
18 February 1827	Eli Smith arrived at Beirut.[195]
18 May 1828	Eli Smith, Isaac Bird and William Goodell departed from Beirut and embarked for Malta.[196]
March 1830	H.G.O Dwight and George B. Whiting arrived at Malta.[197]
21 May 1830	Eli Smith and H.G.O Dwight started their Journey to Armenia.[198]

All these events, shown in chronological order, comprise some aspects of the *story* part of the missionary narrative. Story, as understood in narratological terms, includes chains of events in the form of actions and happenings, and existents such as characters. It is a general outline of what is depicted. It is the content. The way the content is depicted belongs to another

---

190 *ibid.* 214.

191 "Death of Mr. Fisk." *The Missionary Herald*, April (1826): 131.

192 "Thoughts upon the Printing Establishment at Malta." *The Missionary Herald*, July (1826): 211.

193 Josiah Brewer, Elnathan Gridley. "Extracts from the Communications of Messrs. Gridley and Brewer." *The Missionary Herald*, August (1827): 237-239.

194 *ibid.* 237-239.

195 Eli Smith. "Extracts from a Letter of Mr. Smith to the Corresponding Secretary." *The Missionary Herald*, October (1827): 306.

196 Isaac Bird, William Goodell, Eli Smith. "Departure of Missionaries from Beyroot." *The Missionary Herald*, November (1828): 348-350.

197 William Goodell. "Mediterranean: Letter from Mr. Goodell, Dated Malta, July, 1830." *The Missionary Herald*, December (1830): 373.

198 H. G. O. Dwight, Eli Smith. "Letters from Messrs. Smith and Dwight." *The Missionary Herald*, December (1830): 377.

part of the narrative, which is the *discourse*. The narratological understanding of discourse as complementary to story supposes that discourse is how the content of the story is recounted. Metaphors and their conceptual background belong to the discursive level of narration.

The story part of the missionary narrative consists of certain categories. These categories are *activity*, *people* (mainly target groups), *land*, *conditions*, and *purpose* – as the aims and future prospects. Missionaries employed conceptual metaphors to maintain a coherent account of these categories. Often the same conceptual domains are used to narrate more than one category.

Missionary activities were told in diverse ways. Metaphors of cultivation and growth were employed to narrate the distribution of printed materials, printing press, and preaching. Metaphors of war were used to refer to evangelical teaching as a means of submission, of changing demographics through conversion, printing press and propagation, and of the defense of ideas against opponents. Press and propagation/proselytization were also articulated by metaphors of light. The expected course of missionary activities, correct conduct, purposeful activity, and self-orientation were expressed by metaphors of the path. Finally, metaphors of doors and opening were used to explain the distribution of tracts as opening doors of usefulness. Missionaries referred to people who were inclined to listen to their propaganda in terms of metaphors of cultivation. The psychological and social states of the people and societies were articulated by metaphors of cultivation and metaphors of light. Metaphors of war and metaphors of light are conceptual domains used to refer to adversaries and rival groups. The land as a geographical destination belongs to the domains of cultivation, war and light. Social and political conditions were likewise addressed, using metaphors of war and light. As for conditions, favorable and unfavorable conditions belong to the domains of cultivation, light, and opening. Purpose was portrayed in the context of growth by metaphors of cultivation. The aims of altering existing demographics and the final battle were conveyed by metaphors of war. Hopeful indications of future success were portrayed by metaphors of light. Metaphors of path serve as allusions to the course leading to the realization of the Millennium. Finally, metaphors of openings pointed to opportunities that open onto that course.

The following table displays how the distinction between story and discourse was articulated in missionary writings. It also gives a general overview of the metaphorical occurrences mentioned above with some brief examples.

Table 2: Conceptual metaphors

NARRATIVE	
STORY	**DISCOURSE**
Activity (General)	• **Cultivation:** distribution of printed materials/press; speaking and preaching • **War:** evangelical teaching (people should yield); changing demographics through conversion (take possession, occupy); press (artillery of heaven); propagation and defense of ideas • **Light / Darkness**: press (diffuse religious knowledge); propagation and proselytization (enlighten, diffuse spirit of piety) • **Way:** the expected course; correct conduct; purposeful activity; self-orientation • **Door / Opening:** distribution of tracts (opening doors of usefulness)
People / Target Groups	• **Cultivation:** people inclined to listen, to read, to convert (harvest); psychological and social states (fertile soil, propitious sky) • **War:** rival groups, adversaries (enemy, uniting armies) • **Light / Darkness:** people (moral darkness, in darkness, enlightened); adversaries (rulers of darkness)
Land	• **Cultivation:** geographical destination (land, desert, fruitful field) • **War:** geographical destination (dominion

	of Satan, fortress); political situation • **Light / Darkness:** geographical places (land of darkness); social and political conditions (powers of darkness)
Conditions	• **Cultivation:** favorable / unfavorable conditions (fertile soil, desert) • **Light / Darkness:** favorable / unfavorable conditions (a far brighter day, bow in the clouds, storm, clouds, threatening blackness) • **Door / Opening:** favorable conditions as opportunities
Purposes / Aims / Future	• **Cultivation:** theme of growth • **War:** changing demographics; eschatological aims for final battle (ultimate and triumphant success, the battle of the great day) • **Light / Darkness:** hopeful indications for future success (a ray of light already dawns upon our path) • **Way:** leads to the Millennium • **Door / Opening:** opens to prospects and eventually to the way that lead to the end of history

The missionaries were in the Ottoman Empire to propagate and eventually to proselytize. They were looking for a suitable field, a fertile ground, to start their work and sow precious seed. What they found instead was thorny ground. As they were the light-bringers and the light was truth, the opposite party and their adversaries lived in darkness and falsehood. They had to struggle with growing opposition from various opponents, defend their position against them and fight the good fight. This spiritual warfare was the prelude to a final battle before the Millennium. In order to realize their aims, they had to follow a strict course and assume a particular spiritual truth in order to find the right path to continue their journey. They assumed a fixed destination, a fixed point in history and only this way led there: the Millennium. Thus, their activity was supposed to be purposeful. But it also entailed proselytizing. In order to enter the right path, to start mission work, to sow the seed, they were looking for open doors and openings, namely opportunities.

One can summarize the conceptual integration of all these domains by depicting the missionary narrative as a parable: The missionaries arrived in a strange land and they entered a road in a field. During their journey to the ultimate end, they were involved in agricultural activities because they wanted to harvest the crop and bring it with them to the final station. The road and the field around it was not always in the light. This was a hindrance for missionaries and crop alike. Thus, they had to fight the darkness and as a consequence they were involved in a battle with external conditions. In order to win the war and make it to the final point, they constantly looked for openings and open doors to find suitable conditions.

This is an extremely simplified version of the missionary narrative, yet it also provides a powerful hindsight into its conceptual formation. First of all, the conceptual formation is metaphorically oriented. Secondly, conceptual metaphors are interrelated and contribute to the coherence of the narrative. Thirdly, and perhaps most importantly, the narrative has metaphors as its basis but it is more than the conceptual background.

In order to understand what lies beyond or to put it more coherently, over the conceptual background one can go back to the Biblical origins of those metaphors. The parables and other Biblical references also have metaphorical components. Yet the way they function is similar to the simple parable created above. That is, some conceptually grounded stories are projected onto other stories. When a parable refers to a peasant sowing a seed on a field the peasant and other components of the story are not understood literally. Actually, at some point it should be understood literally, so that the literal farmer can be projected onto another conscious (or in creative cases unconscious) being together with other components of the story. Such projections, as displayed above, take place in conceptual domains and produce in turn conceptual metaphors. On a metaphorical level, however, the projections are one-sided, generally positive and move from one domain to the other in a unidirectional fashion. So if the projection of the seed is analyzed it is most likely that one can find the metaphorical projection and conceptual metaphors. When the scope of analysis is extended to include every component, we can see that the story itself is also projected as a whole. In such extensive projections we can see the generic spaces, to return to Mark Turner's scheme, containing general meanings, and if followed these spaces can also open up to certain conceptual domains with a metaphorical character.[199] Yet, when a generic space is used to grasp a specific setting, in other words, when the story is projected onto another story from the real world, a blend is produced. This is why the missionaries did not stop at the general meaning but used its systematicity to bring coherence to their specific stories, as did the first Christians.

If the missionary narrative is regarded in this way, a multilayered narrative connection can be discerned. The very stories they alluded to had already been used. The Biblical stories or conceptual lines had already been projected onto other stories before they were employed by the missionaries. They had their own mental spaces. When missionaries used conceptual metaphors originating from those stories, they adopted the parabolic aspect as well. Thus, they projected an already projected story onto another story to make sense of their actions. The mental space created by the missionaries carried core elements of the original mental space, but it had its own peculiar aspects as well. Thanks to the mutually shared aspects, the missionary narrative remained Christian and could address the notion of the Kingdom of God and the Millennium. The diverging parts were a result of different historical backgrounds and different realities. The eschatological horizon of the missionaries was loaded with ideas like postmillennialism, progress, science, modernity, enlightenment and secularism. These ideas were projected onto a predominantly 'alien' world.

There were two important results. Firstly, the missionaries projected an already projected story onto another reality, so that the general conceptual vein remained intact and enabled the projection, yet the result was an inability at times to comprehend the external conditions. Secondly, by clinging to the religious parabolic realm, the missionaries found themselves in a paradoxical situation. They had to find a way to reconcile ideas of progress, modernity, and secularism with their supernatural beliefs. These topics will be analyzed in the next chapter.

---

199 See Chapter 2, Section "2.4 Blending of Conceptual Domains and The Narrative Element" for Mark Turners theory.

4 Case Studies

In the previous chapter, metaphor networks and their contribution to the missionary discourse were discussed as parts of a greater narrative. This chapter deals with the detection of the same or similar networks and discursive formations in different historical periods and settings. The discursive formations during the founding years of the Ottoman mission display a high degree of systematic and structured usage. During the founding years, the conceptual substrata of the missionary narratives dealt with processes of exploration, learning, sense-making, and alienation. In addition, the missionaries encountered or were involved in a diverse set of activities and events, including propagating the gospel, confrontations with local and central authorities, extensive traveling, and civil or military conflicts. Consequently, their conceptual repertoire dwelled upon a wide range of matters, right from the beginning. This kind of many-sided applicability suggests a well-established conceptual streak in missionary discourse that might have been adopted in the later stages of mission work. Thus, in this chapter, the continuation or discontinuation of detected discursive formations used by the ABCFM will be discussed.

There is a large number of issues of *The Missionary Herald* over the period from the 1830s to the turn of the century. More than seven hundred issued were published over those seventy years. Since it is practically impossible to cover all these issues and periods in the available time and space, case studies will be the preferred medium in this chapter. The choice of case studies is not random. First of all, specific events or processes have been chosen on the basis of their distinct character and their possible impact on missionary responses to these events. Much as in the first decade of the mission, a new establishment, a shift in paradigm or a crisis might have ignited the frequent and coherent use of the conceptual discursive formations of the founding years. With this in mind, two case studies have been chosen.

The first case study is the ABCFM's attempt to launch a mission for proselytization of the Muslims, mainly in Istanbul. Right from the outset, the Board planned to start mission work for Muslims of the Ottoman Empire, but the conditions were adverse and the political climate hostile. They thought that their chance was about to turn for the better in 1856. The Ottoman Reform Edict of 1856 (Islâhat Fermânı) was celebrated by the missionaries and they interpreted the reforms as opening a door for a Muslim mission for the first time since the first missionaries arrived. Thus, not only the attempt but also the historical background is worthy of analysis. Except for minute problems, this period witnessed the first full-scale confrontation, namely the persecution of missionary activities for Muslims, between the Protestants and the Ottoman State as a political and religious entity.

The second case study is the Armenian Massacres of 1894-96 (also known as Hamidiye Massacres, named after the Hamidian light cavalry forces). The Armenian massacres are a highly important event in a global context. Almost all of the major European states were involved in the prior history and aftermath of the massacres and the Western public was deeply interested, involved and informed about the events. Among the Western actors that witnessed the massacres were the missionaries of the Board. The Board had many stations, schools and other establishments in the region and they were immensely taken aback when the events escalated. Consequently, the tragic events initiated a specific response characterized by underlying conceptual metaphors and a related narrative.

When the topics for the case studies were chosen it was not clear whether the missionaries did apply the metaphor networks and discursive formations from the first decade in their narratives. The result is affirmative, albeit with varying conclusions. The conceptual networks and related narrative formations persisted. They referred, however, to a new reality, even in terms of the Protestant discourse.

The analyses start with the historical Congregationalist background, which roughly coincides with the second half of the nineteenth century and thus with the case studies. A good grasp of this background may facilitate a comparative perspective, especially when the Ottoman social or political situations are represented in relation to the case studies. The case studies are presented in chronological order.

4.1 CONGREGATIONAL HISTORICAL BACKGROUND

In *ante-bellum* America, Edwardsian tradition kept its importance for New England Divinity even after its zenith. During this period, social benevolence gained new impetus in Calvinist circles from the aspirations derived from Hopkins' ideas, among many other factors. The foundation of Mount Holyoke Seminary and the discussions on the topic of female piety affected the position of women in a positive way. The missions to Native Americans and the anti-slavery movement underlined the humanitarian aspects of Edwardsians. However, things developed in a different way than they expected, and foreign missions came into question again since more and more importance was attached to them. The Edwardsian tradition lost ground as the nation revised its narratives, in which their invention of the tradition did not fit the schema asserted by the social and political changes.

The evangelist movements in America underwent important changes from the 1840s onward. During the Second Great Awakening, women's position gained more importance as active agents for the success of postmillennialism. Mount Holyoke Female Seminary was founded by Mary Lion in 1837.[1] It was regarded as a sister institution to the Andover Theological Seminary and became an important school for the American Board, like its brother institute. The curriculum was many-sided and the school offered 'ornamentations' such as dancing and the cultivation of gentility.[2] The college "answered an immense need for the schooling of girls and the training of future teachers," and the activities "were focused on the hope that every student would be brought to a personal knowledge of Jesus Christ."[3] The success of Amherst, Williams and Dartmouth in science education was influential since scientific progress was highly valued by the evangelists in

---

1 Joseph A. Conforti. *Jonathan Edwards, Religious Tradition & American Culture*. Chapel Hill: University of North Carolina Press (1995): 87.

2 *ibid.* 87-88.

3 Sydney E. Ahlstrom. *A Religious History of the American People*. New Haven: Yale University Press (1972): 643.

general and Calvinists in particular. The rapid change in *ante-bellum* American society affected the Christian denominations in a peculiar way. The shift from piety to moralism and from Calvinism to religious liberalism started at this period.[4] Andover Seminary remained an important center for overseas missionary activities in many aspects, and the first half of the nineteenth century witnessed the rise of seminaries.[5] Andover was considered to be one of the most influential seminaries. For a long time it was the center of the New Divinity and Edwardsian schools of thought, and took a stance against the Unitarian influence centered at Harvard. Although there were several problems in naming the phenomenon, the so-called New England Theology, which was also named Andover Calvinism, remained powerful until the 1860s. Around this time Old and New school Presbyterians united and curriculum changes were introduced to modernize instruction at Andover.[6] The result was the appearance of 'Progressive Orthodoxy.'[7] As liberal theology gained its stance, "[w]ith the new historical, philosophical, and religious attitudes as common ground, Andover Seminary even returned to Harvard, where for over two decades the joint faculty achieved great distinction and influence."[8]

It is unclear whether Horace Bushnell, Congregational minister in Hartford, was aware of the imminent rift in Congregational theology when he applied the concepts of gradual development and divine immanence.[9] With this, he paved the way for crucial discussions among American Congregationalists that dominated the second half of the nineteenth century as conservative Calvinists were completely against the assumption that insight into religious truth came gradually and that divine influence worked through channels of natural law and natural growth.[10]

The conservative Calvinists protested fiercely and discussions continued from the 1860s to the 1890s. Such celebrated figures among the con-

---

4   Conforti, *Jonathan Edwards*, 88.

5   *ibid*. 108.

6   *ibid*. 141.

7   *ibid*. 141.

8   Ahlstrom, *Religious History*, 778.

9   David Everett Swift. "Conservative versus Progressive Orthodoxy in Latter 19th Century Congregationalism." *Church History*, Vol. 16, No. 1, March (1947): 22.

10 *ibid*. 22.

servatives as Enoch Pond, Edwards A. Park, and George N. Boardman defended the convictions that "[...] the Bible is completed and self-evident revelation," modifications of central doctrines were extremely dangerous, "God's ways need no justification to men," and "conversion is effected by a sudden inflowing of the Holy Spirit."[11] The issue of conversion and the debate over future probation became a central issue for the missionary work since "post-mortem salvation seemed to destroy one of the chief incentives supporting the vast foreign mission enterprise," and the assumption that those who pass away without being converted would undergo eternal punishment would not function.[12]

While all these transformations and discussions were taking place in America, the missionaries were struggling with a different set of problems in Anatolia. The second half of the nineteenth century brought drastic social and political changes which in time escalated into full-scale problems posing both threats to and opportunities for proselytization.

4.2 CASE STUDY I: FAILED CONVERSION OF THE MUSLIMS, 1856-1865

At its commencement, the focus of the Palestine mission was the Jews of Jerusalem and the Middle East, because conversion of the Jews was considered to be a crucial element in the Board's eschatological aspirations. Immediately before leaving Boston to start the Palestine mission, Levi Parsons preached on the "dereliction and restoration of the Jews" and Pliny Fisk delivered a farewell discourse on the "holy land as a field for missionary enterprise."[13] The greater scheme which would lead to the ultimate aim was the "[...] conversion of the heathen and the reformation of the Christian world."[14]

The instructions given to Fisk and Parsons in 1819 by the Board was extensive and covering a multitude of the groups then present in the region:

---

11 *ibid.* 24.

12 *ibid.* 24.

13 "Report from the Prudential Committee." *The Missionary Herald*, December (1820): 70.

14 "Mission to Palestine." *The Missionary Herald*, December (1820): 555.

You [...] will survey with earnest attention the various tribes and classes who dwell in that land, and the surrounding countries. The two grand inquiries ever present in your minds will be, 'What good can be done?' and by what means? What can be done for the Jews? What for the Pagans? What for the Mohammedans? What for the Christians? What for the people in Palestine? What for those in Egypt, in Syria, in Armenia, in other countries to which your inquiry may be extended?[15]

It may be claimed that the Board was not only ambitious in its choice of target range but also clever and careful. The upcoming years testified that trial and error was the most effective method for mission work among the indigenous peoples of the Middle East and failure was the rule rather than the exception. By keeping an eye on diverse groups and conducting flexible missionary activity, the Board created a fertile ground for success. Thus, in the first decade it became clear that work among Muslims was arduous and risky and among Jews to almost no avail. The Armenians, however, proved to be a promising people. As a result, in just 30 years after its start the Protestant Armenians separated from the Armenian millet and this new group was officially recognized as a new entity by the Ottoman state. The Muslims of the empire, however, were mostly unreachable by the missionaries. Although there was no direct mission work to the Muslims, the Board had always kept an eye on this group, waiting for any opportunity to proselytize.

Finally, with the promulgation of the Ottoman Reform Edict of 1856 in February 1856, direct efforts to proselytize Muslims were undertaken by the missionaries.[16] More than 20 Muslims were converted during the following six years and one of them, one Selim Efendi who took the name Edward Williams, was even licensed to preach the Gospel.[17]

Article six of the edict, which guaranteed the freedom of belief and exercise of religious beliefs, was the reason why the missionaries started to

15 Rufus Anderson. *History of the Missions of the American Board of Commissioners For Foreign Missions to the Oriental Churches, Volume I.* Boston: Congregational Publishing Society (1872): 10.

16 William Goodell. *Forty Years in the Turkish Empire.* New York: Robert Carter and Brothers (1876): 425.

17 *ibid.* 426.

operate relatively freely among the Muslim population of Istanbul.[18] The excitement the edict aroused among the missionaries is understandable. The issue of Muslim apostates in the Ottoman legal system had been the major hindrance to the missionaries in approaching Muslims. In 1843, an Armenian and a Greek who turned Muslim but later changed their minds and reverted to Christianity were beheaded in Istanbul. The British ambassador, Lord Stratford Canning de Redcliffe, immediately remonstrated about the case and enforced the proclamation of an edict announcing that no one should be persecuted on account of her/his religious beliefs. The Porte agreed to this outwardly, but the following edict only banned the persecution of born Christians on account of her/his religious beliefs and excluded the Muslims. Accordingly two Muslims were executed in Aleppo and Edirne in 1852 and 1853 respectively.[19] Capital punishment for Muslim converts remained an issue in international politics, and Earl of Clarendon drew attention to the matter when the empire became a member of the Concert of Europe.[20]

According to traditional interpretations of Islamic law, the punishment for apostasy from Islam is execution.[21] There are indications, however, that the Muslim scene was divided into two camps regarding the punishment. The 1843 executions were considered to be a foolish act by the pro-reform circles, and a triumph by the conservatives.[22] During this era and right after the Edict of 1856, official state policy on crypto-Christians reassuming their old faith was to ignore them.[23] Against this background, while the Tanzimât Edict of 1839 promised legal equality to all the subjects of the Ottoman Empire, the Reform Edict of 1856 came up as a more detailed

---

18 Jeremy Salt. *Imperialism, Evangelism, and the Ottoman Armenians, 1878-1896*. London: Cass (1993): 34.

19 Julius Richter. *A History of the Protestant Missions in the Near East*. New York: Fleming H. Revell Company (1910): 171-172.

20 Salt, *Imperialism*, 35.

21 Selim Deringil. "'There Is No Compulsion in Religion': On Conversion and Apostasy in the Late Ottoman Empire: 1839-1856." *Comparative Studies in Society and History*, Vol. 42, No. 3, July (2000): 550.

22 *ibid.* 551.

23 *ibid.* 551.

plan to carry out the promises given in 1839.[24] Despite the reading of some contemporary figures that the edict officially abolishes capital punishment for Muslim apostates, there is no direct reference in the edict to the issue of apostasy.[25] Moreover, due to the dubious wording of the text, the ruling elite was prone to interpret the notion of freedom of religion as freedom to defend religion.[26] Indeed, the British consul Henry Bulwer heavily criticized the missionaries by pointing out that the way they behaved after the proclamation of the edict gave the impression to the state that they were using the edict as a weapon against the sultan and his government.[27] The stance of the government regarding missionary activities was to consider the edict as a charter of rights as well as obligations.[28] Accordingly, openly propagating Protestantism to the Muslims in public places was regarded as offending public order and as an activity that hindered others in the profession of their religion – a clear category of disapproved activity explained in the edict.[29]

In *ante-bellum* America, the evangelists' activities were characterized by active political engagement. Their incentives for involvement in political issues originated from their "endeavor not to be excluded from American Popular Culture" and the "Puritan conception of state as a moral being."[30] They felt the "responsibility as Christians to protect their country's precious but vulnerable experiment in republicanism and representative democracy."[31] The duties of the Christian citizen were "to promote and sustain a moral nation [...] through aggressive soul-saving and thorough active citizenship" since "free government rested on the moral power of an educated, self-disciplined, and religious citizenry."[32] The political engagement of evangelists through the promotion of an ideal middle class Christian citizen

---

24 *ibid.* 556.

25 *ibid.* 556.

26 *ibid.* 556.

27 Salt, *Imperialism*, 36-37.

28 *ibid.* 37.

29 *ibid.* 37.

30 Richard J. Cawardine. *Evangelicals and Politics in Antebellum America.* Yale University Press: New Haven (1993): 17-18.

31 *ibid.* 18.

32 *ibid.* 22-23.

can explain the vision they promoted of the future in the Ottoman Empire as regard missionary activities. These changes were inflected in various ways in the mission field. The formation of a legally recognized community and its legal regulations, which will be discussed below, indicate a high degree of civil character and community involvement which nevertheless resulted in conflict when invisible borders were trespassed.

4.2.1 Conversion of the Muslims

The mild atmosphere in the capital in 1855 was the precursor of a new era. In a letter dated October 19, a missionary reported that "[t]here is a wide door open among the Turks of Constantinople for the sale of the Scriptures." He also added that the prospects of conversing with Muslims had improved and that they had the opportunity to sell books as well.[33] The missionaries were already preparing themselves for the right moment. Hence, the Board was delighted by the edict and the concession the Sultan Abdülmecid I made in it. It was considered to be a foundation stone for "progressive changes, in things spiritual and things temporal, of the highest moment," and "the new magna charta [sic] of his people."[34] The full text was printed in English translation in the June 1856 issue of *The Missionary Herald*. Mr. Schauffler claimed that the edict was considered by Muslims themselves "as opening the door to them to become Christians."[35] One has to rely on Mr. Schauffler's account whether the Muslims actually cherished this new alleged prospect, yet it was clear that the missionaries themselves saw a new door opening, the opportunity they had been seeking since the beginning of the mission to the Ottoman Empire. They commenced a new quest of exploration after years of residence in the capital and other cities of the empire.

The claimed interest of Muslims in the region of Diyarbakır in the summer of 1856 was taken as a "reason to pray in hope that blindness" might be "removed from the eyes of the False Prophet." The interest, however, created unrest among the locals and the missionaries started to com-

---

33 Joel S. Everett. "Constantinople: Letter from Mr. Everett." *The Missionary Herald*, January (1856): 14.

34 "Miscellanies." *The Missionary Herald*, June (1856): 181.

35 *ibid*. 184.

plain that the influence of the new edict could be felt in neither that province nor other interior provinces.[36] Mr. Goodell from the Istanbul station spoke of the abundant reasons to be grateful "for the great magna charta [*sic*.] which secures liberty of conscience for all who dwell under the shadow of the Ottoman Porte" and of the advantages they derived from it in a letter he wrote in December 1856.[37] In the same letter, he also relayed the impressions of a Nestorian convert whose face shone upon seeing the converted Turks and remarked that the Kingdom of God should appear immediately.[38]

As of February 27, 1857, the fact that more than thirty-five hundred copies of the Bible were sold to the Turkish population of Istanbul in 1856 and 1857 was celebrated as an "unexpected opening." Christians of America were invited "to enter upon this great and promising field."[39] The religious interest of the Muslims in the region of Sivas was also attributed to the edict. The edict was regarded as operating silently, but with power. The missionaries expected that their hopes would ripen "into fruition" and that the Muslims would become "the valiant soldiers of Prince Immanuel."[40] Another missionary was also excited by the opportunities to conduct work for the Muslims in the same region and alludes to the "friendly spirit" of the Turks as another "fruit" of the mission work.[41]

The years following the edict also saw a new era of exploration for the Board. The missionaries decided to start a new mission in the Ottoman Balkans. Visiting Edirne in April 1858, one Mr. Morse wrote "[w]e see also Greeks, Armenians and Mohammedans white already to harvest," and the field "should be occupied as speedily as possible." They asked for more resources and helpers and concluded that they were praying for more "labor-

---

36 Augustus Walker. "Diarbekir: Letter from Mr. Walker." *The Missionary Herald*, November (1856): 333.

37 William Goodell. "Northern Armenians: Letter from Mr. Goodell." *The Missionary Herald*, April (1857): 120.

38 *ibid*. 120.

39 H. G. O. Dwight. "Northern Armenians: Letter from Mr. Dwight." *The Missionary Herald*, June (1857): 189.

40 *ibid*. 194-195.

41 Benjamin Parsons. "Northern Armenians: Letter from Mr. Parsons." *The Missionary Herald*, July (1857): 213.

ers to gather his harvest."[42] It was suggested that a Turkish-speaking missionary should be stationed in Edirne as there was an "opening" among the Turks.[43] The new mission enterprise took the recent changes into consideration for future plans. As the Ottoman Balkans became a place of interest for the missionaries, the Board seriously evaluated the region as a field of Christian missions and in an introductory article published in *The Missionary Herald* in October 1858, it was mentioned that the contest with Islam was to be settled there. The policy of concentrating all the missionary forces in Asia was seen to be leaving "an immense extent of territory, and so many strongholds of the enemy unsubdued."[44]

The hopes were not confined to Istanbul and the Balkans, though. They hoped that there were "some Arimathean Josephs [...] among the Turks [...] even in this centre of Moslem darkness," as one Mr. Wheeler reported from Harput in 1859.[45] When Some Muslims showed interest in the missionaries' activities in the region of Maraş, the missionaries evaluated this as "[t]he expectation that a Muslim might be the first fruits of a great harvest. [...] the whole land will be open before us, and we shall be called to go in and possess it. But where is the Joshua, or host who are to do battle?"[46]

The spirit for converting Muslims was likewise present at the recently established theological Bebek Seminary. This center of learning, crucial especially for producing local priests, helpers and preachers, had a defining position in mission policies. Among the students accepted for education, "[s]ome have shown a special interest in the conversion of Mohammedans, and have expressed the intention of devoting their lives, if God will, to that

---

42 Charles F. Morse. "Northern Armenians: Letter from Mr. Morse." *The Missionary Herald*, August (1858): 254.

43 "Northern Armenians: Station Reports." *The Missionary Herald*, September (1859): 277.

44 "Miscellany." *The Missionary Herald*, October (1858): 323.

45 Crosby H. Wheeler. "Northern Armenians: Letter from Mr. Wheeler." *The Missionary Herald*, March (1859): 86.

46 Andrew T. Pratt. "Southern Armenians: Letter from Dr. Pratt." *The Missionary Herald*, May (1860): 152.

work."[47] At the region of Elbistan, southeastern Turkey, calls from Muslims to speak on subjects such as man's sinfulness were celebrated and the Muslims were represented as often saying "we have lost the road, we cannot find God." The missionary, Mr. White, expresses his feelings in a letter written on July 17, 1860, as "some good seed was sown."[48]

Conversion of the Muslims was among the topics in the survey for the year 1860. It was claimed that "[t]he religious movement among Muslims has had a marked development the past year. Doors of entrance to this people have been opening, more or less, in many places besides Constantinople."[49] Yet, the missionaries were not content that "[t]he converts [...] are as yet mostly Armenians."[50] They were also investing more energy in this new field of operations because one Dr. Schauffler was "devoting himself mainly to preparing [...] the scriptures for Mohammedan readers."[51]

Sharing his impressions and experiences, Dr. West, a medical doctor stationed in Sivas, indicated that the medical profession was helpful in reaching people and establishing solid networks. His remarks written in December 1860 are worth noting:

I have the prayers of many Mussulmans. I feel friendship for them in return, and as I continually meet with friendly greetings and kind reception, I feel that I have reason to thank God that he has opened for me so wide a door of usefulness among them. As they gather around me at the shop, or assemble to see me in the surrounding villages to which I am called, or in their homes in the city, I take great pleasure in speaking to them concerning the truths of God's word [...].[52]

---

47 "Northern Armenians: Station Reports." *The Missionary Herald*, September (1860): 269.

48 George H. White. "Southern Armenians: Letter from Mr. White." *The Missionary Herald*, October (1860): 309-310.

49 "Survey of the Missions of the Board." *The Missionary Herald*, January (1861): 4.

50 *ibid.* 5.

51 *ibid.* 5.

52 Henry S. West. "Western Turkey: Letter from Dr. West." *The Missionary Herald*, April (1861): 100.

The survey of the Eastern Turkey Mission for the year 1861 could not produce tangible results because "no cases of conversion" were "reported
among the Moslems; but the missionaries testified, that the evidence accu-
mulated of an interest awakened here and there among them, to inquire into
the truth, which is God's appointed means of salvation."[53] Despite the lack
of results, optimism prevailed.

A missionary from Harput field related the concessions made by Muslims in Peri, a town of 3000 people, and claimed that the Muslims said
"[d]o not suppose that we are ignorant of our condition. We are all eternally
lost, and we know it. We find ourselves in the same state as our fathers
were, and we see no way to free ourselves." The missionary believed that
"with a good helper in Peri he should expect to see the work open rapidly
and that there was an open door in this place, but they cannot enter it till
better times.[54]

Mr. Herrick's letter from Istanbul, titled "Appeal in Behalf of Work
among Mohammedans," asking for helpers and means to conduct work
among the Muslim population of Istanbul, is important in that the letter was
aimed at reminding the Congregationalists of the original missionary plans
for converting Muslims. Mr. Herrick complained that the establishment of
missions among the 'nominal' Christians of Turkey and Persia was within
the proper range of the Board's plan, namely propagating the Gospel in
heathen lands, yet the patrons of the Board might forget the original design
of gaining access to the Muslim mind with the help of these missions. He
asked whether they were losing sight of it at the very moment when the
door was opening for its fulfillment. He asked whether the interest among
Muslims was a fruitful interest and concluded that "the first light was succeeded by a season of darkness." He also inquired if the Board had a wish
to leave "this door of entrance to the Mohammedans" to English societies,
which were less advantageously circumstanced for this work.[55]

---

53 "Survey of the Missions of the Board." *The Missionary Herald*, January (1862):
    11.
54 Herman N. Barnum. "Eastern Turkey: Letter from Mr. Barnum." *The Mission-
    ary Herald*, January (1862): 23.
55 George F. Herrick. "Western Turkey: Letter from Mr. Herrick." *The Missionary
    Herald*, April (1862): 119-120.

The missionary zeal to conduct work among Muslims was not paralleled by their means to carry out this work. They were caught unprepared, and in 1862 a call was made for Istanbul that it was imperative that a missionary to the Turks in Istanbul "should be able to use the language in a style more purely Turkish than that heretofore used and found sufficient among the Armenians," because the difference was not "one merely of the written character." The missionaries were called to become more intimately acquainted [...] with the real state and working of the religious element in the Turkish mind [...]."[56] By way of conclusion it was stated that "gather[ing] a harvest of matured, ripened fruit, not from that tree which is wild by nature but from that which is renewed by grace," had to be preceded by "the preparation of the soil, the planting, the watchful, patient tending and watering."[57] It seems that the lack of helpers or people with adequate knowledge of the Muslim groups was not the only problem for the missionaries. They were not familiar with the culture and the ways of thinking among this group of people. Considering that, right from the beginning the missionaries relied mainly on learning the intricacies of other cultures in order to persuade, this drawback might have been at the heart of their general failure. The door was open but they did not exactly know how to get in.

In another reference to the Turkish mentality, it was considered that a change of some kind was "gradually going on in the Turkish mind." The reference was related to the interest of the Muslims in Protestantism in Merzifon.[58] Rather hopefully, the missionaries were detecting "a waking up of the Turkish mind to feel at least the advantages of literature, the science and the arts of Christian Europe."[59] Understandably, wishful thinking had been a part of the missionary discourse when appealing to their followers and benefactors, and likewise when motivating the field workers. But past experience had taught them about the possible frictions their activities might engender, and they insightfully estimated that "[t]he stern battle in

---

56 *ibid*. 120.
57 *ibid*. 121.
58 "Miscellanies." *The Missionary Herald*, September (1862): 292-293.
59 "Western Turkey: Station Reports." *The Missionary Herald*, September (1863): 268.

Turkey" was "yet to be fought" when Muslims began "to give heed to the truth."[60]

The new period created new chances for the mission work. The references to interaction with Muslims in the missionary writings increased in number. This might suggest that they felt more confident and less threatened. Despite the increase, such reports and references remained secondary to work among Armenians. One can find metaphors of growth, light, war and opening in their reports. Yet, they too are not equally distributed. The dominating metaphorical concept is opportunity in the sense of opening/open door. The efforts that went into proselytizing Muslims were still not well founded. The missionaries saw the 'opening' and they were struggling to 'enter.' Apart for in Istanbul, there was no established mission work for Muslims, and this work in Istanbul was confined to a limited number of mission staff. Thus, all the other metaphorical expressions are secondary to the metaphors of opening. They were articulated as subsequent occurrences, or possible outcomes of advantageous situations that had been used well. The missionary reports not only evaluated the situation. Narrating encounters and defining them as opportunities is a simple but effective missionary tool for appealing to public interest. As can be seen, there was a constant call for more workers. One aim was to persuade the Board's headquarters for further investment in this new field. The other was to create financial income through donations from the readers. The majority of the instances related are, however, solitary events. They do not exhibit a long-lasting story that would get more attention. There are few stories that found a place in *The Missionary Herald* for a couple of issues. Some of these events are handled below. There is one story that was widely covered in the missionary letters, though. This story first appeared in the April 1859 issue of *The Missionary Herald*. It is the story of Ahmed Agha, a Muslim convert from the city of Kayseri, who was persecuted by his people and the government following his conversion. His story coincided with the new phase of mission work for the Muslims and as such, it either appeared as a major narrative of persecution and conversion, or as a complementary narrative to them.

---

60 "Items of Intelligence." *The Missionary Herald*, February (1863): 41.

4.2.2 The Story of Ahmed Agha

> His name must at present be suppressed
> [...] He had three daughters nine, eight and
> five years of age respectively as of 1861.[61]

The story of Ahmed Agha related here is a summary of the missionary texts about him. Ahmed Agha chanced to meet a native helper visiting Kayseri as early as 1852. Having frequently listened to his discussions with the Armenians, he decided that the helper's religion is the true religion. He received a copy of the New Testament and started reading it in his free time. One day while reading the Testament in his vine garden, he was overcome and started weeping. On that occasion, his wife asked him what was wrong and he had to confess his conversion. In time, his wife embraced the new faith as well. In 1858, some of his neighbors, reportedly Armenians, reported to the Turks that he read the Gospel and had been seen with the missionaries. He was threatened by his fellow coreligionists and started thinking about moving away from Kayseri to Istanbul in order to evade persecution or even possible death. To this end, he sold his house, shop, vineyard, and part of his lands.[62] Ahmed was denied a passport by the city and, according to the missionary accounts, was repeatedly threatened with death.[63] Since he could not leave the county of Kayseri he moved to Muncusun, where there was a small Protestant community. There he met with other Protestants for prayer, which he could not do in the city.[64]

In 1860, Ahmed Agha left his family behind and managed to go to Istanbul to look for prospects, but to no avail. The missionary accounts claim that after his return from Istanbul, an Armenian incited Muslims against Ahmed Agha and certain men were reported to be planning to murder him. On hearing this, the civil head of the Protestants went to the pasha, the ad-

---

61 "Recent Intelligence." *The Missionary Herald*, June (1861): 188.

62 Julius Y. Leonard. "Northern Armenians: Letter from Mr. Leonard." *The Missionary Herald*, April (1859): 115-116.

63 "Northern Armenians: Station Reports." *The Missionary Herald*, September (1859): 273.

64 Wilson A. Farnsworth. "Northern Armenians: Letter from Mr. Farnsworth." *The Missionary Herald*, January (1860): 18.

ministrative head of the district, and requested protection for him. The pasha consented. Right after this incident, Ahmed declared his apostasy from Islam by proclaiming it on one of the busiest main streets of Kayseri. Ahmed and his family left Kayseri secretly on November 27, 1860, and set off for Samsun. After spending two days at the English consul's house for his protection, Ahmed and his family were put on board a French steamer bound for Istanbul by the consul himself.[65] Their stay proved to be hard for Ahmed Agha and his family. He had economic problems and could not conduct his line of work, fabricating articles of iron, because there was more supply in Istanbul than demand.[66]

Social integration was another problem. The family was located in Bebek, far from the main Muslim quarters of Istanbul, and Ahmed's wife had problems finding company. She started seeing relatives from Kayseri who lived in Istanbul and eventually in 1862, her relatives convinced her to sign a petition in which Ahmed was accused of deceiving his wife. After the petition was delivered to the authorities, Ahmed was summoned before the Minister of Justice. Ahmed confessed that he was a Christian and a Protestant. He was instructed as to the amount of money he was to pay his wife, and after the formal ratification of divorce as a Muslim apostate, he was divorced ipso facto from his wife. But because he was unable to raise enough bail, had 10,000 piasters debt and refused to sign a paper ratifying the divorce, he was imprisoned. Meanwhile, his wife changed her mind and escaped from her relatives' house. Ahmed was released on the intervention of the English Embassy and the family happily reunited.[67] The story of Ahmed Agha does not finish there. But before continuing with his story, a closer look at the persecution of Muslim converts is necessary.

---

65 Wilson A. Farnsworth. "Western Turkey: Letter from Mr. Farnsworth." *The Missionary Herald*, March (1861): 73-74.

66 *ibid.* 75.

67 George F. Herrick. "Western Turkey: Letter from Mr. Herrick." *The Missionary Herald*, November (1862): 353-355.

4.2.3 Persecution

Despite new legal regulations, the conversion of Muslims continued to be a legal and social issue in the ensuing years. The first reference to the persecution of Muslim converts after the Edict of 1856 appears in 1857, when members of a family of Muslim converts were examined at the house of Cyrus Hamlin. The two officers examining the family came to the conclusion that no coercion had been used and that the accusations of the convert's mother were false. They added that every subject of the sultan was allowed to enjoy religious freedom.[68] Their attitude, however, could not stop the persecution. Although the Porte stopped investigating the case, some influential officials stirred up public Muslim discontent over the peril posed by converts, who fled for safety. Cyrus Hamlin recounted that the gathering storm looked "so lowering." In accordance with the usual optimism of the missionaries of the Board, however, he estimated that the "the storm" might soon pass over and they might have "tremendous and destructive storms, and then a clear sky to work in."[69] This early instance of a legal case shows the intricate web of actors that determined the outcome. The state officials acted according to the new edict, but it is not clear if their attitude was a decoy. Public sentiment, aroused by conservative officials, threatened the family. Thus, although the state did not persecute the converts, the social setting was a great hindrance and seems to have been orchestrated as *de facto* persecution. Indeed, the missionaries were wary of public unrest. Tensions escalated as a result of a conflict at a burial place for Protestant Armenians in July 1860 and Gregorian Armenians resorted to violence.[70] One missionary portrayed the scene as a "lowering sky" and added that their "few converts from Islamism appeared firm, intending to meet the storm if it must come."[71]

---

68 "Recent Intelligence." *The Missionary Herald*, November (1857): 379.

69 Cyrus Hamlin. "Northern Armenians: Letter from Mr. Hamlin." *The Missionary Herald*, December (1857): 390-391.

70 H. G. O. Dwight. "The Northern Armenians: Letter from Mr. Dwight." *The Missionary Herald*, October (1860): 311-313.

71 William G. Schauffler. "Mission to Western Turkey: Letter from Mr. Schauffler." *The Missionary Herald*, November (1860): 342-343.

The government was also taking steps to curb missionary activity. Customs officers in Edirne did not allow Turkish and Persian books on religious subjects to pass through on direct orders from Istanbul in April 1858. The missionaries brought the matter to the Porte and the English consul, as a result of which the books were given back. This success was important for the missionaries since it showed that "when the Turks had taken a stand they gave way." The part of the letter relating to this incident was titled "Turkish Bigotry Yielding."[72] Backed by the English consul, the missionaries seem to have assumed an attitude of superiority. Moreover, the case was depicted in terms of rivalry and submission.

There is a similar story to that of Ahmed Aghas in the missionary letters from the field. Hasan, a Muslim convert in Ankara, became a matter of concern when the authorities decided to persecute him following his conversion. Hasan, openly professing his new religion, was put into prison in 1861. The local helper, one Abgar, who related Hasan's persecution in his letter, was distressed and remarked that the Turks had all become their enemies.[73] He was considered to be "fully enlightened" as a result of his conversion to Protestantism. When he was brought before the pasha, the pasha cited that "[r]eligion is free," but he was in any case imprisoned on grounds that he was still married to a "faithful woman." After his release, Hasan was exiled to Yozgat, a provincial city under the jurisdiction of the pasha in Ankara. The missionaries were worried about his fate and his case was brought to the ambassadors of England and Holland.[74] Having spent twelve days in Yozgat, Hasan made his escape and arrived at Istanbul on June 2, 1862.[75] Unlike Ahmed Agha, Hasans's story does not occupy a huge place in the Herald or cover a long period. One reason might be that the incidents he went through were not as dramatic as Ahmed Agha's.

The above mentioned cases soon turned out to be minor events in the larger scheme of things for the mission. Although the missionaries were not capable of starting a full-scale mission to the Muslims due to a lack of re-

---

72 "Northern Armenians: Letter from Mr. Morse." *The Missionary Herald*, August (1858): 251.

73 "Miscellanies." *The Missionary Herald*, May (1862): 163-164.

74 Benjamin Parsons. "Western Turkey: Letter from Mr. Parsons." *The Missionary Herald*, August (1862): 242-243.

75 "Items of Intelligence." *The Missionary Herald*, August (1862): 239.

sources, they were optimistic. The door was open and they were getting ready to enter and claim the land. Therefore, they were shocked on July 17, 1864, when Turkish converts in Istanbul were arrested and imprisoned. According to the missionaries, the charge against the converts was professing Christianity. This time the persecution did not stop there. The state was openly targeting the mission headquarters in Istanbul. On July 18, the police closed the mission's bookshop, which was also the treasurer's office, the office of Mr. Bliss, the agent of the American Bible Society, and the office of Dr. Thompson. The printing office was also closed. Upon Mr. Brown's protest, acting as charge d'affaires for the United States, the government seal was removed from the door on July 20.[76]

The unexpected swoop forced the missionaries to look for a possible explanation. One Mr. Herrick stated his belief that "certain frantical [sic] Turks" provoked by Catholics and members of other rival Christian sects had spread the rumor that thousands of Turks had turned Protestants and thus influenced the opinion of high ranking officials and even the sultan himself.[77] Herrick indicated the reformist-conservative split between the Muslim factions as a possible reason for such rumors. The missionaries believed that the order for the operation was obtained directly from the sultan in consultation with the British ambassador, Henry Bulwer, and with his tacit approval.[78]

Ahmed Agha was also among the seven or eight Turkish converts who were arrested. He was at Mr. Herricks' house when the officers took him.[79] The missionaries could not establish Ahmed's whereabouts for three days. Later, they communicated with him and the rest of the converts by mail because they were denied every attempt to see them in person. The converts were not charged with any crime "except that of being Christian and endeavoring to induce other Turks to embrace Christianity."[80] Both American and English missionaries were disappointed by the lack of support from the British ambassador Henry Bulwer, because Britain was seen as "the

---

76 "Monthly Summary." *The Missionary Herald*, September (1864): 278.

77 George F. Herrick. "Letter from Mr. Herrick." *The Missionary Herald*, August (1864): 306.

78 *ibid.* 306.

79 *ibid.* 306.

80 *ibid.* 307.

acknowledged protector of Protestantism" in the Ottoman Empire.[81] As a result, they made an open call to the ambassador:

The Universal voice of Christians in Constantinople, both native and foreign, cries against this detention, in close custody, now for two weeks, of those whose only crime is that they are Christians; and every eye looks to your Excellency and to English influence, speaking through you, to effect their release, both from prison and from exile.[82]

Sir Bulwer responded to this appeal by delivering a communiqué via the chaplain of the embassy.[83] He stated the government's accusations against the missionaries and suggested that the missionaries confined themselves to the discussion of Christianity.[84] He also informed the missionaries that the government had justified the arrest of some of the converts as an act of protection, saying that their lives were threatened.[85] The Board implicitly accepted the counterproductive methods of the Church Missionary Society as "the real occasion, though not cause, of the recent violent proceedings of the government."[86]

To the missionaries' mind, Henry Bulwer had acted together with the Porte in the organization and execution of this persecution. He simply had joined "the Turkish officials in a crusade against Protestant missionaries," and the reason they gave for this "Anglo-Turkish coalition" was that Britain pursued the policy of strengthening Turkey politically in the family of European nations. The Board did not approve the precedence of politics over religion. The measures of the government, aided by the British consul, were believed to have quenched the "feeble light Christianity had caused to shine

---

81 *ibid.* 306.

82 *ibid.* 306.

83 *ibid.* 307.

84 *ibid.* 308.

85 George F. Herrick. "Letter from Mr. Herrick." *The Missionary Herald*, August (1864): 308.

86 *ibid.* 311.

in the minds of" imprisoned Turkish converts and "laid a heavy, crushing hand upon their forming, unfortified faith."[87]

What happened to Ahmed Agha? The missionaries specifically addressed a note concerning Ahmed Agha to the American Embassy and they were guaranteed that their note would be sent to the Porte with a further note added by the embassy.[88] Yet Ahmed Agha was the only convert still detained in prison in October 1864, despite the fact that the other converts who were arrested had been allowed to go free.[89] Having spent three months in prison, Ahmed Agha was depressed and he felt too exhausted to remain cheerful.[90] The prison superintendent refused the request for permission to send him a copy of the Gospel.[91] Meanwhile, according to missionary accounts, his wife bore the hardships "in a commendable and Christian spirit."[92]

Ahmed was later called before a pasha, the head of police.[93] At that meeting, the pasha examined him in a kindly manner for two hours and learned about him, his family, and his past. He tried to convince Ahmed Agha go back voluntarily to Kayseri and promised a good government office if he complied. Ahmed Agha stated his personal reasons for leaving Kayseri and refused the offer on the grounds that he felt comfortable in Istanbul.[94]

Before the end of October, Ahmed Agha was sent into exile in Tekirdağ.[95] The situation was not at all favorable for the missionaries. Mr. E. E. Bliss, who arrived in Istanbul on October 15, 1864, stated that the

---

87 George F. Herrick. "Western Turkey: Letter from Mr. Herrick." *The Missionary Herald*, December (1864): 376-377.

88 George F. Herrick. "Letter from Mr. Herrick." *The Missionary Herald*, August (1864): 311.

89 George F. Herrick. "Western Turkey: Letter from Mr. Herrick." *The Missionary Herald*, January (1865): 16.

90 *ibid.* 16.

91 *ibid.* 16.

92 *ibid.* 16.

93 *ibid.* 16.

94 George F. Herrick. "Western Turkey: Letter from Mr. Herrick." *The Missionary Herald*, January (1865): 17.

95 "Monthly Summary." *The Missionary Herald*, January (1865): 24.

persecution had been a great blow to the work among the Muslims: no Muslims attended their services, and when the missionaries tried to proselytize them, the Muslims declined their attempts, pointing to the recent persecution, arrests and exiles.[96] Ahmed Agha spent a month in Tekirdağ before being seized and sent to prison for a short while by the local governor. The Protestant Armenian pastor at Tekirdağ sent a telegram to Istanbul and the British Embassy informed the Porte on the matter. As a result, the Porte sent a telegram ordering his immediate release and the local governor was asked to account for his "unwarranted interference."[97] Ahmed Agha spent the second month of his exile at Edirne. The governor of Edirne treated him with kindness and he was allowed to travel and act freely within the city. The governor also promised to provide him with money for his journey back to Istanbul.[98] Finally, in December 1864, Ahmed Agha returned from exile and was united with his family in his own rented house in Istanbul.[99]

The missionaries drew attention to the fact that the sultan accorded freedom of faith and worship to his subjects under the protection of the Edict of 1856. Their resentment was deep. For them, "the dawn of Christian intelligence, penetrating and arousing the Moslem mind, and the growing conviction of many a Turk" that the doctrines of Protestantism were "of divine authority [...] had at length created among the ignorant and fanatical masses an apprehension [...]."[100] The demand that the missionaries ceased their activities of propagation in places of public worship was considered to be "closing the great door of access to the Turkish mind." They complained that the news of man's salvation might not be peacefully proclaimed "to the millions who sit in darkness." From the missionary perspective, the adopted measures were "a barrier to the spread of the gospel, set up by an act of arbitrary power."[101]

---

96 *ibid.* 24.

97 George F. Herrick. "Western Turkey: Letter from Mr. Herrick." *The Missionary Herald*, March (1865): 79.

98 *ibid.* 79.

99 *ibid.* 79, 87.

100 "Annual Meeting of the Board." *The Missionary Herald*, November (1864): 337.

101 "Annual Meeting of the Board." *The Missionary Herald*, November (1864): 338.

The missionaries claimed that they did not "preach or lecture against the Mohammedan religion." In response to the charges that they were distributing anti-Islam books and tracts, they accused the Church Missionary Society and Rev. Dr. Pfander of producing and circulating these documents, and pretended to have assumed a moderate view on Islam in the public sphere and in their propagation activities.[102] It is ironic that while attacking the Muslim faith incessantly from the beginning of the missions to the Ottoman Empire, the missionaries had advertised and praised the books and pamphlets on the many occasions on which they were mentioned in *The Missionary Herald*. Despite these hindrances, the missionaries had hopes for the future of their work among the Muslims. They called the process a "crisis," yet as one missionary stated, they had "strong and cheerful confidence" that there would be "a real advance" in their work among the Muslims.[103] The short term indications, however, were not favorable. In a letter written on October 15, 1864, the persecution was regarded as a "great blow to the work among Mohammedans" and increased the elusiveness of Turkish targets to the missionary advances.[104]

The persecution abated slowly, and the imprisoned converts were exiled. Yet, government intervention against the missionary activities among the Muslims continued. The following extract summarizes the missionary sentiment:

Fearful that the advancing light of Christianity, entering the darkened minds of the Mussulman population, may weaken the spiritual authority of the Turkish rulers, the government, by its acts during the past six months, has given abundant proof that it would gladly put an end to the whole protestant reformation.[105]

This statement grasps the gist of the discontent on the government side. The missionaries were well aware of the fact that it was a struggle of legitimacy for the state. By undermining the most important and well-established as-

---

102 George F. Herrick. "Western Turkey: Letter from Mr. Herrick." *The Missionary Herald*, October (1864): 308-309.

103 *ibid*. 311.

104 "Monthly Summary." *The Missionary Herald*, January (1865): 24.

105 Joseph K. Greene. "Western Turkey: Letter from Mr. Greene." *The Missionary Herald*, April (1865): 113.

pect of public legitimacy and support for the state, that is Islam, the missionaries became competitors in this field. Their feigned surprise and the hypocrisy apparent in their statements is contradictory, to say the least, to their previous conduct and quite astonishing. Claiming to hold Islam in respect at the height of the persecution, they resorted to their original discourse, in this instance by calling the Muslim mind darkened, perhaps considering that English-language publications were exempt from this moral attitude of showing respect to the society they lived in.

4.2.4 Metaphors

The attempt to start a mission to the Muslims was articulated in terms of metaphors, as shown above. The use of linguistic metaphors indicates a pattern similar to those observed in the metaphor networks of the founding years. To start with, linguistic metaphors belonging to the same group of conceptual metaphors were used to refer to very similar situations. Secondly, the metaphor networks were used in a complementary manner to each other. Lastly, despite some exceptions, the use of metaphors was diachronic and the beginning, development and final phases of the attempt to start a mission to the Muslims can also be marked by the dominance of certain metaphor networks during the various phases.

Metaphors of doors and opening make up the larger part. Especially at the beginning, the missionaries used these metaphors to refer to new opportunities or favorable conditions. Linguistic metaphors such as "a wide door opening," "to enter this great and promising field," "whole land will be open before us," "doors of entrance opening," "God has opened a wide door of usefulness," "the door of entrance," operate on the same level. First, they refer to the visible opportunities evaluated by the missionaries. Yet these opportunities were not considered in isolation from the missionaries' aims. Thus, secondly, the metaphors imply the furtherance of missionary activities if these opportunities should be utilized. The teleological nature of the missionary point of view is represented as entering a field or a path. Opportunities and taking advantage of opportunities were regarded as the entrance points which the missionaries considered as inevitably leading to the coming of the Kingdom. These notions can be seen in the conceptual metaphor **Progress is Forward Motion**, which is a subcase of **CHANGE IS MOTION**. The conceptualization of motion can be seen in the importance of opportunities as facilitating and thus aiding mission work. As such, the use of these linguistic metaphors can be regarded as instances of **Aids to Action are Aids to Motion**. Given that missionary activities were directed to a specific aim, the commencement of the conceptualized motion is **Starting a Purposeful Action is Starting Out for a Destination**. Both metaphors originate from **Purposeful Action is Directed Motion to a Destination**, destination being the Kingdom of God.

Following on from metaphors of openings and doors, the missionaries also resorted to metaphors of agriculture and cultivation. They were optimistic that hope would ripen into fruition, and described positive outcomes from encounters with Muslims as fruit for mission work. When they assessed a community or a group of people ready to receive their message, they applied the term of gathering a harvest. Harvest here stands for the community that is ripe or mature enough to listen to and understand missionary propagation. Proselytizing was articulated as sowing seeds, and favorable conditions were identified as prepared soil that had been improved by planting, tending and watering. All these metaphorical usages can be related to the conceptual metaphor **BELIEFS ARE BEINGS WITH A LIFE CYCLE**. This very general metaphor includes **BELIEFS ARE PLANTS**. To see how the linguistic metaphors function against the background of these metaphors, we can look at more specific instances of these conceptual metaphors, which are **Encouraging Beliefs is Cultivating a Plant** and **Development of a Belief is Growth of a Plant**. Moreover, as the missionary mind was constantly scanning and evaluating favorable conditions prior to starting mission work, which were also represented in the form of metaphors of cultivation, one can take into consideration the conceptual metaphor **Necessary Prerequisites are Necessary Prerequisites for Plant Life**.

The third cluster of metaphors are metaphors of light and darkness. The classic examples of the light/darkness dichotomy can be seen in expressions such as "blindness," "shadow of the Ottoman Porte," "center of Muslim darkness," "season of darkness," "light of Christianity" and "dawn of Christian intelligence," and "darkened minds." The dichotomy is present in the conceptual metaphor **GOODNESS IS LIGHT / BADNESS IS DARKNESS**. The dichotomy also points to a set of conceptual metaphors that originate from **DISCOURSE IS A LIGHT MEDIUM**. The missionary activity predominantly relied on the application of missionary discourse as propagation, and the metaphors lead to **IDEAS ARE LIGHT SOURCES**, which in turn involves the metaphor **IDEAS ARE PERCEPTIONS**. Two related subcases of this set of metaphors that are closely connected to the missionary applications of linguistic metaphors are **Understanding is Seeing** and **Aids to Gaining Awareness are Aids to Vision**. The negative formulations of these metaphors are **Not being Aware of Reality is not Seeing Reality**, and **Impediments to Awareness are Impediments to Seeing**. As such, the dichotomy of good and bad was articulated on a conceptual level. In two instances, the missionaries used metaphors related to weather conditions to refer to unfavorable conditions and state persecution. These are metaphors of storm, lowering sky, and clear sky. These metaphors also function on the presupposition that dark sky is bad and a clear sky is good. Thus, they and other metaphors mentioned above are related to **DARKNESS IS A COVER**. As the metaphors were used to express persecution, storm and lowering sky can be seen as instances of **Adversity is Adversity due to Bad Weather** and thus **EXTERNAL CONDITIONS ARE CLIMATE** as well.

The fourth set of metaphors consists of metaphors of war. The missionaries used these metaphors to refer both to the aggressive expansion policy of the Board and to unfavorable conditions arising from centers of power, predominantly the state. They refer to fields or lands, both metaphorical and real, and convey the intention of taking hold of, possessing and occupying them. Phrases such as "subduing the strongholds of the enemy," "fighting the stern battle," "taking a stand" and "enemy yielding" are other uses. In one instance, the missionaries complain about the impact of the persecution of Muslim converts by stating that the persecutors impaired the forming, unfortified faith of the converts. It may be assumed that the fortification that is alluded to is a mental state or level of knowledge, and the faith that is needed to be able to defend one's beliefs and ideology in a coherent manner without losing it. Although sometimes the boundary between spiritual and real warfare became blurred, the missionaries mainly stayed within the confines of spiritual warfare in their language. Thus, metaphors of war can be seen in the general context of **THEORETICAL DEBATE IS COMPETITION**. Which leads respectively to the conceptual metaphors **COMPETITION IS WAR, ARGUMENT IS WAR, Theories are Fortifications**, and **Attacking a Theory is Attacking a Fortification**.

4.2.5 Conclusion

During this period, the missionaries were involved in a different type of work, namely proselytizing Muslims. The first reason for this difference comes from the fact that the legal and political climate had been different up until the Edict of 1856, despite previous government attempts at reform. Secondly, and consequently, missionaries of the Board found themselves in a similar situation to that of the founding years. Despite the fact that the missionaries were acquainted with Turkish and other Muslim peoples in the empire, they realized that their acquaintanceship with them was superficial. Thirdly, the new era that started with the Edict of 1856 not only brought optimism and opportunities for the missionaries, but also initiated significant and crippling events, such as civil unrest and massacres in Syria in 1860 and the power struggle between the conservative and reformist camps in the capital. These events consequently provided the basis for the suppression of missionary work among Muslims, because the Ottoman state made it clear that equality is a community-based equality and religious propaganda threatened the well-being and peace of society in general.

It is not surprising then that the missionaries started to evaluate these changes by resorting to metaphors of opening, an open door, and entering. The possibility of mission work among Muslims was regarded as an open door. Other conceptual metaphors of cultivation, war, and light/darkness are also in accord with previous missionary uses of conceptual language. There is, however, one metaphor network that is missing; the metaphors of path and road. Although opening suggests forward motion and entering the field or land is reminiscent of making one's way along a path, those conceptual metaphors were not directly applied in this period when referring to the attempts at converting Muslims. Multiple reasons can be given as the cause for this lack of metaphors of path and road. To start with, the missionaries were not prepared to start a mission to the Muslims. They had limited access to Muslims and consequently lacked invaluable cultural information, including linguistic competency, to facilitate the process. Secondly, they probably could not foresee the outcome of their attempt, because they were going at it hesitantly. Lastly, and as a result of the previous causes and the final blow from the Ottoman Porte in 1864, the missionaries failed to enter the field, pass through the open door and start a proper mission. Hence, there was no road to walk on.

As a result, the missionary narrative was also not coherent in temporal terms. The metaphor networks were complementary but at the same time they were not well developed. There are two main reasons for the weak narrative, and they are interrelated. As stated above, the attempt to proselytize among Muslims started late in mission history on account of historical, political and legal issues, and when it started, it was with limited temporal span and limited success. In their attempt to narrate the new situation, the missionaries had insufficient experience of the real world to put the linguistic and conceptual metaphor networks into a more developed parabolic narrative. There is a narrative, but it is not as powerful as the narratives and parabolic connections of the founding years. Secondly, the timid start and its humble continuation might indicate that the missionaries had doubts about the future of a possible mission to the Muslims. It is true that they referred to opportunities as openings and invited missionaries and patrons of the Board to take advantage of favorable conditions, but they do not seem to have referred to what happened after they entered into the field. As such, the missionaries chose to restrict their conceptual discursive formations to the real life events they encountered; they did not employ them to allude to a better articulated, and more extensively discussed teleological agenda. All in all, a lack of external data, namely real life encounters, a relatively reserved and cautious attitude on the part of the missionaries, and ultimately persecution by the state hindered this interesting and specific period of ABCFM activity in the Ottoman Empire. Otherwise, it could have developed into a full-scale narrative relying on conceptual networks, but surpassing them by comprising coherent and full stories that could be projected onto other stories.

4.3 CASE STUDY II: MISSIONARY RESPONSES TO THE ARMENIAN MASSACRES OF 1894-1896

4.3.1 Historical Background

In this case study, the missionary discourse will be analyzed by looking at how the missionaries and the Board responded on a discursive level to an unusual set of events. The events are known as the 'Hamidian Massacres' or 'Armenian Massacres of 1894-1896.' To be more specific, the massacres that took place at the end of 1895 and beginning of 1896 and other incidents occurring until 1897 will be placed under scrutiny. The reason for limiting the number of cases is to allow us see the employment of missionary discourse in all its many facets. For this, the volumes chosen from *The Missionary Herald* are those of 1896, 1897 and 1898. In these issues, the main allusions to the massacres are almost without exception to those that took place during this period, because these were the most widespread and devastating. Also, this choice makes sense because the first comments and responses in *The Missionary Herald* start to appear in the January issue of 1896, and by the end of 1898 the events and their shocking results abated to such a degree that the missionary discourse was channeled into other topics not immediately related to the massacres.

The period that finally reached its climax in the massacres started with the signing of the Treaty of Berlin in 1878.[106] During this period, British policy towards the territorial integrity of the Ottoman Empire changed with William Ewart Gladstone's administration after the Liberal Party won the elections in 1880.[107] London's suspicions about the expansion of Russian and German power were of crucial importance to this policy shift.[108] The Gladstone administration saw the demise of the Empire as inevitable and in order to curb Russian power in the region, decided to take control of key points in the Ottoman Empire.[109] Moreover, the 1880s saw a rise in the anti-Muslim and anti-Turkish sentiments in British and Western public opinion.[110] Finally, Gladstone demanded the implementation of article 61 of the Treaty of Berlin, which guaranteed improvements in the living conditions of the Armenians living in the six districts (Vilayet-i Sitte) of Erzurum, Bitlis, Van, Harput, Sivas, and Diyarbakır.[111] The Porte feared that such a process might ultimately lead to an independent Armenia at the expense of Ottoman territorial integrity.[112]

---

106 Kemal H. Karpat. *The Politicization of Islam.* Oxford: Oxford University Press (2001): 208.
107 *ibid.* 208.
108 *ibid.* 208.
109 *ibid.* 208.
110 *ibid.* 209.
111 *ibid.* 209.
112 *ibid.* 209.

London was also aware that an autonomous administration for Armenians might lead to civil and military strife and end in massacres.[113] The Armenians made a false analogy between their cause and that of the Bulgarians, who actually won Bulgarian autonomy with the help of Russia in 1878. This occurred after the Bulgarians, together with the Russians, embarked on a campaign in 1877-78 to get rid of the Muslim population in the Balkans before the implementation of the Treaty of San Stefano and Treaty of Berlin.[114] Their aim was to gain the demographic advantage and thus guarantee autonomy according to the regulations imposed by the treaties, even though Muslims were already in the minority in most places in Bulgaria.[115] But in the six districts with a considerable Armenian population Armenians did not constitute the majority, despite claims to the contrary by Armenian nationalists.[116] Armenian patriarch Nerces helped rig the figures about the population of the region, which were immediately accepted by Western powers and Russia.[117] Although Nerces later admitted to having manipulated the population data, those powers never brought it to the attention of the public.[118] Under such circumstances, the Muslim communities started to feel uneasy following rumors of imminent atrocities similar to those in the Balkans.[119]

Against a background of internal and international power games, the Armenian question evolved into a secular issue dominated by Armenian nationalist organizations rather than traditional ecclesiastical circles.[120] Those organizations quickly adopted the policy of grabbing the attention of European powers and, by exhibiting the horrors committed by Muslims and Turkish despotism, invoking foreign intervention, because this policy had

---

113 Davide Rodogno. *Against Massacre: Humanitarian Interventions in the Ottoman Empire, 1815-1914*. Princeton: Princeton University Press (2012): 190.

114 Karpat, *Politicization*, 209.

115 Rodogno, *Against Massacre*, 187.

116 *ibid.* 187.

117 Karpat, *Politicization*, 210.

118 *ibid.* 210.

119 *ibid.* 209.

120 Rodogno, *Against Massacre*, 185.

worked well in the Bulgarian example.[121] But once again, they ignored the fact that Christians were the majority in Bulgaria.[122]

There was yet another side to the story. In the nineteenth century in Eastern Turkey, the Armenian farmers and shepherds, and the Kurdish nomadic tribes lived in an equilibrium that rested on the payment of feudal dues to Kurdish tribal chiefs in exchange for vows of protection.[123] Following the rise of successful separatist movements in Bosnia, Serbia and Bulgaria, Armenian nationalist and socialist organizations appeared in the 1870s and 1880s and confronted the Kurdish suppression and the underprivileged legal state of the Christian subjects in the Ottoman Empire.[124] The Hunchak Party, a socialist group founded in 1887 in Switzerland, started organizing the farmers in Sason district of Bitlis province (vilayet).[125]

In 1893, 3,000 or 4,000 pastoralist Kurds attacked the Armenians living at Talori in the Sason district, and the Armenians arrived at the opinion that the Turks were not employing everything within their power to prevent these attacks.[126] In 1894, the government asked for taxes from the inhabitants of Talori but they refused, claiming that the Kurdish attacks meant that they lacked the financial means to satisfy the demand.[127] The local authorities sent troops but the troops were repulsed by the Armenians.[128] The governor of Bitlis gained permission for a more comprehensive operation and the Armenians of Sason found themselves confronted with the Hamidian regiments and regular troops from Bitlis and Muş garrisons, reinforced by

---

121 *ibid.* 187.

122 *ibid.* 187.

123 Ann Marie Wilson. "In the name of God, civilization, and humanity: The United States and the Armenian massacres of the 1890s." *Le Mouvement Social*, No: 227 (2009/2): 29.

124 *ibid.* 29.

125 *ibid.* 29.

126 Roy Douglas. "Britain and the Armenian Question, 1894-7." *The Historical Journal*, 1976, No: 19, 1, p. 116.

127 *ibid.* 116.

128 *ibid.* 116.

the Fourth Army corps.[129] A twenty-three day operation ensued starting on August 18. The death toll was high. The European powers protested against the treatment of the Armenians after the massacre and the Porte appointed a commission of inquiry. The way the commission conducted its inquiry and the promotion of the responsible officers drew a strong reaction from the European powers, who demanded that the Ottoman government institute the reforms agreed on in the treaties of San Stefano and Berlin in 1878, which had not been put into practice until then.[130]

The Ottoman Government decided that the reforms were to go into effect in October 1895, but the widespread massacres throughout the Ottoman Empire obstructed their implementation.[131] The Hunchak party organized a procession in Istanbul on September 30, 1895. The ostensible aim was to present a petition to the grand vizier, but beneath that the Hunchakists wanted to underline the demands of the European powers. Probably afraid of an Armenian uprising in the Eastern provinces, and furious with Armenian collaboration with Macedonian revolutionists, the government responded harshly. Hundreds of people were killed. Within a short time the events spread to the rest of the empire, mainly to places with a considerable Armenian population, and above all to the six provinces. These were the 'vilayets' with the largest Armenian populations for which Britain, Russia, and France had endorsed the package of reforms relying on the above mentioned treaties.[132] Starting at Akhisar and Trabzon on October 3 and 4, massacres took place at more than forty locations between October and December and ceased briefly after an outbreak at Birecik on January 1, 1896."[133] Later, on August 24, 1896, Dashnaksutyun, Armenian Revolutionary Federation, seized the Imperial Ottoman bank in Istanbul in order to protest at the massacres and prompt external intervention. The event gained international attention and the revolutionaries were allowed to leave. Yet

---

129 ibid. 116; Robert Melson. "A Theoretical Inquiry into the Armenian Massacres of 1894-1896." Comparative Studies in Society and History, Vol. 24, No. 3 (1982): 487.

130 ibid. 487-488.

131 ibid. 488.

132 Wilson, "In the name of God," 29.

133 Melson, "Theoretical Inquiry," 488.

approximately 6,000 Armenians were killed in Istanbul in the ensuing attacks on the community.[134]

4.3.2 Missionary Response

The massacres were a great shock to the missionaries. They were expecting a continuation of unrest and even an outbreak of violence, but the dimensions of the events were beyond their comprehension. One of the earliest comments, which appeared in the January issue of 1896 (still before the massacres came fully to a halt) was as follows:

Speaking after the manner of men and without thought of a superintending Providence, it must be said that never since Protestant missions began has a disaster so appalling overtaken any missions as that which has occurred in Turkey within the past few weeks. It is difficult to speak in measured words of what has transpired.[135]

Unable to make comparisons and appalled by the extent of events, the missionaries stated that "never in the history of any person" then now living had "there been such a disaster"[136] and that "[t]he century has seen nothing to compare in horror with the facts which are certified to by innumerable witnesses."[137] The shock was so great that the missionaries were unable to make up their minds, and report and evaluate the events properly in their writings over the following two months. The reason for their silence and confusion was explained in a missionary letter: "The trials of the last two months might be considered as constituting a reason for more full and frequent writing, but the effect has rather been to strike us dumb [...] [i]n the midst of the awful judgments of God, we have kept silence. These have been solemn days indeed."[138] The missionaries' claim was that never in the lifetime of any one then alive had there been a more piercing call for chari-

---

134 *ibid.* 488-489

135 "Editorial Paragraphs." *The Missionary Herald*, January (1896): 2.

136 "Editorial Paragraphs." *The Missionary Herald*, February (1896): 47.

137 "The Massacres in Turkey." *The Missionary Herald*, February, (1896): 54.

138 "Western Turkey Mission." *The Missionary Herald*, March (1896): 105.

ty, and it was inconceivable that another call like this should come in that generation.[139]

After the events "[c]harges have been made by high Turkish officials" that missionaries had "incited the Armenians to sedition." In response, the missionaries "demanded an official investigation of these charges."[140] The charges were "repeatedly denied" and thought to be "credited by some who" did "not know the character of the men" and who had "no conception of the benevolent and Christian work" in which the missionaries were engaged.[141] Although the missionaries were wary of the revolutionary movements, they were aware of another aspect of their involvement in the tension between the Muslim and Christian populations. The Board was of the opinion that they had come "under obligations to the Christians of Asia Minor." The reason was that with the aid they had given them, the Christians had made great advances along every educational and religious line, and "largely because of these advances," they had "fallen into dire stress."[142] These lines can be read as proof that philanthropic reasons were secondary for the Board because they never considered the equally underprivileged Muslim communities as worthy of proper education. The Muslims were mostly unreachable as prospective converts due to both the religious indifference of the community itself and the threat of state persecution. Moreover, according to their own statements, the missionaries were aware that providing one portion of the community with better means would result in social conflict.

Although the massacres took place in a number of places throughout Anatolia, Eastern and Southeastern Turkey were the regions most affected. The Eastern Turkey Mission gathered itself towards the summer of 1896 and started to take immediate steps for recommencing widespread missionary activity in the region. The steps to be taken were explained by a missionary from the region in the following lines:

I would like to emphasize also two or three leading principles which direct all our efforts in this difficult task of resuscitating and reorganizing our field work. First, we

---

139 "Editorial Paragraphs." *The Missionary Herald*, April, (1896): 136.

140 "Editorial Paragraphs." *The Missionary Herald*, March (1896): 90.

141 "Editorial Paragraphs." *The Missionary Herald*, May (1896): 179.

142 "Editorial Paragraphs." *The Missionary Herald*, June (1896): 222.

keep the front to the fact that all this work of evangelization and education is God's work and theirs primarily, and quite subordinately that of the American churches through their missionaries. [...] Second, necessarily connected with the first is the vital importance of reaffirming, as strongly as ever, the principle of self support. [...] Third, directly in the line of the two preceding principles, and their legitimate development, is the future extension of the work from these churches as subordinate centres, rather than from the one centre in Harpoot.[143]

The paragraph is an indication that the missionaries were recovering after initially being caught off their guard. In a couple of months, they evaluated the situation and displayed their resilience with new plans for the future.

Despite their optimism, though, the missions in the region suffered from a lack of resources. Missionary narratives were widely read by the American public. They had an extensive network of mission stations in the region and controlled the flow of information. Thanks to their privileged position and their cooperation with other organizations, they contributed heavily to the narrative surrounding the 'Armenian Question.' When the mission's work was disrupted by the massacres and the ensuing financial problems, the missionaries started to make calls for donations and made it clear that the mission was suffering from a lack of financial means. The call might be in the form of asking whether the readers could afford to replace a pastor who had become a martyr rather than abandon his faith,[144] or general complaints about the shortage of staff and helpers brought about by these tribulations.[145]

Towards the end of 1898, the atmosphere had returned to normal. The missionaries were returning to Turkey, new missionaries were sent, and this occasion was a matter of celebration: "This fact shows that the outlook for the missionary work in Turkey has vastly changed within two or three years. [...] It is ground for profound gratitude that the aspect of affairs is so different from what it was at the time of the 'events' in the Ottoman Empire [...]."[146] It was thought that widespread quiet and peace had "succeeded to the storms and distress of the past years" and confidence was reviving,

---

143 "Eastern Turkey Mission." *The Missionary Herald*, June (1897): 240.

144 "Word of Cheer and Cries for Help." *The Missionary Herald*, June (1898): 177.

145 *ibid.* 179.

146 "Editorial Paragraphs." *The Missionary Herald*, October (1898): 381.

business was resumed, prostrated communities and shattered households were gathering themselves together and adjusting to the new conditions, and the semblance of prosperity already began to appear.[147]

4.3.2.1 Some Metaphors

The missionaries, appalled by the atrocities, wrote extensively on the topic. Their writings depicted the situation, evaluated circumstances, explained plans and asked for help, which soon turned into a full-scale campaign. As with their endeavors, their language reflected the mission's many-faceted activity. Conceptual formations are one of the underlying elements that relate all these issues broadly and coherently to one another and convey them to the reader. Referring to the massacres, one of the metaphors that emerged was the metaphor of storm. The violence that terrorized Talas was referred to as a cyclone that struck Talas.[148] When explaining how a member of the Merzifon Church lost his life, the imagery used was of a "storm bursting on him."[149] Insecure and horrified, the missionaries were uncertain whether "the bolt" might not fall any day.[150] The missionaries described themselves as protectors and a "shield during that awful storm of blood."[151] All in all, what happened was breaking storms[152] until finally "[w]idespread quiet and peace" had succeeded "the storms and distress of the past years."[153] Two years later the missionaries explained the situation of the Armenians as a people "gathering up and securing what remains to them after the storm."[154]

It has been shown in the previous chapter that weather metaphors are used in the missionary discourse and have a meaningful place in the metaphor network. Previously they were applied to unfavorable situations, but

---

147 "Annual Survey." *The Missionary Herald*, November (1898): 443.
148 Wilson A. Farnsworth. "What Shall the Missionaries in Turkey Do?" *The Missionary Herald*, February (1896): 57-58.
149 "Editorial Paragraphs." *The Missionary Herald*, March (1896): 95.
150 "Eastern Turkey Mission." *The Missionary Herald*, March (1896): 106.
151 "A Martyred Preacher in Turkey." *The Missionary Herald*, February (1897): 84.
152 "Editorial Paragraphs" *The Missionary Herald*, July (1897): 263.
153 "Annual Survey." *The Missionary Herald*, November (1898): 443.
154 "Central Turkey Mission." *The Missionary Herald*, December (1898): 508.

here the massacres triggered their use. The storm or bad weather metaphor is based on the metaphor **Adversity is Adversity due to Bad Weather** and it is a case of the **EXTERNAL CONDITIONS ARE CLIMATE** metaphor.

Actually in the previous instances from the 1820s it was shown that the storm metaphor had a connection with metaphors of light and darkness. Might the missionaries have had a similar type of connection in mind? The following lines bear testimony to this relation: "Notwithstanding the clouds that darken the outlook in Turkey [...] they are wonderfully sustained in their work and confident that light is yet to break through the clouds."[155] It is now possible to assert that the storm metaphor is also based on the conceptual metaphors **GOODNESS IS LIGHT / BADNESS IS DARKNESS, GOODNESS IS WHITE / BADNESS IS BLACK** and perhaps, **DARKNESS IS A COVER** as well, because of the implication of clouds covering the sky. In all these cases, the idea of storm is used to refer to the massacres and the subsequent turmoil.

The missionaries also used metaphors of light and darkness. When they defended the decision to stay as the right choice, they alluded to their presence for the Armenians as the "last ray of hope,"[156] and in their despair could see "no ray of hope" in their future.[157] The notion behind the metaphorical expressions is the concept that **LIGHT IS A LINE** and **HOPE IS LIGHT**. As it is a ray, another conceptual base might be the metaphor **LIGHT MOVES FROM A LIGHT SOURCE**, i.e. the evangelical Christianity and the missionaries. This conceptual background can also be seen in the following passage:

If there has been a country during the nineteenth century which has had a darker outlook than Turkey has to-day, I do not know what one it is. From whatever point of view it is regarded, there is not a ray of light from any quarter, except as one looks up and remembers the divine promises and the divine love.[158]

---

155 "Editorial Paragraphs." *The Missionary Herald*, April (1896): 136.

156 "Eastern Turkey Mission." *The Missionary Herald*, March (1896): 107.

157 *ibid*. 107.

158 Herman N. Barnum. "The Outlook in Turkey." *The Missionary Herald*, April (1896): 147.

In this example one can see the underlying conceptual metaphors clearly. Their discourse omits the actual background and equates a whole country to a source of darkness. The binary opposition of light and darkness is a powerful metaphor that incites positive and negative feelings in the reader without inviting them to consider the situation in a broader context. The missionary claim that there was no country with a darker outlook than Turkey thus gains credibility.

The missionaries explained their help as "the only bright spot in this, their darkest and most terrible experience,"[159] or while describing their mood as sad after a field trip, the adjective they used in contrast was bright.[160] If they believed the events they expected to happen were negative "the outlook was dark,"[161] and unwanted elements were "dark features."[162] A similar use can be seen in the lines "[b]right as the promises of God is the outlook for Christ's work in these and other cities in Turkey."[163] Here too the conceptual metaphor **GOODNESS IS LIGHT / BADNESS IS DARKNESS** is applied.

A good illustration of how the missionaries employed light is the way they refer to the "light of the gospel."[164] It is easy in this example to trace the conceptual metaphors **LIGHT MOVES FROM A LIGHT SOURCE** and **IDEAS ARE LIGHT SOURCES**. Moreover, if the ideas emanating from the gospel are understood as a consistent set of messages, the conceptual metaphor **DISCOURSE IS A LIGHT MEDIUM** can also be seen in the background. In line with this metaphor, the missionaries referred to the members of the Armenian Apostolic Church as "receiving truth and enlightenment to a degree that will make the former condition of their church forever impossible."[165] Again, **IDEAS ARE LIGHT SOURCES, DISCOURSE IS A LIGHT MEDIUM** and **LIGHT MOVES FROM A LIGHT SOURCE** constitute the substrate. Viewed in the light of this ex-

---

159 Grace N. Kimball. "Relief Work at Van, Eastern Turkey." *The Missionary Herald*, June (1896): 235.

160 "Eastern Turkey Mission." *The Missionary Herald*, February (1897): 61.

161 "Editorial Paragraphs." *The Missionary Herald*, April (1897): 132.

162 "Editorial Paragraphs." *The Missionary Herald*, July (1897): 258.

163 "Eastern Turkey Mission." *The Missionary Herald*, February (1897): 62.

164 "Editorial Paragraphs." *The Missionary Herald*, April (1897): 135.

165 "Editorial Paragraphs." *The Missionary Herald*, May (1897): 174.

planation, both metaphorical expressions, light of the gospel and enlightenment, are instances of **Aids to Gaining Awareness are Aids to Vision**, thus **Understanding is Seeing**, which is covered in turn by **IDEAS ARE PERCEPTIONS**. Using this conceptual background, the missionaries called themselves the "light of the world,"[166] talked of people longing for "more light,"[167] and portrayed their activities as casting "a pleasing light upon a scene otherwise most dark and pathetic."[168]

4.3.3 Enter, Walk, Reach: Openings, Future Plans and the Kingdom

4.3.3.1 Teleology and the Millennium

One can roughly identify three ways of comprehending the world in the West before Darwin. The first view is that the world was recently created and constant, namely the Christian Orthodox dogma. The second view assumed an eternal world which was either constant or cyclical, operating on the principles of chance and necessity and leaving no place for a teleological interpretation. The third view supposed a world of long duration or even eternal that is progressing in the direction of improvement and perfection. This view is represented in Christianity through ideas of the Millennium and resurrection. Of the three world views, the last is the underlying view for missionary discourse and ideology, with its peculiar interpretation. The missionary world view was teleological, hence finalistic and based on the ideas of progress and perfection.[169]

Their main inspiration was the spirit of 'disinterested benevolence' articulated by Jonathan Edwards.[170] The Protestant endeavor was aimed at

---

166 "Western Turkey Mission." *The Missionary Herald*, October (1897): 396.

167 "Eastern Turkey Mission." *The Missionary Herald*, July (1897): 276.

168 "Annual Survey." *The Missionary Herald*, November (1897): 441.

169 Ernst Mayr. "The Idea of Teleology." *Journal of the History of Ideas*, Vol. 53, No. 1 January - March (1992): 117.

170 Marwa Elshakry. "The Gospel of Science and American Evangelism in Late Ottoman Beirut." *Past and Present*, No. 196, Aug. (2007): 173.

creating a new man abroad.[171] The force behind the inauguration of the missions was millenarianism.[172] As a committee of the Board announced:

For some time before the Messiah came a light to lighten the Gentiles and the glory of his people Israel, an expectation extensively prevailed, that a glorious luminary was about to arise, and an important change to commence. Prophecies to this effect were on record, and the providence of God strikingly indicated their approaching fulfillment. Something very similar to all this is manifest in the present age. If the Messiah was then the Desire of all nations, his millennial reign is no less so now.[173]

According to the head of the committee, Jedidiah Morse, "the Papal and Mohammedan impostures were both established in 606 A.D. and their demise was expected to take place in 1866 to be followed by the millennium."[174]

As stated above, the missionaries were postmillennialists. This philosophy, which dates from the late eighteenth and early nineteenth centuries – although the ideas of the Millennium and the resurrection of Jesus had already been previously developed – became more than a tool to guess the date of second coming and defined the way people understood the events in a historical context and against a conceptual background of gradual improvement and rational laws.[175] In a nutshell, postmillennialism "[...] was the faith that the Kingdom of God would be gradually realized in this world; justice, peace and love would eventually reign supreme" and the world would be the gradually redeemed "under the influence of Christ's spirit rather than his physical presence."[176]

---

171 *ibid.* 174.
172 Ira V. Brown. "Watchers for the Second Coming: The Millenarian Tradition in America," *The Mississippi Valley Historical Review*, Vol. 39, No. 3, December (1952): 450.
173 *ibid.* 450.
174 *ibid.* 450.
175 James H. Moorhead. "Between Progress and Apocalypse: A Reassessment of Millennialism in American Religious Thought, 1800-1880," *The Journal of American History*, Vol. 71, No. 3, December (1984): 526.
176 Jean B. Quandt. "Religion and Social Thought: The Secularization of Postmillennialism," *American Quarterly*, Vol. 25, No. 4, October (1973): 391.

The idea behind this understanding was the working of the moral government of God on the framework of time.[177] Putting the ways of God on a time schedule was a way of justifying his ways by showing that God will win out over evil.[178] Yet the postmillennialists were aware that this justification required a great deal of happiness for people rather than anguish on the temporal level.[179] As a consequence, postmillennialist ideals assured that the end would not come at a time when the majority of humanity ceased to exist or were destined to go to hell.[180] Postmillennialism entailed "the belief in the imminence of the transformation, the reliance on providential agencies, and the confidence put in the total spiritual regeneration of society."[181]

Mid-century America witnessed the rise of topics that were equally important for both religious and social thought.[182] The most important was the merging together of postmillennialist expectations with the acceptance of civil institutions and technological developments as facilitators for the coming of the Kingdom.[183] The postmillennialists saw the ever-increasing volume of advanced technology, social welfare and progress in the arts and sciences as indications of the Millennium.[184] These secular advances were seen as cornerstones in the triumph of Christianity.[185] The completion of the transatlantic cable in 1858 was celebrated by the Protestant community with these ideas in mind.[186] Advances in printing, the steamboat, and merchandise were the means of conveying evangelical teaching and influence.[187] Yet, technological and social advancements were only one aspect of the postmillennialist aspirations. Steamboats and cables were balanced with the eschatological imagery from the Bible, such as in the cosmos of

---

177 Moorhead, "Progress and Apocalypse," 528.

178 *ibid.* 528.

179 *ibid.* 528.

180 *ibid.* 528.

181 Quandt, "Religion and Social Thought," 392.

182 *ibid.* 392.

183 *ibid.* 392.

184 Moorhead, "Progress and Apocalypse," 533.

185 *ibid.* 533.

186 *ibid.* 533.

187 *ibid.* 533.

John's Revelation consisting of angels, on the one side, and on the other the rising dead and eternal flames for the wicked.[188] Postmillennialist thought was full of the antinomies that inhered to its conceptualizations.

In the second half of the nineteenth century, the religious impulse known as 'liberalism' in the United States was on the rise. It tackled the social, moral, ecclesiastical and the theological issues of the era.[189] Right before the rise of liberalism, the changes in society had severe effects on traditional preaching and teaching.[190] In addition to which, new scientific discoveries, religious scholarship, and shifts in moral and religious attitudes initiated intellectual difficulties.[191] Darwin's Theory of Evolution, and consequently the rise of positivistic naturalism and the cumulative result of modern methods of acquiring knowledge, together with historical research, posed questions about the Bible and the history of doctrine. As a result, the liberal theologians had to grapple with an intellectual challenge of vast magnitude.[192] There were several varieties of religious liberalism and the Northeast regions played an important role.[193] Although Congregationalist groups were the directly linked to the Board, the impact of several other groups cannot be overlooked. Thus, besides Andover and Bangor, the contributions of Harvard, Yale and the Union Theological Seminary to the creation of a liberal intellectual corpus were crucial.[194]

The liberals called themselves 'progressive orthodoxy' and they set up the authority of Christian consciousness beside the already existing authorities of the Bible and Christian theology.[195] The interpretation of the Bible was supposed to be conducted by Christian consciousness, an idea which aimed at refuting the conservative view that the "meaning of Bible verses is evident and its message constant."[196] They modified the Hopkinsian view of divine sovereignty and concluded that God is immanent in the created

---

188 *ibid.* 525.
189 Ahlstrom, *Religious History*, 763.
190 *ibid.* 763.
191 *ibid.* 763-764.
192 *ibid.* 774-778.
193 *ibid.* 774-778.
194 ibid. 774-778.
195 Swift. "Conservative versus Progressive," 23.
196 *ibid.* 23.

world, God is Christ-like and, as a consequence, "a theology which teaches divine attributes or actions which offended the Christian consciousness needs to be modified."[197] John Edwin Smylie draws attention to the fact that this notion "changed providence from God's action '*upon* history' to his action '*within* it'" (italics in the original).[198] He cites Josiah Strong as an example of this point of view: "Science, which is a revelation of God's laws and methods, enables us to fall into his plans intentionally and to co-operate with him intelligently for the perfecting of mankind thus hastening forward the coming of the kingdom."[199] Yet the most problematic aspect was the belief in future probation, according to which "those who have not experienced Christ in this life will meet him in the next" and "the spiritual development may carry on beyond death into the intermediate state."[200] In short, as far as human nature was concerned their emphasis was on man's freedom and his capacity for altruistic action. For that reason, sin was considered to be an error or limitation which can be corrected by moral education and the example of Jesus, or by social reform. Original sin or human depravity was not accepted.[201]

What was the underlying reason for the rift in Congregationalist Theology? David Everett Swift answers this question by pointing to sources of progressive orthodoxy:

In part it stemmed from the manner of thought of America as a whole around the middle of the 19th century. Gabriel, Curti and Hofstadter have shown that the tendency to think in terms of development was characteristic of the American mind at this time. Americans extended this to a general optimism about the future possibilities of individual human beings and of society. Also prevalent was a faith in reason and law as fundamental characteristics of the operation of universe. Progressive orthodoxy assimilated a measure of all these intellectual tendencies. It also inherited the experiential and ethical emphases to new purposes. In part progressive ortho-

---

197 *ibid.* 23.
198 John Edwin Smylie. "Protestant Clergymen and American Destiny: II: Prelude to Imperialism, 1865-1900." *The Harvard Theological Review*, Vol. 56, No. 4, October (1963): 299.
199 *ibid.* 300.
200 Swift, "Conservative versus Progressive," 23.
201 Ahlstrom, *Religious History*, 779-781.

doxy was an attempt to combat skepticism and indifference by making Congregational theology more practical and more relevant to the needs and thoughts of latter 19th century Americans.[202]

John Edwin Smylie's notions on the changes in Protestant theology in the second half of the nineteenth century show how this process could also be understood in its proper historical setting:

Such were the basic ideas of history and the role of American nationality in history as expounded by northern Protestant clergymen in the decades following the Civil War. They harmonized with the historical philosophies of the times, and furnished the categories in which many of those same clergymen were later to interpret the Spanish American War and Philippine annexation [...] If it is correct to assume that "all great human causes turn on theories of history," [...] these patterns of interpretation go far to explain the temper of Protestant America on the eve of Imperialism.[203]

The need to respond to the realities of the era was not ignored by the Congregationalists. Their understanding of social and political transformation was articulated in a specific type of discourse laden with religious language which was characterized by extensive use of old metaphors in a new setting with new meanings. The missionaries were no exception and applied, appropriated and reinvented that rhetoric as they conducted overseas mission work. Since that discourse was already influenced by its context, which manifested itself as profound transformations, and since it claimed to be influential on those transformations, the missionary discourse was likewise equipped with new means of expression to respond to specific settings and world views in this era.

Despite certain theoretical rifts in Congregationalism, the coming of the Millennium was always the focus of the missionary work. The link between the aim and the ways to attain this aim, or certain steps that would contribute to the realization of this aim, is one of the most important defining elements of the missionary discourse. At the time of the crisis, alongside extensive comments and observations, the set of metaphors referring to the

---

202 Swift. "Conservative versus Progressive," 23-24.
203 Smylie, "Clergymen," 310-311.

areas of purposeful activity and a final goal was applied in a meaningful manner.

The final aim, the end of history or the Millennium, not only entails a conceptualization of the future as a notion but also elicits constant reference to that notion in the discourse. The references to future in the missionary writings appear to be mainly in three domains: Kingdom of God as an abstraction, the future as a notion, and practical opportunities before the missionaries as predictions (or in some instances expressing the inability to predict due to a lack of data). As can be expected, these issues were expressed by different discursive strategies. First of all, the notions were stated directly in the majority of articulations. It had to be done that way, otherwise the audience might find it hard to understand what is at stake. Secondly, metaphorical expressions were applied. These expressions are coherent, to the point, and full of various meanings which could be immediately understood by the audience, thus enhancing the impact of a limited vocabulary on the discursive level.

Reflecting on future possibilities and whenever possible predicting the near and distant future is central to the missionary discourse. In the course of the three years following the massacres, this principle tenet of the discourse mainly evolved around the opportunities offered in the aftermath of a humanitarian crisis. But there is more to it than meets the eye. Opportunity seeking is just one aspect of the teleological discourse.

4.3.3.2 Kingdom of God

Among the various ways of coping with the attacks on a discursive level was the highlighting of the idea of Kingdom of God. The notion is articulated at different levels and against different conceptual backgrounds. As a goal to be achieved and as an ultimate end to evangelistic missionary work, the idea of the Kingdom of God is central to missionary discourse. In a very early reaction to the massacres, the missionaries were praised for their response by stating that "[t]he only gleams of light which appear to human vision in the midst of the disaster are found in the courage and faith of our missionaries" and for their "conviction that God has some wise though hidden purpose in these events by which he is hastening the coming of his Kingdom."[204] This response in its vagueness is a testimony to how per-

---

204 "Editorial Paragraphs." *The Missionary Herald*, January (1896): 2-3.

plexed the Board was at the beginning regarding the massacres. With limited data, the missionaries were encouraged in their conduct and the situation, despite being a hindrance to missionary work, was regarded as facilitating the final goal without any definite foundations other than the will of
God.

In the light of previous data regarding missionary conceptualizations
and source domains such as purpose, opportunity etc., this reaction is striking. It is as if the Board vaguely detected or even sensed the positive traits
of the disaster or promoted a discourse that looks at the 'brighter' aspect,
thus affecting the general mood and orientation. In the same spirit, it is alleged that the massacres are "but part of the coming forward of the kingdom for which you and we have prayed and worked so long [...]."[205] The
positive stance is reinforced further as they claimed that "God's hand is in
all this movement and that whatever may happen he will see that no grave
mistakes are made."[206] The events are seen through the looking glass of the
Kingdom. Referring to out stations in the Eastern Turkey Mission, one missionary depicted the state of these peripheral posts as "[t]hough sorely
stricken [...] these Christian communities, when looked at from the standpoint of the Kingdom of God, are being built up as never before."[207] It will
be seen in the upcoming section on opportunities that actually the Board
gained an unimaginable benefit from the massacres once the missionaries
evaluated the events from a broader perspective with more data. It might be
argued that the first response is more elaborate than it might seem.

The comment in the February 1896 issue of *The Missionary Herald* is
more balanced and laden with data than the first reactions mentioned above,
because the missionaries were encouraged to "prosecute their noble work."
Now the importance of missionary intervention is underlined in the belief
that "[a]ll these things being done, we may expect with confidence to re-
joice, and that in the near future, at seeing a glorious advance of the Kingdom of our Lord."[208] The Board specifies that the road to be followed and
the formula to attain the Kingdom involves human intervention. The mis-

---

205 *ibid.* 4.

206 "Editorial Paragraphs." *The Missionary Herald*, January (1896): 4.

207 "Eastern Turkey Mission." *The Missionary Herald*, June (1897): 237.

208 Wilson A. Farnsworth. "What Shall the Missionaries in Turkey Do?" *The Missionary Herald*, February (1896): 59.

sionary work is highlighted as part of the equation. The missionaries were "strong in the faith that" God would "overrule these disasters for the advancement of his Kingdom."[209] Reminiscent of Hopkinsian ideas, such lines indicate a dichotomy between the will of God and human intervention. It has been shown in many instances that the missionary discourse is as precise as possible when there is enough data to make good evaluations or very fitting predictions. Yet, when the future is unclear, the will of God appears as a *deus ex machina* to fill in the blanks, and optimism is the price they pay for their lack of information.

4.3.3.2.1 God's Hand

The lines "[t]he people are excited, but we are not, for we are sure that God's hand is in all this movement and that whatever may happen he will see that no grave mistakes are made," which appeared when the missionaries had a thorough view of the atrocities and the situation in the aftermath of the massacres, reflect that they could see the gravity of the situation but were unable to suggest a comprehensive explanation for what had happened and why it had happened.[210] Trying to resume an optimistic attitude and a passable explanation, they shifted the notion of agency. The agency in such instances shifts from the missionaries to God. For instance, the credit in these lines is given to divine power: "We may not live to see the consummation of God's purpose, but he will accomplish his plans, and they will be good."[211]

Human agency in postmillennialist thought can be considered as an instrument for bringing about the Kingdom of God, which actually serves the purpose of creating a defense for God's purpose against 'enlightened' reason.[212] The reason for highlighting human agency in this way was the inheritance of enlightenment philosophy by orthodox clergy, especially through Scottish Commonsense Philosophy, despite the fact that they were wary of the excesses of rationalism.[213] The result was the emergence of the moral

---

209 "Editorial Paragraphs." *The Missionary Herald*, April (1896): 136.

210 "Editorial Paragraphs." *The Missionary Herald*, January (1896): 4.

211 "Editorial Paragraphs," *The Missionary Herald*, March (1896): 94.

212 Moorhead, "Progress and Apocalypse," 528.

213 *ibid.* 528.

government of God as a central theme in theology.[214] According to this view, God ruled the universe based on the idea of benevolence to the benefit of the majority of humans and did this through persuasion rather than arbitrary interference; an opinion that guaranteed the rationality of the universe.[215] It was hard for the followers of reason and law to come to terms with a God who governs the realms with supernatural short cuts.[216] Similar ideas can be perceived in the background of missionary discourse. For them "the best policy" was "to go on as far as possible in our customary way and wait for such results."[217] Despite their trust in their established ways, the missionaries did not take credit. These lines ended with the statement, "as a just and wise [...] and a loving God shall prescribe."[218] The missionaries attributed the outcome of their activities to the completeness of "God's sustaining power."[219]

In Maraş, one missionary, confronted with the question 'Has such a thing ever happened in the world before?' asked by one of her students, said that she had "tried so much to lead them to see God's hand in history" and "by adding to their faith knowledge" they had come to feel that "[s]omehow, good shall be the final goal of ill."[220] The missionaries knew that God was "working out his own great designs" and they "should not lose confidence" as it was their "duty and privilege to trust him, and to do the work that he requires" because the future was his.[221] When Armenians belonging to the Armenian Apostolic Church benefited from the charity of the missionaries after the massacres, the idea was to help, and leave "[t]o sift out those spiritually hungry from the multitude who seek loaves and fishes [...] to the hand of the Master."[222] This is a clear separation of the

---

214 *ibid.* 528.
215 *ibid.* 528.
216 *ibid.* 528.
217 "Western Turkey Mission." *The Missionary Herald*, April (1896): 154.
218 *ibid.* 154.
219 *ibid.* 155.
220 "Central Turkey Mission." *The Missionary Herald*, August (1896): 334.
221 Wilson A. Farnsworth. "The Armenians." *The Missionary Herald*, February (1897): 58.
222 "Western and Eastern Turkey Missions." *The Missionary Herald*, April (1897): 154.

fields. The missionaries, with an optimist spirit, were responsible for conducting necessary work. The spiritual results were attributed to the intervention of God. The propagated idea was that "all this work of evangelization and education is God's work and theirs primarily, and quite subordinately that of the American churches through their missionaries."[223] The missionaries had "a duty and an opportunity" and God was leading them, letting them go forward.[224] All in all, to the missionary mind God alone knew what the end would be, but the end was in his hands and he opened before them an empire, and it was not theirs to question the way he was leading.[225]

This paradoxical view is best exhibited by Yale professor Samuel Harris, an ardent follower of the belief that progress was the essence of time and the United States was crucial for the cause of progress.[226] In his 1870 lectures at Andover Theological Seminary, Harris proposed that events in human history unfold in an orderly manner and that the Kingdom of God is imposed through persuasion rather than arbitrary means.[227] Yet, he also stated that unaided human agency was not enough for the realization of this aim and it entailed "a divine energy super-naturally flowing into the history of man."[228] The earth was considered a "battleground for the soul of man between the powers of heaven and hell."[229] The Board believed in God's ability to tell and decide the outcome of their actions and the protection and success of the missionaries were entrusted to God's hands.[230]

They were not, however, fatalists, and active involvement was encouraged by the Board by giving to these "missionaries the solemn and deliberate pledge of the American Board to stand by them in the maintenance of their work with [...] constant sympathy and prayers and gifts till the whole

---

223 "Eastern Turkey Mission." *The Missionary Herald*, June (1897): 239.
224 "Western Turkey Mission." *The Missionary Herald*, October (1897): 396.
225 "Annual Survey," *The Missionary Herald*, November (1898): 447.
226 Moorhead, "Progress and Apocalypse," 541.
227 *ibid.* 541.
228 *ibid.* 541.
229 *ibid.* 541.
230 "The Outbreak at Van, Eastern Turkey." *The Missionary Herald*, September (1896): 356.

land" was won for the Kingdom of Christ.[231] Thus, they believed that "[t]he providence of God points but one way, and that right onward until Christ is Lord in all the land."[232]

Allusions to Biblical parables were also used. In order to show the importance of work done before the massacres it was stated that "[t]he larger work is the quite unobserved influence of the leaven of the gospel" and "[t]his leaven is working among the millions of Armenians and Greeks and, to some extent, among the Turks."[233] On another occasion, it was stated that the leaven of the gospel had been introduced to the Armenians and had been permeating the whole Armenian community.[234] In these instances, the audience was reminded of the work already done and the enduring effects of this work – most probably in order to prevent the idea that it was to no avail.

Missionaries publicized the renewal of faith among the victims and their proximity to the Kingdom of God in their writings.[235] They also saw the remaining churches and infrastructure as the nuclei of a new beginning for the establishment of the Kingdom in what they called "this part of the Land of Eden."[236] The idea was to attract people again to the notion of the Kingdom and propagate it accordingly.[237]

Where are the metaphors then? It is already stated that the notion of the Kingdom of God is perhaps the most important subject in the missionary discourse, and its conceptualizations regarding the missionary activities are abundant. It is exhibited that the main body of metaphorical allusions to the Kingdom of God is related to Biblical parables. The source domain is nature, specifically cultivation. The missionaries employ the agricultural metaphors again on different occasions to depict or explain events. The meta-

---

231 "Editorial Paragraphs" *The Missionary Herald*, November (1896): 436.

232 "Annual Survey." *The Missionary Herald*, November (1897): 441.

233 Wilson A. Farnsworth. "Some Results of Missionary Work in Turkey." *The Missionary Herald*, March (1896): 102.

234 Herman N. Barnum. "The Outlook in Turkey." *The Missionary Herald*, April (1896): 148.

235 "Central and Eastern Turkey Mission." *The Missionary Herald*, May (1897): 192.

236 "Eastern Turkey Mission." *The Missionary Herald*, June (1897): 240.

237 "Eastern Turkey Mission." *The Missionary Herald*, July (1898): 278.

phorical expressions are complementary to the direct references to the Kingdom of God. The Kingdom of God is the aim, but all their activities are steps toward that aim. The missionaries were inclined to conceptualize their activities and their results by referring to the imageries derived from the tradition of the parables. Consequently, while referring to the Kingdom directly without in some instances applying metaphors too extensively, they also reminded the reader that the missionary work was conducted with that aim in sight by using metaphorical expressions derived from the parables, and thus these metaphorical expressions were inherently reminiscent of the Kingdom in its very context.

The calm and firm response of the pupils in Harput at the time of the massacres was praised by a missionary by stating that even in extreme peril, the schoolgirls "showed the fruits of their Puritan training."[238] The desolation, massacres and lack of means similarly elicited the use of the metaphor of the Kingdom. One Mr. Ellis described everything as dark, yet concluded that "it seems as if some great spiritual harvest must be at hand; the dawn must be nigh."[239] Satisfied with the interest of the people in religious affairs after hard times, the missionaries had joy to "learn of the spiritual fruit now being gathered in many parts of Turkish mission."[240] Probably the most distinctive example of the employment of the metaphors of Kingdom can be seen when the missionaries refer to the supreme aim:

It is well to remind us the supreme aim of Christian missions,- to plant the Christian Church. The missionary has the priceless privilege of [...] leading men to a saving faith in Christ. [...] The aim of missions culminates in the purpose to plant a native evangelical church [...] self governing under Divine guidance [...].[241]

As a projection of the future, the agricultural metaphor also proved apt. For instance, during the period of recovery at the Eastern Turkey Mission, the

---

238 John K. Browne. "Modern Martyrdom in Armenia." *The Missionary Herald*, February (1896): 88.

239 "Eastern Turkey Mission." *The Missionary Herald*, March (1897): 113.

240 "Editorial Paragraphs." *The Missionary Herald*, April (1897): 134.

241 George E. White. "The Supreme Aim." *The Missionary Herald*, April (1897): 141.

importance of centers for the study of the Bible was pointed out and the missionaries believed that "this [...] must bear its fruit."[242]

One of the results of the massacres was a softening in the attitude of the Armenians of the Armenian Apostolic Church toward the Protestants. The Board was willing to make the most out of this occasion but the financial crisis obstructed their efforts because it proved difficult for them to employ more workers. One pastor depicted these Armenian Apostolic Church members as "all ripe for garnering if we had workers,"[243] and another missionary was crying with impatience that "not a man step in and gather this great white harvest of souls for Christ and heaven!"[244] Despite these obstructions, the missionaries were yet to see "the encouraging truth that seed sown in faith may, after years, bear good fruit" and "[o]ften the ground on which the seed is sown may appear stony, but there is stony ground that may be crumbled to rich soil by frost and rain, or even violent storms- severe trials, indeed, but 'blessings in disguise.'"[245] So when the mission field was calm and the dangers for conducting missionary work abated, the missionaries were free of concerns for their safety and could go to the field "with the assured conviction that they go to help in gathering a great harvest in that land."[246]

Once again, the discourse pertaining to the eschaton was deeply immersed in the metaphors of cultivation. Equating the church, people and processes with agricultural terminology is reminiscent of the postmillennialist ideas of abundance of crops resulting from technological progress in the imminent Kingdom. Yet, the metaphors were functioning on an abstract level of connotations. Related to parables, the allusions are about belief in general, and one of the first metaphors that can be detected is **Encouraging Beliefs is Cultivating a Plant**. In relation to it, the metaphor **Development of a Belief is Growth of a Plant** is also used. Both of them emanate from **BELIEFS ARE PLANTS**, which in turn comes under **BELIEFS ARE BEINGS WITH A LIFE CYCLE**. Lastly, references to conditions that might facilitate or hinder the agricultural growth mentioned in the mission-

---

242 "Central Turkey Mission." *The Missionary Herald*, June (1897): 236.
243 "Eastern Turkey Mission." *The Missionary Herald*, July (1897): 277.
244 "Eastern Turkey Mission." *The Missionary Herald*, August (1897): 316.
245 "Eastern Turkey Mission." *The Missionary Herald*, August (1898): 315.
246 "Editorial Paragraphs." *The Missionary Herald*, October (1898): 381.

ary discourse are cases of **Necessary Prerequisites are Necessary Prerequisites for Plant Life**.

Another effect of constantly repeating the religious-teleological aim and the involvement of God in the course and outcome of events was the reinforcement of the religious character of missionary activity. Missionary plans, actions and reactions, articulated predominantly in reference to these fields, can easily be differentiated from philanthropic work conducted by any other agency. In times of a huge catastrophe, they saw opportunities and it was immediately made clear that what they thought and did was not in the realm of secular ideas. If the Board took credit for everything the missionaries achieved, they would have risked subordinating the ultimate purpose and making it seem to be of secondary importance. The purpose permeated their discourse to such a degree they barely hid their pleasure at the opportunities arising from the massacres.

4.3.3.3 A Special Case: Seed of the Church

In 1824, the missionaries came up with a radical idea. They had hit against important obstacles in their search for a way to create contacts and eventually convert the Muslim population. Moreover, the intricacies of the millet system that provided the Christian groups with autonomy in internal group affairs proved to be a hindrance as well. Goal-oriented and cold-blooded, they proposed a possible way to overcome these obstacles:

My mind dwells with deep interest on the question "how is the Gospel to be preached to the Mussulmans"? According to the established law, and a law which to the extent of my information is rigidly executed, it is immediate death for any Mussulman, of whatever rank in whatever circumstances to renounce his religion. Undoubtedly God can so pour out his spirit upon men that they shall embrace the Gospel in multitudes even with the certainty of immediate death. But has he ever done thus? Has the Gospel ever prevailed where this was the case? Under the pagan emperors fiery persecutions were endured and the Gospel still prevailed. But in these persecutions, it usually was only some of the principal persons, or at least a part of the Christians, that were put to death. Perhaps, if a few conversions should take place, and be followed by immediate martyrdom, the blood of the martyrs would again prove the seed of the church, and the persecutors cease from their opposition. Possibly the bloody and fiery scenes of the first centuries are to be acted over again.

Possibly some great political revolution is to open the door for the free preaching of the Gospel to the followers of the false prophet.[247]

The idea of martyrdom was seen as a lever. The expected or longed-for-deaths were envisaged as part of a bigger scheme rather than as individual occurrences. The missionaries were well aware of the political turmoil between the Greeks and the Turks in the Eastern Mediterranean, along with the Greek claim to independence. Probably influenced by the atmosphere, they saw a way out in the notion of martyrdom and an ensuing political unrest that would result in revolution.

As they kept conducting their field trips and extensive observations, the missionaries also kept the idea of political change in their minds. This extract from 1827 shows how this idea was articulated in a specific context in the light of specific observations:

The Armenians, who come more especially into Mr. Goodell's sphere, have their origin in the ancient country of Armenia, and from thence derive their name. The vast territory east and northeast of Syria and Palestine is occupied by the Armenians, in company with other sects. In Palestine, they have four monasteries, the one at Jerusalem, of which more will be said by and by, being the most splendid and opulent in the holy city. In Constantinople, there are supposed to be not less than 100,000 Armenians, among whom, as they are a body of enterprising merchants, there is immense wealth. The Armenians are the bankers of the East, and rule the mercantile republic, from Constantinople to Calcutta; and traveling much, for the purposes of trade, they have become the most intelligent of the oriental sects, and on that account are the most likely subjects for reform.* — Mr. Goodell thus speaks of them in his letter of latest date.[248]

The keen missionary eye detected a suitable subject for the longed-for change in the Armenian community. The notion of reform was thought to suit the Armenians of the Ottoman Empire, and not without foundations, such that the missionaries knew that it was more than wishful thinking, as

---

247 Pliny Fisk. "Palestine Mission: Journal of Mr. Fisk." *The Missionary Herald*, October (1824): 306.

248 "State and Progress of the Palestine Mission." *The Missionary Herald*, April (1827): 105.

events in the succeeding years were to show. They did not mean a general walkthrough for their purposes. Almost prodigiously they foreshadowed a change in a twenty-five-year time period for the Armenian reformation:

> There is something pleasant in the thought, that you and we may be permitted to live, and to look at the expiration of the twenty-five years, upon those bright scenes of Armenia, and of the countries around her, which seem even now to be unfolding. But that the life of all of us should be thus prolonged, is hardly to be expected. May we so live as to be always able like Paul to feel, that to depart and to be with Christ is far better.[249]

Given that in 1850 the Ottoman State officially recognized the Armenian Protestant community as a separate community, one can see that the missionaries' plans were not only well-founded but also well-applied and carried out.

The missionaries attached transformational value to the notion of martyrdom. The idea of reform was a priority and the means to achieve that goal were crucial for the missionary enterprise. They hoped martyrdom would facilitate religious reformation and legal reform in the Ottoman Empire. For instance, as the struggle for Greek independence heated up, the missionaries could not help but state that "the time of political revolution should also be a period of religious reform."[250] Although they distanced themselves outwardly from mundane politics and unrest, their presentation of martyrdom indicated a contrary stance. Their zeal for the coming of the Kingdom was so great that they literally yearned for the slaughter of converts. Martyrdom in the missionary discourse was a foundational element for the order they wanted to constitute, and this perspective can be seen in the following paragraph:

> Fire, or sword, or poison may destroy the converts, who have already become the proofs and pledges of missionary success; but belonging, as they do, to all the principal denominations in Syria, and representing all, the news of their martyrdom

---

249 "Great Meeting of Armenians at Constantinople." *The Missionary Herald*, April (1827): 115.

250 Pliny Fisk. "Western Asia: Letter of Mr. Fisk." *The Missionary Herald*, September (1827): 267.

would every where become matter of conversation and inquiry, and their blood would be like good seed sown in a prolific soil.[251]

Once again, cultivation is used as the conceptual background to address to the audience. Martyrdom as a seed needed blood rather than water. The analogy was clear. If the converts were persecuted the "consequences would be as in ancient times" as "[t]he converts by mutual prayer and exhortation would encourage and strengthen each other to die nobly; and they that were scattered abroad, would everywhere preach the word."[252] From a missionary point of view persecution was not understood as a process that would "destroy the spirit, or silence the voice of free inquiry," but as an important step once it had been awakened with regard to "the subject of religion" that would raise the spirit of the persecuted to a "greater determination, and hastened and multiplied its blessed results." Hence the maxim: "the blood of martyrs is the seed of the church."[253] Years later the missionaries got what they asked for: revolutionary resistance, massacres and thus 'martyrs,' and a reform coerced by the Western powers that could not be implemented.

One might assume that the missionaries celebrated the massacres not only as opening up new opportunities for mission activity, but also as the fulfillment of a prophecy they made decades ago which was also based on the Christian history of the martyrs.

4.3.3.3.1 Martyrdom

After the massacres, one of the primary tenets of the missionary discourse was 'martyrs' or 'martyrdom.' There had been cases of 'martyrdom' before in the history of the Ottoman missions, but none of them was comparable to what happened in the massacres of 1894-96. It is fitting to discuss this specific topic under the heading of the Kingdom of God because the notion of martyrdom articulated in the relevant issues of *The Missionary Herald* is

---

251 "Great Meeting of Armenians at Constantinople." *The Missionary Herald*, April (1827): 115.

252 "Obstacles to the Growth of Evangelical Piety in Syria." *The Missionary Herald*, April (1828): 114.

253 *ibid*. 114.

believed to be founded on the preceding conceptualization of this institution as the seed of the church. In addition, other metaphors were utilized as well.

The missionary position in this regard was to promote and praise the deaths and to present martyrdom as a device that would make the propagation of certain ideas and the inducement of emotions possible. When the missionaries decided to stay at their posts wherever possible, the Board applauded this decision, saying that they stayed "for the work to which in more senses than one they have given their lives."[254]

The story was constructed in appropriate fashion from the very beginning, with the seminal idea being that many in Eastern Turkey had "boldly endured martyrdom for Christ's sake."[255] Accepting the Muslim faith as a deal for surrender was unacceptable to the missionary mind. Responding to the forced conversion of many Armenians in Harput, a missionary statement conveyed this attitude quite clearly: "I am sorry to say many of them consented to become Moslems, though one Gregorian priest chose and suffered death."[256] The Armenians killed in the incidents were called "the noble army of martyrs" and they were believed to have received "the martyr's crown."[257] The deaths were cherished and the sentiments were declared in an optimistic way: "Let there be no fear for the church of Christ when his followers witness for their Lord after the fashion shown us in recent months."[258]

The massacres and the death toll certainly alarmed the missionaries about the results of their work. Thus "when nearly every missionary station in Asia Minor" had been "baptized in blood," the question that was asked was "what are the results of sixty years of missionary work in that land?"[259] The missionary discourse was aptly orchestrated to make the most out of the losses. The Christian cause had to be brought forward and the notion of martyrdom was a ready tool and a weapon in missionary conceptualization.

---

254 "Editorial Paragraphs." *The Missionary Herald*, January (1896): 3.

255 "Editorial Paragraphs." *The Missionary Herald*, February (1896): 47.

256 *ibid.* 47.

257 "Editorial Paragraphs." *The Missionary Herald*, March (1896): 95.

258 *ibid.* 95.

259 Wilson A. Farnsworth. "Some Results of Missionary Work in Turkey." *The Missionary Herald*, March (1896): 99.

In these lines, the audience was informed in such a way as to assure them that the people had not lost their lives in vain:

Word comes to us from Central Turkey that many of the Moslems have expressed great wonder that the Christians have so generally met death "unresisting, and with their hands over their eyes." They also came to the Christians asking, "What is the meaning of the word 'Hesous' that so many of these men pronounced just before we killed them?"[260]

Here we see explanations for the American public and the answer to the question whether years of missionary activity had been to any avail. It was suggested that people displayed a true Christian character in the face of death, and part of the credit for their firmness goes to the Board. Being Protestant was considered to be influential in displaying the 'right conduct,' namely choosing death: "[...] this noble man, who sealed a most exemplary Christian life with a martyr's death, was an arch-persecutor of Protestants before his conversion."[261] In another occurrence it was said that many people misunderstood the call for surrender (*teslim* in Turkish, coming from the Arabic word stem 'slm' which is also the root for the word Islam) and instead of turning Muslim chose death.[262] As a result, "all the Syrian, Armenian, Armenian Catholic, and Protestant churches" were ruined or received serious outward injury, and might truly be called martyr churches.[263] The missionary analogy to the persecution of the first Christians was applied again.

The advantages of life losses were not viewed on the level of simple propagation by the missionaries. The Board was an activity-based organization and any factor that would further their work was well appreciated. They realized that the sorrows brought Armenian Apostolic and Protestant Armenians close, whereby the loss of beloved people played a major role: "It is not long since such a mingling of Gregorians and Protestants would have been impossible, and would have deemed a pollution of the old

---

260 "Editorial Paragraphs." *The Missionary Herald*, May (1896): 180.
261 "Central Turkey Mission." *The Missionary Herald*, May (1896): 207.
262 *ibid.* 206.
263 *ibid.* 206.

church. In the congregation were many whose husbands and fathers were among the recent martyrs for their faith [...]."[264]

The missionaries created a unique narrative and nourished it with accounts of singular incidents that would trigger an emotional response in the reader. The story of a mother in Urfa, whose two sons were caught by the mob, was one of them. The crowd demanded that the young men turn Muslim, and seeing that the mother allegedly cried "[d]ie, but don't deny the Lord." As can be expected, the two were slain because "they stood firm."[265] Such stories were plentiful and they helped the missionaries connect with their followers and elicit responses. For instance, "[t]he story of the martyred pastor at Oorfa [...] has touched many hearts, and several generous gifts have been received by us to be used for the support of his six orphan children."[266] This period in the missionaries' letters are full of stories of people "wearing the martyr's crown,"[267] attending "the glorious army of martyrs,"[268] and "sealing their faith with blood."[269]

In this context, the missionaries, although at first appalled by the possible impact of losses on what they had already achieved, detected a ready motif to produce a heart-moving story that was Christian in its very essence. It was indeed the realization of a prior aim, albeit stated in the context of converting Muslims by gaining the sympathy of the masses after the possible persecution and death of converts. Moreover, since the missionary narrative was a multiplicity of many narratives and Biblical stories, including the parables via conceptual metaphors, they managed to project the story of early Christians persecuted and killed by the authorities on to a modern event.

4.3.3.4 Teleology, Future, Plans

The Board responded swiftly to the massacres and one of its reactions was to attempt to guess what the near future might bring:

---

264 "Editorial Paragraphs." *The Missionary Herald*, June (1896): 221.

265 *ibid.* 225.

266 "Editorial Paragraphs." *The Missionary Herald*, March (1897): 88.

267 "Central Turkey Mission." *The Missionary Herald*, May (1896): 207.

268 *ibid.* 206.

269 "Editorial Paragraphs." *The Missionary Herald*, June (1896): 224.

If they are able to maintain in the land [...] there is a noble future before them. All the Armenians in the empire [...] are ready, as never before, to accept the messengers of the gospel. We hope [...] that in the near future a most glorious reformation is to be seen in the Turkish Empire.[270]

The future estimates, which concurred with the mood promoted among the field workers, were optimistic. Despite "the clouds that darken the outlook in Turkey," they were "wonderfully sustained in their work and confident that light [was] yet to break through the clouds."[271]

As already mentioned in the previous section, it became an important issue for the Board that missionaries should not leave their posts. Not that the Board weighed up the pros and cons of missionaries staying in the field from a sentimental point of view. In many instances, the idea was promoted so as to elicit an emotional response from the reader by referring to the heroic deeds or stance of the missionaries. But beneath this emotional tone, there were important calculations from the institutional viewpoint:

The objection that men and women ought not to be exposed to certain perils is really part of a much larger question. How far are risks lawful in any enterprise? [...] Enterprise usually involves risks. No progress of any kind is possible without it. If immunity from danger had been made a condition of enterprise, the development of civilization would have been arrested long ago.[272]

Even when "[t]he future [was] uncertain" and nobody could "draw a bright" picture "from the human point of view," the missionaries stuck to the notion that "God is good" and one of them expressed his feelings by saying "I have a firm faith that in some way, how I do not know, good is to come out of all this evil, order out of chaos."[273]

It had always been the goal of the missionaries to create self-supporting communities so that they could achieve the evangelization of the world.

---

270 Wilson A. Farnsworth. "What Shall the Missionaries in Turkey Do?" *The Missionary Herald*, February (1896): 58.

271 "Editorial Paragraphs." *The Missionary Herald*, April (1896): 136.

272 "Editorial Paragraphs." *The Missionary Herald*, April (1896): 137.

273 Herman N. Barnum. "The Outlook in Turkey." *The Missionary Herald*, April (1896): 149.

The mission work was seen as a necessary but temporary stage, not the sole aim. Reverend George E. White of Merzifon station reminded the missionaries that "[t]he aim of missions culminates in the purpose to plant a native evangelical church in every land, self-governing under Divine guidance, self-supporting and self-propagating" and "[w]hen that is attained missionary work will be done, and not before."[274]

One important result in the aftermath of the massacres was that the wall between Armenian Apostolics and Protestant Armenians was torn down. Hard times drew these groups closer. In Kayseri, Armenian Apostolics and Protestants came together on the Sabbath and organized a 'self improvement circle.' To the missionary "[i]t was very refreshing, and suggestive of 'good times coming' to find such an audience." This rapprochement was believed to have the power to change the future of the missions: "Christianity has yet a future in this land, and it is not too much to hope that many a small, despised Protestant community of to-day will become the propagating centre of this new regenerated life."[275]

Some predictions for the future were still vague as of 1897. The mood of optimism was highlighted and the urgency of recommencing work was brought to mind in these lines: "[T]he field [...] has been loudly calling for the work of construction. [...] We attempt no prophecy; we cannot see into the future, nor can our missionaries at the front. They are content if they can see one step ahead and if can know that the Master is leading them. [...] They must have reinforcements at once [...]."[276] One of the reasons for acting with such deliberation when making decisions and predictions might be the lack of information and a confused state of institutional mind. These elements, however, did not exclude the possibility that the missionary discourse, as publicly displayed in *The Missionary Herald,* also internalized the notion of the future as an opening and the opportunities as open doors; hence choosing strictly to follow one path might have caused the problem at this point of overlooking diverse opportunities. Moreover, in order to make the right decision in times of turmoil, being able to see one step ahead and making short-term plans is a clever response so as to avoid losing track

---

274 George E. White. "The Supreme Aim." *The Missionary Herald,* April (1897): 141.

275 "Western Turkey Mission." *The Missionary Herald,* May (1897): 190-191.

276 "Annual Survey." *The Missionary Herald,* November (1897): 433.

of the field work. The confused state of the missionaries' minds can be observed when they mention that God would lead the way and make things happen, but at the same time demand new field workers and means to commence work. Deliberate action is planned, but when that cannot be achieved, certain prerequisites such as more workers are demanded. The theoretical background for this dichotomy has been explained above.

Their uncertainty about the future does not mean that the missionaries lost track of the realities surrounding them. They were well aware of the situation in general terms. The vulnerability of the Armenians was clearly observed, the sympathy of the Armenian Apostolics was taken notice of, and the missionaries were counting on the outcome of this humanitarian crisis for the realization of their future aims. The missionary discourse pointed to a bright future. For the Board there was "no single feature of missionary work in Turkey at the present time that makes so resistless an appeal to the benevolence and sympathy of Christendom, that yields so much immediate returns, or that promises so great things for the future."[277]

One year later, while evaluating the Central Turkey Mission, the Board was more definite in terms of the future, while still leaving the uncertainty as a part of the equation. Regarding the missions' educational establishments, it was stated that "[t]he higher schools of the missions attract a large body of picked youth [...] [t]he future in this field, though not without clouds and uncertainties, is bright with promise and hope, and we do well to plan for it with large thoughts and courage undaunted."[278] In this instance not only the field to be operated, i.e. education, was expressly stated, but also the meticulous efforts that went into its planning.

Futurity is mentioned on multiple occasions by using the word 'future.' The catastrophe gave urgency to the issue of the forthcoming days, months, and years, together with plans, incidents and investments. Future itself had become a central tenet for the discourse. Along with these general references to 'future,' there was a more specific way of responding to the problems. The missionaries kept the notion of 'future' alive as a discursive category by continually referring to it. This is no surprise because the underlying theological premises are teleological in essence, and the Board as an organization and Congregationalism as an institution were evolving around

---

277 "Annual Survey." *The Missionary Herald*, November (1897): 441.
278 *ibid.* 445.

the idea of the coming of the Kingdom of God. Use of metaphors of light and darkness (including weather conditions) was one way of linking the religious character of the future. Metaphors of cultivation intrinsically suggested a change in quality and quantity (of what is cultivated), and thus a direct reference to future for its own sake. Biblical relations to the conceptual metaphors and the general narrative based on a highly religious discourse created a series of stories and sub-discourses. The parabolic nature of these was projected onto the notion of futurity. Thus, future as referred to by the missionaries was not only a possibility in the linear flow of time, as understood in scientific or more accurately secular terms, but a flow of ideas, actions, certainties and uncertainties affected by human action, but ultimately defined and determined by the supreme will of God. The human action part involved one important skill; opportunity-seeking.

4.3.3.5 Opportunity

From the beginning of its establishment, the missionary discourse in *The Missionary Herald* about the missions to the Ottoman Empire was laden with concepts, conceptual metaphors, and their linguistic articulations, that were directed to the notion and occurrence of opportunities. The main body of conceptual metaphorical expressions referring to the idea of opportunity is given in Chapter 3.

The first missionary reaction to the massacres was to stay at their posts wherever possible. In Talas, two American women who ran a boarding school refused to leave. This case was described as follows:

We dare not say that these women are not acting in the wisest way by remaining at their posts and grappling bravely with the peculiar duties that the times lay upon them. This is their supreme opportunity. [...] These are the great opportunities of their lives and nobly are they meeting them.[279]

Although widely discussed, the first reaction was seen as a proper way of coping with the situation and an opportunity to show perseverance in their missionary work. What exactly was meant by the notion of opportunity? Was it a mere personality test to endure hardships? Although the mission-

---

279 Wilson A. Farnsworth. "What Shall the Missionaries in Turkey Do?" *The Missionary Herald*, February (1896): 58.

ary character was believed to be undergoing a test through the massacres, the main line of opportunities was in the benefits for the missionary work itself. One Mr. Wingate, a young and inexperienced missionary located in Kayseri, acted cool and collected and not only ensured the safety of the mission premises but also saved many civilians. He was active in the field. It was stated that his actions "won for him golden opinions" from the people and they would "greatly increase his influence for good."[280]

The Board quickly grasped the importance of staying in the field. Careful observations resulted in short to middle term future projections for missions:

> An interest has been awakened in the Armenians such as never existed before. [...] [T]he hundreds of thousands receiving aid from those in the ends of the earth must be drawn to the gospel as never before. We are told that in the great oil regions, where a well [...] becomes less productive, it is found to be profitable to put in dynamite and have an explosion. Of late there have been fearful explosions in the regions where the most successful missionary work has been carried on. It is reasonable to expect that these explosions are [...] to be followed by an evangelical work [...].[281]

The crudeness of the imagery is shocking, but it is a good example of the pragmatic, opportunity-seeking missionary mind. For the missionaries it had become their "duty to stay and make the most of [...] opportunities, trusting God for the future."[282]

Soon another prospect was discovered. The massacres brought Protestant and Armenian Apostolic communities closer and the missionaries were fond of this rapprochement. For them the new situation brought "opportunities without a parallel in the history of these missions" and "[t]o leave the field now would be to give up the possibility of a stronger position and wider influence than has ever before been possible in the history of these missions."[283] In this new era, the "door of welcome to the whole Ar-

---

280 *ibid.* 58.

281 Wilson A. Farnsworth. "Some Results of Missionary Work in Turkey." *The Missionary Herald*, March (1896): 102.

282 "Eastern Turkey Mission." *The Missionary Herald*, March (1896): 107.

283 "Editorial Paragraphs." *The Missionary Herald*, April (1896): 136.

menian people for spiritual work" was "wide open" and it was referred to as "an opportunity quite unexampled in the history of our work for that race, an opportunity practically without limit."[284]

Several missionaries of the Board left Turkey for the United States during and after the incidents. The decision to 'occupy the field' was strong and the return of the missionaries was much celebrated and encouraged because for the Board, "[t]he need of these laborers in their several fields" was very great and they went "with courage, believing that the Lord" was calling them and was "opening before them a wide door of usefulness."[285]

One Dr. Fuller of Antep points out that "[e]very barrier on the Armenian side is down for the time at least, and we have the freest access and most cordial welcome everywhere"[286] As the Board was coping with the financial crisis, the work load increased for the limited number of field workers and in Arapkir the 'Biblewomen' stated that they were "overwhelmed by the work now opening before them."[287] Despite all the hindrances, the missionaries assumed an optimistic attitude and one missionary from Malatya expressed his feelings as "[b]right as the promises of God is the outlook for Christ's work in these and other cities in Turkey."[288]

Despite this optimism and the zealous efforts of missionaries towards the end of 1896 and at the beginning of 1897, the missionaries in the field bitterly felt the results of global budget cuts following decisions made in Boston. The very best way, as it had always been, was to appeal to the feelings of solidarity among fellow Christians in the United States. Seeing many prospects before them, they raised the question "[c]an Occidental Christians fail to stand by a sister church in such an hour of extremity and opportunity?"[289]

Seeing that the new situation might not be exploited to the utmost due to a lack of necessary means, they also made appeals to the Board itself: "Oh why does not our Board seize the opportunity for reaping seed long

---

284 "Editorial Paragraphs." *The Missionary Herald*, May (1896): 183.

285 "Editorial Paragraphs." *The Missionary Herald*, September (1896): 348.

286 *ibid*. 350.

287 "Eastern Turkey Mission" *The Missionary Herald*, February (1897): 60.

288 *ibid*. 62.

289 "Western Turkey Mission." *The Missionary Herald*, March (1897): 112.

since sown in weariness, faintness, drought, and desert?"[290] In Antep, the Rev. M. Sanders drew attention to the same problem and described the situation as a lifetime opportunity and "a glaring contrast between the opportunities presented" and "the support received from America."[291] Mr. Fowle of Kayseri shared the feelings of his fellow missionary brother and, regarding favorable conditions in rural Kayseri, expressed his discontent: "It cannot be that the Lord is opening these doors to mock us; but without men or money how can we enter in and occupy?"[292] One Mr. Browne situated in Eastern Turkey joined the chorus by demanding new people to work and said "I am deeply impressed with the rare opening here for a faithful worker, but where is such to be found?"[293] The missionaries at Urfa shared the mutual feeling of disappointment over the lack of means:

> The work is far beyond the capacity of the laborers, and the call for reinforcement is incessant. [...] To human appearances we are passing over unimproved opportunities such as are very seldom given to the church [...] It seems to me there never were such opportunities to work for the Master as there are in Oorfa to-day.[294]

Finally when the mission stations in the region received financial help and more helpers in 1897, the missionaries called it the great event of the year and the realization of the long desired aim to open of a new and vast possibility of influence.[295]

The missionaries evaluated the circumstances as "open doors" for their preaching and evangelistic efforts, and the vulnerability of the Armenian Apostolic Church as "presenting open doors" to their "preaching and evangelistic efforts." Not being able to make the most of this troubled state among the Gregorians, the missionaries had the feeling that with more resources, a reformation could occur, and a new era would begin in the histo-

---

290 "Editorial Paragraphs." *The Missionary Herald*, July (1897): 260.
291 "Editorial Paragraphs." *The Missionary Herald*, August (1897): 300.
292 "Western Turkey Mission." *The Missionary Herald*, August (1897): 314.
293 *ibid.* 316.
294 *ibid.* 340.
295 "Editorial Paragraphs," *The Missionary Herald*, February (1898): 63.

ry of their mission.[296] Celebrating the fifty years of the Central Turkey Mission, President Fuller stated, "never in the history of the world [...] was there a people more wonderfully prepared to heed the voice of preachers and teachers than now."[297] Once again, the missionaries saw the opportunity arising from the calamity. The rapprochement was attributed to the fact that the Armenian Apostolic Church was shaken to its foundations and learned a lesson only disaster could teach.[298] Finally, the evangelical preachers were welcome and "in the fires of persecution animosities melted away."[299]

In its assessment of missionary activity more than two years after the massacres, the Board was satisfied with the work done, despite the troubles:

With the county far from quiet, multitudes of people in despair, and dire uncertainty overhanging all, our missionaries have taxed every resource at their command to keep every department of work in full operation, and at the same time to seize the new opportunities opened to them.[300]

In the aftermath the mission celebrated the "openings and a vast field to be occupied" in the line of education, and called the victims of the massacre a rich harvest ready to be gathered.[301]

4.3.3.5.1 An Opening: Orphans

Soon the missionaries realized that an unimaginable opportunity was there before them. The massacres had left many Armenian children without parents. The children were in dire need of basic requirements which the Armenian community was unable, and the Ottoman Government unwilling to

---

296 "Eastern Turkey Mission." *The Missionary Herald*, September (1897): 353-354.

297 "Fifty Years of the Central Turkey Mission." *The Missionary Herald*, October (1897): 393.

298 "Triennial Statement Made by the American Board to the National Congregational Council, Portland, Oregon, July 11, 1898." *The Missionary Herald*, August (1898): 304.

299 *ibid.* 304.

300 "Annual Survey." *The Missionary Herald*, November (1898): 447.

301 "Editorial Paragraphs." *The Missionary Herald*, December (1898): 485.

provide. The well-established missions and above all the educational infrastructure enabled the missionaries to take the situation in hand. For the Board it was "a form of charity which appeals most strongly to the instincts of young and old."[302] The orphan work was described "as an opportunity and a blessing to both missionaries and people."[303]

Nazan Maksudyan points out that the missionaries remained indifferent to the victims of the Crimean War (1854-56) and the Russo-Ottoman War of 1877-78 as they "subconsciously" knew that they had no chances of converting Muslims.[304] As far as the massacres of 1894-96 were concerned, this approach gave way to an intense commitment:

In contrast to this previous disengaged attitude towards humanitarian relief, the Armenian massacres [...] evolved into a major arena, where many actors fought for legitimacy, power, prestige, and hegemony over a seemingly philanthropic field of the opening of orphanages.[305]

As of 1896, there were 50,000 Armenian orphans below the age of 12 in Turkey.[306] The inability of Gregorian Armenian patriarchate to provide orphanages left the field open for foreign intervention and the Board managed to open 80 orphanages housing 10,000 orphans in more than 30 districts.[307]

The education in the orphanages consisted of common school education, vocational training and religious education.[308] The boys were trained in tailoring, shoemaking, carpentry, bookbinding, and cabinet-making, while the girls had courses in weaving, rug making, sewing, needlework, embroidery in silk, lace work, quilt making, and hemstitching.[309] As those jobs turned out to be more suitable for an urban environment, the missions

---

302 "Editorial Paragraphs." *The Missionary Herald*, January (1897): 9.
303 "Western Turkey Mission." *The Missionary Herald*, October (1897): 397.
304 Nazan Maksudyan. "Being Saved to Serve: Armenian Orphans of 1894-1896 and Interested Relief in Missionary Orphanages." *Turcica*, Vol. 42 (2010): 50.
305 *ibid*. 51.
306 *ibid*. 51.
307 *ibid*. 52, 55.
308 Maksudyan, "Saved to Serve," 58.
309 *ibid*. 62.

started to open agricultural departments to avoid unemployment.[310] In the meanwhile, the missionaries did not forget their primary aim of converting orphans. They were well aware of the ease of converting helpless orphans. The following lines, quoted by Maksudyan, are written by a missionary from Mardin station:

> Truly this is a hopeful and blessed work. Hopeful, because the children are so young. They are the little twigs which we may bend in the right direction. They are virgin soil in which we may sow seeds of truth and righteousness. They are lambs of the flock, and in doing for them we are obeying the command: "Feed my lambs."[311]

The missionaries explained their work as a philanthropic venture and noted that they were "under obligation to do the work of the Good Samaritan."[312] They justified their incentives to start helping orphans by referring to the Bible, as is usual in missionary discourse: "We read in James 1: 27, 'Pure religion is this, to visit the fatherless and the widows in their afflictions'."[313] However, mission work is principally goal-oriented and well planned with regard to the future of any scheme or establishment. Following the humanitarian explanation and Biblical justification, they mention the importance of working for orphans for their future aims by stating that "[t]his work of caring for orphans is one that with God's blessing may in a few years make that land as the garden of the Lord."[314]

One Dr. Raynolds explained the tactical importance of taking and educating children as follows: "While it is worth much to be able to keep the multitudes from starving, little can be done to lift them out of their filth and ignorance. But the children can be put under such influences as may change their whole destiny for time and eternity."[315] The contrast between general charity work conducted to help the desolated Armenians and the specific and well-organized orphanage establishment is striking. Such an attitude

---

310 *ibid*. 62.
311 *ibid*. 66.
312 Wilson A. Farnsworth. "The Armenians." *The Missionary Herald*, February (1897): 58.
313 *ibid*. 58.
314 *ibid*. 58.
315 "Editorial Paragraphs." *The Missionary Herald*, March (1897): 90.

raises doubts about the primacy of humanitarian motives for charity work in the first place:

When one sees the number of orphans from the mountain villages enjoying the advantages of a Christian education, he might well bring to mind the old legend of Satan, who in order to destroy God's gift of flowers carefully buried all their seeds underground, and then sent the sun and rain to complete their destruction, with the result that *they grew!*[316]

Is it too much to say that the children were ornaments, pawns in a far-reaching missionary plan or tools used to realize goals? For although it would be unfair to underestimate the emotional involvement of the missionaries with these children, the institutional approach surpassed the individual one. As the Board decided that the children should be acquainted with "such a style of living, in the way of food, clothing, and customs, as shall not put them out of touch with their countrymen, or unfit them to resume life in their villages, while at the same time habits of personal neatness are inculcated, to serve as a lever for gradually elevating the people," one might consider that the plan was not merely to provide the children with what the Board might offer, but with what the Board chose to give them. When understood in this way, it is no wonder that they explained this decision by stating that "[w]e seek to avoid giving so high an education as to awaken a longing for life outside their own country."[317] The Board aimed at creating self-sustaining, self-supporting Protestant communities. In a similar vein, they were afraid that by receiving a Western style superior education, the orphans might leave their lands and go abroad. This was not commensurate with the goal of creating local Protestant communities. The children were seen as a guarantee for the future and as mentioned by a missionary in the field, "[t]hese orphans must be cared for [...] till they are older and more capable of self-support [...]."[318]

Despite these plans, the missionaries complained of accusations from the Armenian Apostolic Church questioning their reasons. In Bursa, one Mr. Baldwin reported that "[s]ome of the clergy have been unwise enough

---

316 "Central Turkey Mission." *The Missionary Herald*, January (1898): 25.
317 "Eastern Turkey Mission." *The Missionary Herald*, July (1897): 278.
318 "Editorial Paragraphs." *The Missionary Herald*, July (1898): 257.

to stir up a sectarian agitation and impugn the motives of the missions in undertaking to do so much for orphans [...]."[319]

Towards the end of 1897, *The Missionary Herald* could write that "[o]rphanages are established at almost every station, and add greatly to the cares of missionaries, but also to the interest of their work."[320] Fully functional, the missionaries were providing the children with proper school education and introducing trades such as cabinet-making, shoemaking, sewing, cooking, weaving, thus teaching "each according to natural ability and taste of the child."[321]

Mr. Hubbard of Sivas mentioned that he had never seen anything that fills him "so completely with satisfaction as the sight of these contended, obedient, enthusiastic children gathered in their large schoolroom for their Sabbath-school [...]."[322] He was well aware of the importance of influencing young minds, as can be understood from the way he describes the orphans: "They are specially open to spiritual leading and teaching."[323] Without parental supervision and the interference of the Armenian Apostolic Church, the missionaries enjoyed the freedom of imposing evangelistic faith on these children while offering comfort, vocational education and safety.

In their writings they did not hide the way the orphans were given religious education. Dr. Barnum of Harput expresses his feelings regarding the religious awakening of the orphan children in these words:

This is a very touching sight to us all, especially when we remember that thirteen months ago not one of these boys and girls who are now so much interested in spiritual things knew how to pray, or had any knowledge of Christ and his salvation. One of the little girls [...] said that she was glad she had lost everything, for in that way she had found Christ, whom she could not lose.[324]

---

319 "Western Turkey Mission." *The Missionary Herald*, October (1897): 397.
320 "Annual Survey." *The Missionary Herald*, November (1897): 441.
321 "Central Turkey Mission." *The Missionary Herald*, January (1898): 24.
322 *ibid.* 24.
323 *ibid.* 24.
324 "Editorial Paragraphs." *The Missionary Herald*, April (1898): 129.

Thirteen months was enough time for the missionaries to affect the way the children think. The missionaries were right in their estimation that the orphan work would be an important investment for the 'Christian cause.' This incident in Harput was not a single example of how fast the missionaries indoctrinated orphans. At Van, Dr. Reynold related his astonishment "at the acquaintance which many of the orphans show with the Bible and religious truth, gained by them during the few months of their residence in the orphanage."[325] This quick change and transformation is not a coincidence because the children in the orphanages of the Board were "taught reading and Bible truths" every day.[326] The description of how the orphans were treated and how they responded to their means in the orphanages in Western Turkey might explain the mechanisms behind these quick results:

A peculiar interest gathers about the orphanages and the hapless youth who find in them a home and comfort, education, and an outlook for the future. They respond quickly to the influences that surround them; they take kindly to the necessary discipline of the homes in which they reside; they soon become skillful in the industrial arts which are taught; their scholarship is good; and best of all, most of them are earnestly walking in the Christian life.[327]

For the pragmatic and goal-oriented missionary mind, to which anything other than achieving the final goals was secondary, orphanages were the birthplaces of a new generation which would facilitate the coming of the Kingdom and "[b]eneath this kindly charity, so wisely administered, a new nation" was "rising up to bless the land and to glorify God."[328] The way the orphans were treated and transformed was considered to be an element of pride and publicity for the Board. In Merzifon, one missionary stated: "Their home behavior was also very much praised as greatly improved, and their testimony of the way they were treated in Marsovan was good for our reputation."[329]

---

325 "Eastern Turkey Mission." *The Missionary Herald*, July (1898): 277.
326 "Eastern Turkey Mission." *The Missionary Herald*, August (1898): 314.
327 "Annual Survey," *The Missionary Herald*, November (1898): 444.
328 *ibid.* 445.
329 "Western Turkey Mission." *The Missionary Herald*, March (1898): 111.

4.3.4 Conclusion

When the massacres started, the missionaries were caught unprepared for a humanitarian tragedy of such scale. It was not only the horrors they witnessed that account for the initial psychological confusion they experienced and reported in their writings. Since the 1830s, Armenians were the main targets for missionary work and the massacres chiefly took place in the regions with a considerable Armenian population. It was precisely these places where the Board had invested extensively in terms of work force, local networks and infrastructure, including mission stations, schools and medical centers. Thus, they were confronted with the huge risk of losing everything they had worked for. Such a result might have been difficult to account for after decades of promising work. Moreover, the destruction of their accomplishments could have been detrimental to their future work, because it would have been hard to convince the American public which favored overseas missions about the Board's prospects of success. This would have caused a drop in donations. The first reports show that they were unable to explain the situation coherently. However, the dramatic tone soon gave way to a professed optimism. Without a bright, promising outlook, the missionary discourse would have had to confine itself to its present and past, the nemesis of an organization that is primarily defined through its purposeful activity and teleological ideology.

Metaphors were present from the very beginning and most of them were used to explain the adverse circumstances. Along with optimism came metaphors that were more promising. Yet, the missionary discourse was also abundant with the agency of God in what had happened and what would happen in the future. It was hard to provide a thorough and satisfying explanation of the events by simply alluding to the realm of the secular. This seems to be a part of the transition from perplexity to optimism as God's agency, together with the involvement of the missionaries, could account for the prospects of the mission as well. God's power compensated for their weakness.

Having observed and understood the situation fully, the missionaries started to discern the potential for further work. The humanitarian crisis deprived the missionaries of a peaceful environment and many local helpers, some of whom were slain during the massacres. The Armenian population was in dire need of basic needs. Optimists as they were, the missionaries were constantly looking for opportunities to develop their work among the masses in miserable conditions.

The purpose, namely the Kingdom, was articulated at length. It is no surprise that the missionaries resorted to referencing the Kingdom since the ultimate aim of the Board was to facilitate its realization. In addition, the Kingdom was likewise an element of missionary narrative, both in terms of story and discourse which was heavily backed by a web of conceptual metaphors and parables. The Kingdom was a way of writing about the future in an encouraging way. The initially perplexed missionaries were reminding their readers of their mission and purpose.

The allusions to the Kingdom alone, however, were not enough to write about or to endeavor for the realization of a future that promised success. Everything was God's deed, but they also believed in the importance of human agency aided and favored by God. For human agency to function properly, the missions relied on opportunities from the very beginning. Their conceptual repertoire for conveying their ideas on opportunities was well established and in accordance with other metaphorical expressions. Missionaries in the field quickly detected the main fields for openings. The foremost field was humanitarian work to help the Armenians. Secondly, they also detected a need for spiritual help. Moreover, in times of an extraordinary catastrophe Armenians of the Armenian Apostolic Church, who had kept their distance, proved friendly to their advances. Perhaps most important of all the openings was the work for the orphans. Armenian children who had lost their parents were seen as an excellent target for conversion.

Once again, the conceptual formations appear as constituting parts of a series of stories and series of narratives. The linguistic metaphors, as shown in the previous chapter, were derived from Christian sources, the Bible being the primary source. The parables, Biblical eschatology, and other narratives and notions related to Biblical eschatology are thus also present in the writings published in the issues of *The Missionary Herald* from this period. Consequently, single, individual metaphors or conceptual domains were not the only tools for conveying stories, ideas, and events. By applying these domains, the stories in which they took place were also projected onto real-life events.

Along with the parables, one can also detect another story that was projected with great determination and power. The discourse on martyrs drew heavily on Christian history. To start with, the persecution and killing of

Christians is a topic that recurs on many occasions in the New Testament. Indeed, the first cases of persecution can be found in the Gospel of Luke. Chapter 4:14-30 deal with the hardships Jesus Christ faced (the people of Nazareth unsuccessfully tries to throw him off a cliff after he preaches) and parts 6:22-23 refer to the hardships his followers suffered. Sections on Jesus' questioning by Pilate and Herod, on his death sentence, crucifixion and death were later followed in the Acts, which was believed to be written by the same author who wrote the Gospel of Luke. This connection suggests a continuity in the issues discussed. The Acts of the Apostles expands the context for the issue of persecution. The book is full of references to the persecution of the early Christian church – the death of Stephen, considered to be the first Christian martyr, in 6:8 and 8:1, being one of them.

Another Biblical source pertaining to persecution and martyrdom is the Book of Revelation. The author, John (not to be confused with John the Apostle), addresses the seven churches of Asia Minor on matters of persecution. In 6:9-11 and 20:4 he also writes on Christians who were tortured and killed. The original name of the book is *apocalypsis*, which means revelation in ancient Greek.[330] The book was the revelation of the final aim, the coming of a new age and therefore a new heaven and new earth.[331] The final chapters, 21 and 22, are about these themes. Thus, John speaks of suffering and patience as a response. He promotes the idea that "the time is near."[332] Finally, there is direct reference to the importance of martyrs as initiators of the Christian church. Tertullian's line "the blood of martyrs is the seed of the Church" was quoted by the missionaries. The reference employs a metaphor of cultivation. Yet, more importantly, it also links the massacres to early persecutions and Tertullian's idea that Christians should embrace hope and faith in the face of persecution and death.

The common point to all the stories and missionary accounts is martyrdom. Martyrdom is the starting point for projection. As the Missionaries gradually gained confidence and calculated the situation better after the first months following the initial massacres, they adopted a noticeably hopeful tone when they started to articulate notions of an inevitable future, the end

---

330 Anthony Ernest Harvey. *A Companion to the New Testament: The New Revised Standard Version*. Cambridge: Cambridge University Press (2004): 783.

331 *ibid.* 783-784.

332 *ibid.* 785.

of times, and the realization of the ultimate aim in connection with the opportunities they detected. The projection of expectant ideas expressed in the Book of Revelations or writings of Tertullian reinforced the formation of missionary discourse. Even in the face of death, Christians had reason to be confident. The walkthrough proposed by the missionaries overlapped with the early stories in which persecution and death were supposed to be followed by a struggle between good and evil and the ultimate victory and reign of God. All in all, the blends produced by the projection of previous parables and stories on real life events functioned as excellent tools for bringing coherence and orientation to missionary discourse.

5 Modernity and Ottoman Reactions to Missionary Activities

5.1 MODERNITY AS A KEY CONSTRUCT

This chapter explicates the greater background in which the missionary narrative was produced and the missionaries conducted their activities. By the help of this explication, the missionary narrative of above mentioned historical processes can be reviewed and better understood in retrospect. Among other characteristics, nineteenth century is a period of modernization for the Ottoman Empire and the world. The missionary narrative was created in the context of that modernization process. Since the analysis of the subject matter also revolves around the vague concept of modernity, it would be best to discuss the evaluation of missionary activities in this specific context. The term modernity is laden with a vast number of meanings and connotations, depending on the specific instance in which the term is applied. It is even possible to speak of 'modernities' rather than an all-encompassing concept.[1] But that is not to say that the many inflections and articulations of the term applied to the analyses of different epochs and diverse geographical locations do not have any overlapping features.

To start with, modernity is accepted to have its origins in, and to have been diffused from, the 'West.' The main reason for this approach is the association of modernity with the Enlightenment. To illustrate, while writing on different topics related to modernity, Punter, Himmelfarb, Goody and

---

1 For a through discussion of the notion of 'multiple modernities' see: S. N. Eisenstadt. "Multiple Modernities." *Daedalus*, Vol. 129, No. 1, Winter (2000): 1-29.

Barnett relate the discussion of the term modernity to Enlightenment ideals, whether approvingly or otherwise.[2] For Goody, "[m]odernity has also been identified with the rise of capitalism, and connected with the growth of rationality and of secularization, more recently with urbanization and industrialization."[3]

David Punter offers five initial hypotheses about modernity, some of which may be useful in explaining the concept of modernity for the Board and the religious tradition it represents. Three of them are particularly important. In the second hypothesis, he claims that "[m]odernity has a particular relation to culture and [...] to the literary" since "culture is always striated by the past and the future; where the world of labour may feasibly thrive on stasis and the need for stability in order to assess and fulfill economic need, the world of culture exists in part as a testing-ground of possibilities."[4] The second hypothesis helps define the background against which the Board conducted its activities. Their access to the New Divinity tradition was mainly through texts and educational institutions, and their aim to convert the world according to this tradition was mainly carried out through education in their schools and the distribution of the books and pamphlets printed in mission printing houses. In this way, they connected past to future through cultural events and activities which relied mainly on education and printed texts. The third hypothesis is about the complex relation of modernity to the 'foreign.' For Punter, "cultures evolve at different rates in different places; thus 'imports' of foreign artifacts, whether these are from other 'civilized' cultures or from cultures perceived as primitive, will often be crucial as ways of voicing that within the host culture which might otherwise appear unable to be voiced."[5] The issue of 'foreign' in the framework of American missionary endeavors in the Ottoman Empire speaks for

---

2   David Punter. *Modernity*. New York: Palgrave Macmillan (2007): 13-23; Gertrude Himmelfarb. *The Roads to Modernity: The British, French, and American Enlightenments*. New York: Alfred A. Knopf (2004): 3-235; Jack Goody. *Capitalism and Modernity: The Great Debate*. Cambridge (UK): Polity (2004): 16-17; S. J. Barnett . *The Enlightenment and Religion: The Myths of Modernity*. Manchester: Manchester University Press (2003): 1-224.

3   Goody, *Capitalism*, 6.

4   Punter, *Modernity*, 8-9.

5   *ibid*. 9.

itself. In this particular instance, doctrinal knowledge and the methods of dissemination can be given priority over artifacts as elements that emphasize their 'foreign' character. The fifth hypothesis is on the political trait of modernity:

Modernity is always and everywhere political; it is also consequently inseparable from economic and technological conditions. Walter Benjamin in his crucial essay "The Work of Art in the Age of Mechanical Reproduction" (1935) suggests that the moment of modernity is the moment at which the work of art loses its 'aura', its uniqueness, becomes reproducible, but we may say that the history of western culture is striated by many such moments [...].[6]

According to the fifth hypothesis, it can be claimed that the American missionaries coming from a print culture encountered a calligraphic culture at the early phase of their activities. It should also be noted that the rate of literacy in Ottoman Empire in 1800 was 1% and barely reached 5-10 percent in 1900.[7] The missionaries had dominant religious motives, yet the encounter transformed their intentions, discourses, and activities into political ones independent of their motives.

Modernity and religion may seem controversial at first glance. M. A. Gillespie's comments on Karl Löwith's book *Meaning in History* is pretty interesting in this regard:

[...] Karl Löwith argued in *Meaning in History* that modernity was the result of the secularization of Christian ideals and that it was thus not ultimately distinct from the Middle Ages [...] For example, from this perspective the notion of progress, which is so essential to the modern self-understanding, appears to have been the secularization of Christian Millenarianism. Seen in this way, the traditional account of the emergence of modernity as the triumph of reason over superstition seems to be seriously flawed.[8]

---

6   *ibid.* 9-10.
7   Carter V. Findley. *Bureaucratic Reform in the Ottoman Empire: The Sublime Porte, 1789-1922.* New Jersey: Princeton University Press (1980): 139.
8   Michael Allen Gillespie. *The Theological Origins of Modernity.* Chicago: The University of Chicago Press (2008): 11.

The relation of millenarianism to modernity is striking when evaluated in light of the postmillennial idea of progress held by the missionaries.[9] It is hard to accept a simplified secularization theory, but the theological origins of modernity should not be ignored. These origins are stressed by Gillespie when he states "the shapes that modern thought subsequently assumed were not arbitrary reoccupations of medieval positions but a realization of the metaphysical and theological possibilities left by the antecedent tradition."[10] However, it should not be ignored that rigorous 'secularization' does not apply to Missionary thought and activities, which were religious in essence. The content was disseminated with the help of modern, scientifically-influenced means such as the printing press, modern teaching techniques, and teaching equipment.[11]

Although not specifically connected to the topic, Calinescu's opinions on the utopian imagination as related to Christianity exhibit the interrelatedness of Western cultural paradigms, modernity, religion, and utopianism:

Utopian imagination as it has developed since the eighteenth century is one more proof of the modern devaluation of the past and the growing importance of the fu-

---

9 A brief historical background to Congregationalist theology in the second half of nineteenth century is given at the beginning of Chapter 4. Moreover, the same chapter contains a thorough discussion of the paradoxical coexistence of religious and secular stances in Congregationalism and postmillennialist thought. The current section develops on what was already discussed in Chapter 4 and expands on this by means of further examples by concentrating specifically on the secularization process that took place in the second half of the nineteenth century. It is assumed that the gradual rise of secular traits in postmillennialist thought has a direct link with the discussion of modernity in missionary context.

10 Gillespie, *Theological Origins*, 12.

11 Albert Barnes' lines, published in 1868, display the complex relationship between the religious and the secular: Christianity, more than science, has secured the press. It early seized upon it as a most important auxiliary; it made it tributary to its own great work in diffusing the doctrines of the Reformation; it now employs it in the work of diffusing the truths of revelation in a large part of the languages spoken on the earth. It takes the press with it wherever it goes; it forms no plan for its own propagation or perpetuity except in connection with it (Albert Barnes. *Lectures on the Evidences of Christianity in the Nineteenth Century*. New York: Harper's (1868): 395).

ture. Utopianism, however, would hardly be conceivable outside the specific time consciousness of the West, as it was shaped by Christianity and subsequently by reason's appropriation of the concept of irreversible time. The religious nature of utopianism is recognized by both its adversaries and advocates.[12]

Calinescu's points can be regarded as a gateway to the utopian nature of the millennial ideas of the missionaries as well as to their associations with modernity (it is no coincidence that the postmillennialist idea also appears in the utopian novels of Edward Bellamy and Ignatius Donnelly from the second half of nineteenth century).[13] Calinescu's summary of the bourgeois idea of modernity is particularly important since what he explains bears a striking resemblance to the values and ways of New Divinity thought and missionary enterprise:

The doctrine of progress, the confidence in the beneficial possibilities of science and technology, the concern with time (a *measurable* time, a time that can be bought and sold and therefore has, like any other commodity, a calculable equivalent in money), the cult of reason, and the ideal of freedom defined within the framework of an abstract humanism, but also the orientation toward pragmatism and the cult of action and success – all have been associated in various degrees with the battle for the modern and were kept alive and promoted as key values in the triumphant civilization established by the middle class.[14]

The moral values of the missionaries can be seen as a reflection of these traits. Even the 'cult of reason' with a theological inflection can be placed among these values and, as far as missionary activity is concerned, 'the orientation toward pragmatism' best characterizes the orientation of missionary activities in the Ottoman Empire.

It can be assumed that Congregationalist modernity is the result of their conservatism. The Calvinist reaction against the shift in the social and political structure above all forced the evangelists to find new ways of articulat-

---

12 Matei Calinescu. *Five Faces of Modernity: Modernism, Avant-Garde, Decadence, Kitsch, Postmodernism*. Durham: Duke University Press (1987): 63.

13 Jean B. Quandt. "Religion and Social Thought: The Secularization of Postmillennialism," *American Quarterly*, Vol. 25, No. 4 (Oct., 1973): 394-395.

14 Calinescu, *Five Faces*, 41-42.

ing their ideas. The most important figure in this respect was Timothy Dwight. Dwight was the president of Yale College and consequently the head of Connecticut's ecclesiastical establishment.[15] The hopes that arose after the Great Awakening, that America was the harbinger of the Millennium and the new Protestant country was destined to save the world, were threatened by the skeptical philosophy and liberalism of the Enlightenment.[16] Moreover, the 'ungodly' revolution in France appalled the Protestants. Being a millennialist, Dwight placed liberal democracy and pluralism in the context of millennialist philosophy, which interprets history as a continuous war between the faithful and the followers of satanic delusion.[17] The main idea was to transpose Calvinist theology to the new secular environment and for that purpose Dwight formulated a practical Calvinism by discarding the supernaturalism of the Great Awakening.[18] Stephen E. Berk asserts that "[t]he Second Great Awakening, an evangelical movement which began at Dwight's Yale, was the outgrowth of his enterprising approach to religion."[19] Dwight's concern was the merging of Federalists and Congregationalists against the Jeffersonians.

Although he was unsuccessful in this attempt, it can be said in light of what subsequently occurred that he unintentionally made the new evangelical orthodoxy a part of the emerging American nation, which in turn contributed to Protestant modernity. One clear indication of this is that "[i]n the new orthodoxy, voluntary associations and persuasion replaced coercive ecclesiastical establishments."[20] This fact is extremely important to understand the missionary establishment. Unlike their predecessors, the American Protestant missionaries were less aggressive toward their target groups. As can be seen in their activities in the Ottoman Empire, the foundation of Bible societies, voluntary associations in nature, and the constant attempts to persuade individuals or groups indicate that within a short time after the Second Great Awakening, the practical and pragmatist adaptation of per-

---

15 Stephen E. Berk. *Calvinism versus Democracy: Timothy Dwight and the Origins of American Evangelical Orthodoxy*. Connecticut: Archon Books (1974): x.

16 *ibid*. ix.

17 *ibid*. ix.

18 *ibid*. x.

19 *ibid*. x.

20 *ibid*. xi.

suasion and voluntary societies were internalized and became a part of their philosophy. Thus, it is possible to claim that evangelist Congregationalists and their missionaries had become conservative elements in the equation of emerging modern American society.

The kingdom theology of 1850s, which accepted science, technological advancements and culture, the rise of New Theology and religious liberalism, contributed to the secularization of American Christianity.[21] The postmillennialist perspective of New Theology, which considered Christ's spirit and human activity as the main contributors for the coming of the Kingdom, was central in this respect.[22] Andover Theological Seminary, one of the main centers of liberalism, took a position that supported the immanence of God in nature and society (a notion partly derived from the doctrine of evolution), and conversion as gradual improvement of the individual.[23]

Although, modernity as a concept eludes general definition due to the infinite attributes one can find among its various geographical and temporal inflections, in the case of American missionaries in the Ottoman Empire, the concept can be seen through a comparative eye. The concept originated in the West and its attributes are strictly Western oriented and related to the social, political, and cultural transformations and paradigms that occurred in the Western world. Despite this, any attempt to analyze the term and the historical processes associated with it is doomed to failure if it keeps generating the *sui generis* explanation of the Western character of modernity.

It is true that the existence of certain structures and material advances comprise a considerable part of the characteristics of what is called modernity. Yet, the same applies to the absence or lack of these or other traits in other spatial and historical situations. Thus, the manifestations of modernity in the construction of roads and other infrastructures, educational facilities, military establishments or bureaucracies (which, in the Ottoman case can also be called patrimony) are significant. These facts are related to the way of thinking of a certain period. Besides this diachronic aspect, there comes the fact that there were no proper roads in the Levant, as for instance near Beirut: a synchronic occurrence which also makes the discourse of moder-

---

21 Quandt, "Religion and Social Thought," 393.

22 *ibid.* 394.

23 *ibid.* 394.

nity meaningful. For that reason, a comparative approach is not only useful, but also inevitable, because as Peter Burke claims, "thanks to comparison [...] we are able to see what is not there, in other words to understand the significance of a particular absence."[24] Burke draws attention to the danger of ethnocentrism in a comparative approach:

It may well seem odd to point out such a danger, since the comparative analysis has long been associated with the increasing awareness of non-Western cultures on the part of Western scholars. All the same, these scholars have often treated the West as a norm from which other cultures diverge. 'Feudalism', for example, like 'capitalism', is a concept originally formulated on the basis of Western experience. There is an obvious danger of trying to force other people's history into Western categories of this kind.[25]

The application of the term 'feudal' to Ottoman society may cause complications. Yet, in a time when the central authority constantly attempted to 'modernize' the military, education, bureaucracy, and law by taking the Western models as examples, it is not forcing other people's histories into Western categories, but merely seeing the inflection of what is asserted by the West in some parts of the East under the specific condition of missionary activities and discourse.

One advantage of analyzing a historical period is that the events that occur subsequent to the examined period are known to the writer. Thus, the concepts of modern and modernity are not only key constructs for making a meaningful and coherent study of missionary narrative. They also provide historical and cultural analysis with a useful theoretical background, since beginning in the eighteenth century the problem of modernization became the major issue for the Ottoman Empire, while remaining a central issue for the 'modern' Near and Middle East.

In order to understand and piece the events of the Middle East mission together, the writings of the missionaries are of utmost importance. The Christian postmillennialist orientation of their discourse is teleological and places emphasis on the importance of a predicted and predestined future. The historical process is seen as culminating in the inevitable end of the

24 Peter Burke. *History and Social Theory*. Cambridge (UK): Polity (1992): 23.
25 *ibid*. 26.

Millennium and constant progress in modern terms is foreseen through human agency. The result is an idealist understanding of human actions and history. As for the activities in the Ottoman Empire, they were driven by notions originating from that discourse.

Discourse cannot be alienated from the activities of the missionaries, and the events that occurred as a result of mission work also need to be explained. To a certain extent the events intermingled with the discursive foundations of the missionaries. The outcome of missionary activities was connected to the stance of the Ottoman state as well as the cultural background of the indigenous people. Discourse was not the only thing the missionaries brought to the Middle East. They were present with their clothes, hairstyles, language, presses, books, and even their style of horseback riding. They furnished their houses with a different taste, their gardens reflected their cultural background, and their activities were conducted through that background against that of the indigenous people. Discourse was the abstract idea behind what was tangible or met the eye. Thus, it was an encounter of cultures and the encounter of the material and immaterial peculiarities of cultures.

The term encounter is aptly discussed by Peter Burke. He establishes a connection between the notions of 'frontier' and 'encounter.'[26] The following passage also offers an insight into the missionary activities in the Ottoman Empire:

The view from outside needs to be supplemented by one from inside, stressing the experience of crossing the boundaries between 'us' and 'them' and encountering Otherness with a capital O (or perhaps with a capital A, since the French were the first to produce a theory of *l'Autre*).We are dealing here with the symbolic boundaries of imagined communities, boundaries that resist mapping. All the same, historians cannot afford to forget their existence.[27]

For him the frontier is in essence a cultural frontier. He refers to certain ideas of Fernand Braudel in his discussion. The following passage from

---

26 Peter Burke, *What is Cultural History?* Cambridge (UK): Polity (2004): 116-119.

27 *ibid*. 117.

Braudel can be linked to the idea of a cultural frontier, which in turn can be linked to the geographical borders:

The mark of a civilization is that it is capable of exporting itself, of spreading its culture to different places. It is impossible to imagine a true civilization which does not export its people, its way of thinking and living [...] A living civilization must be able not only to give but to receive and to borrow [...] But a great civilization can also be recognized by its refusal to borrow, by its resistance to certain alignments, by its resolute selection among the foreign influences offered to it and which would no doubt be forced upon it if they were not met by vigilance or, more simply, by incompatibility of temper and appetite.[28]

Burke gives the example of the resistance to print in the Islamic world and concludes that "the world of Islam has been viewed as a barrier separating the two zones in which books were printed" and states that it was "only in the nineteenth century that Islam and print negotiated an alliance."[29] This example is particularly important considering that major activities of the American missionaries were dependent upon presses to produce books, tracts and other documents to be distributed and used as teaching material.

The figure who connects the relationship of American Protestantism to secularism and modernity to the Ottoman Empire and missionary work in the Empire is famous American Social Gospeller Josiah Strong. Strong's ideas were the pinnacle of Congregationalist secularism for he advocated the importance of science and the advancement of communications technology and industry, together with the moral improvement of believers.[30] Strong's moralistic and cultural postmillennialism was down-to-earth and his millennialist aspirations were closely related to the missionary work of the churches. He even worked on a plan for visiting city dwellers lost in the vastness of modern urban life in order to invite them to conversion and Christianity and change public opinion on religious matters[31] (The reason behind his urban missionary attempt resembles what Marshall Berman sees

---

28 Fernand Braudel. *The Mediterranean and the Mediterranean World in the Age of Philip II*. London: Collins (1973): 763-764.

29 Burke, *Cultural* History, 11.

30 Quandt, "Religion and Social Thought," 398.

31 *ibid*. 398.

as the paradoxes of modern urban life, as expressed in the works of Baude-laire).[32] Strong's attitude suggested a primacy of moral effort should be placed on conversion, and he promoted the idea that the Kingdom was to come through the deeds of people who were ennobled by "Anglo-Saxon culture, Christian morality and organizational genius."[33]

Strong's appearance in the story of ABCFM in the Ottoman Empire is closely tied to his ideological and theological views, which can be charac-terized secular and American in character. During and after the Armenian massacres of 1894-96, the Board conducted a widespread and influential campaign in the United States.[34] Indeed, the Board's opinions on interna-tional events was evaluated with due regard and seriousness by decision-makers at the highest levels of the American government.[35] The Board had a network of personal connections and a missionary lobby to assert its poli-cies on such levels.[36] Josiah Strong organized a subcommittee for the Evangelical Alliance in order to coordinate the political activities of ABCFM in the Ottoman Empire.[37] When several missionary schools were destroyed in the events of 1895, the Board demanded indemnity and the Secretary of Defense, Richard Olmey, discussed the plausibility of landing American Marines on the Anatolian coast and moving inland as a protec-tive measure.[38] Olmey later informed the Board that the plan was not deemed to be feasible.[39] When the Ottoman state delayed payment of a $100,000 indemnity, Strong and the Board gradually resorted to more ag-gressive methods between the years 1896 and 1898.[40] Missionaries had a meeting with President Cleveland, who told them that an American gunboat

---

32 Marshall Berman. *All That is Solid Melts into Air*. London: Verso (1983): 141-142, 159-160.

33 *ibid*. 399.

34 James Eldin Reed. "American Foreign Policy, the Politics of Missions and Josi-ah Strong, 1890-1900." *Church History: Studies in Christianity and Culture*, Vol. 4, Issue 02, June (1972): 235.

35 *ibid*. 232.

36 *ibid*. 233.

37 *ibid*. 236.

38 *ibid*. 236.

39 *ibid*. 236.

40 Reed, "Foreign Policy," 237.

had been sent to the Bosphorus as a display of power and will, yet the missionaries were not content with that measure either.[41] As the Board repeatedly demanded drastic action against the Ottoman State, Josiah Strong visited Washington in the spring of 1897 together with a committee of missionaries and tried to persuade politicians to take military action.[42] William E. Dodge, a wealthy New York merchant and diplomat, as well as an associate of the Board, was also among the group of men visiting Washington. He did not support military intervention and opposed Strong, asking "[h]ave Christians a right to compel other nations to accept their teaching?"[43]

The question actually represented the deep paradox the missionaries had been struggling with for quite a while: the seemingly irreconcilable attitudes of gunboat diplomacy and spreading the religion of love. The missionaries, together with Strong, came up with a solution that was more political in essence than religious. Missionaries were first and foremost evangelists. Yet, they were also American citizens. As such, they had no right to coerce others to comply as evangelists, but they had the right to demand protection as American citizens.[44] The position of the Board can be seen in the following passage:

Our readers do not expect us to say all that is in mind concerning affairs in Turkey. We presume that the reasons for this reticence are well understood. There is no reason, however, why we should not here say emphatically that should there be any truth in the report that the Turkish government purposes to expel all missionaries from the empire, such a purpose will be in direct violation of treaty rights and must never be permitted by our government. We have no thought whatever that our government will consent that its citizens be driven from positions which, by the explicit pledges of Turkey, they have been allowed to occupy. Our citizens in Asia Minor who are engaged in commercial enterprises, such as dealing in rugs or cotton, could not be expelled without international complications in which Turkey would not wish to involve herself. Our citizens dealing in books and in other matters connected with education have the same right to remain where they are, and should enjoy fullest

---

41 *ibid*. 237.
42 *ibid*. 238.
43 *ibid*. 238.
44 *ibid*. 239.

protection. We have no doubt whatever that our government will maintain this position.[45]

As the massacres came to a halt in 1896 Washington and the missionary lobbyists alike lost interest in such fierce and ambitious interventionist projects.[46]

In James Eldin Reed's words, Strong was "at once a humanitarian and an aggressive nationalist, an internationalist and a jingo."[47] His millennialism had two sides, the first being a millennialist Christian internationalism and the second a fervent American nationalism.[48] As in the paradoxical concurrence of Enlightenment values, the acceptance of scientific development, the idea of progress, and irrational eschatological beliefs and imagery, the partial secularization of American Protestantism and the missionary establishment struggled with the paradox of a religion of peace and the politics of war and intervention. It is hard to ascertain to what degree the Board was aware of its increasingly 'mundane' schemes and involvements. In retrospective, despite the alleged general mission policy of political nonintervention and indifference, the Ottoman mission staunchly set foot on highly political fields, such as education, and became rivals with political entities; namely other religious beliefs and groups at the beginning, and the Ottoman State in the second half of the nineteenth century. The main context of rivalry was the interpretation of what this chapter calls 'modernity' by those entities, and the outcome of the corresponding work and consequent frictions was highly secular and political. In order to examine the other side of the coin and the development of a modern state (which later evolved into modern Turkey) in its relation to missionary modernity (and vice versa), the transformation of the Ottoman State and its reaction to American missionary activity will be reviewed in the next section.

---

45 "Editorial Paragraphs." *The Missionary Herald*, May (1896): 179.
46 Reed, "Foreign Policy," 240-241.
47 *ibid*. 242.
48 *ibid*. 242.

5.2 FROM INTRUDERS TO ENEMIES: OTTOMAN MISSIONARY RELATIONS

5.2.1 A Period of Great Expectations

The nineteenth century was a period of constant and drastic change for the Ottoman Empire. The attempts at modernization initiated by Selim II at the end of eighteenth century were brought to another level. The turning point was the disbandment of the Janissary Corps by Sultan Mahmud II in what was called the "Auspicious Incident" in 1826. This incident cleared the way for a period of drastic reforms and fundamental changes in the very fabric of the state. The declaration of the Imperial Edict of Reorganization (Tanzimât Fermânı) of 1839 saw the commencement of a new era that lasted from 1839 to 1876 which is known as Tanzimât (reorganization). In 1856, the Sublime Porte felt the need to express the ongoing changes via a new imperial reform edict, Ottoman reform Edict of 1856. The new reforms aimed at enabling the Ottoman administration and eventually society to catch up with the necessities of being 'modern,' albeit only in appearance and with timid steps. The social, legal and political transformations of Tanzimât culminated in the First Constitutional Era, 1876-1877, and the first constitution, Kanûn-u Esâsî (the basic law).[49] The experiment was short-lived. The newly inaugurated Sultan Abdulhamid II ended the First Constitutional Era and the period of Tanzimât effectively by shutting down the parliament.[50] Abdulhamid had his own agenda and set of reforms to implement.

The missionaries witnessed every stage of this century-long quest and were certainly not bystanders watching from a distance. The more they got involved in the social, religious and political life of the rapidly transforming Ottoman Empire, the more they became active elements of transformation. From the point of view of the Ottoman State, they remained interfering outsiders from the beginning, and as the missionary establishment grew stronger they were regarded as adversaries.

---

49 M. Şükrü Hanioğlu. *A Brief History of the Late Ottoman Empire*. Princeton: Princeton University Press (2008): 113.

50 Karpat, 125.

The missionaries came to the Ottoman Empire with pre-conceived and pre-established ideas and long-term aims. These ideas were a combination of "strong, unbroken religious faith with the postulates of the Enlightenment and the successful American experience of having set up what was broadly acclaimed in the west as the most modern and democratic state on earth."[51] This missionary theology and ideology and the notions surrounding them arose from a strong historical background including the Declaration of Independence, 1776, the Second Great Awakening, 1790-1840, and the resulting anticipation of the coming of the Kingdom.[52] The first missionaries assumed the beginning of a new era in which the fall of Islam, the demise of papacy, and the restoration of the Jews to Palestine and to Jesus would occur. They took the Near East as a central scene for the new era.[53]

The first ten years proved especially hard for the first missionaries. Pliny Fisk and Levi Parsons not only encountered many problems, they also met with early deaths within a couple of years as a result of poor conditions. Persecution was another major problem. Yet, direct state persecution was an exception thanks to the quasi autonomous position enjoyed by religious communities. Hence, as the missionary work in Mount Lebanon, Syria and Palestine swelled, religious communities of the region issued complaints to local authorities and chose to deal with individual converts within the confines of their own internal administrative mechanisms. As a result of the appeals, local representatives of the central government and in some cases the Porte occasionally interfered. It should be noted that the missionaries enjoyed British protection wherever they went, and British consular protection was a restricting element for the Porte.[54] Moreover, the Ottoman state had more important problems to deal with at that time. When the political unrest resulting from the Greek Revolution erupted in full scale turmoil in Beirut in 1826, the houses of the missionaries were also plundered. The Maronite bishop (patriarch) came down from his monastery in Mount Leb-

---

51 Hans-Lukas Kieser. *A Quest for Belonging: Anatolia Beyond Empire and Nation*. Istanbul: Isis Press (2007): 15.

52 *ibid*. 14.

53 *ibid*. 18.

54 See Chapter 1, footnote 54 for detailed information on British protection.

anon and told his community to drive out the missionaries.[55] In 1841, the Maronite bishop asked Zekeriya Pasha, the governor of Syria, to curb or suspend destructive missionary activities among the local population. Subsequently, the Porte delivered a verbal note to David Porter, the United States minister resident in Istanbul, in May 1841, asking him to coerce the missionaries into leaving Lebanon. The growing influence of American missionaries among the Armenians elicited a reaction as well. As of 1839, there were already 800 Armenian converts and the Armenian patriarchate was alarmed by the rapidly growing numbers. Armenian patriarch Matheos issued a complaint to the Sublime Porte and resorted to the threat of excommunication in order to prevent close contact with the missionaries. Following a public campaign launched by the patriarchate, Armenians from Erzurum, Trabzon and Bursa sent petitions to the Porte targeting missionary activities in their cities. Rifat Pasha, the minister of justice, sent a note to the American legation, once again asking for the withdrawal of the missionaries and for the second time the American authorities replied that they had no authority to do so. The Porte assumed a different attitude and ordered local authorities to prevent proselytism among the Armenians, thus proclaiming Protestantism among Armenians illegal, but to no avail.[56]

The incidents in the first twenty-five years of the mission indicate that although the state was well aware of the missionary establishment, it regarded and handled the matter within the confines of the *millet* system. The involvement of the state varied, but the underlying motive was to prevent social disruption and flaws in the established order. The complaints mainly arose from local communities or religious groups rather than the state itself. It can also be seen that the mid-40s marked the rise of the mission among the Armenians, and in turn a severe reaction from the Armenian millet at the highest level. The growing discontent caused the state to intervene more actively, yet it could not prevent the establishment of the Protestant community. The role of the British embassy should also be taken into consideration in the recognition of the Protestant community by the Porte.[57]

---

55 Çağrı Erhan. "Ottoman Official Attitudes towards American Missionaries." *The United States and the Middle East: Cultural Encounters.* Eds. Abbas Amanat, Magnus T. Bernhardsson. New Haven: YCIAS (2002): 320.

56 *ibid.* 320-322.

57 See section "1.4. The Armenian Reformation".

One year after the first missionaries landed in Izmir, in 1821, the Greek revolution began.[58] This was foreshadowed by Sultan Mahmud's campaign against Tepelenli Ali Pasha, who had created an autonomous administration at Yanina in Epirus.[59] Ali Pasha was an Albanian-born Muslim well acquainted with regional politics. He adopted Greek as the language of instruction and Greek schools flourished under his rule. Thus, Mahmud's campaign hastened the Greek revolt (1821-1827). Losing power against his adversaries, including his vassal, Mehmet Ali Pasha of Egypt, Mahmud implemented military reforms. The Janissary Corps rebelled but Mahmud resolutely declared war on them, and on June 14, 1826, the Janissary Corps was destroyed. Throughout the 1830s Mahmud introduced new reforms, such as re-fashioning central agencies as European-style ministries, expanding the translation office of the Sublime Porte (Bab-ı Âli Tercüme Odası) to become a center for modernization and diplomacy, and reorganizing civic offices and provincial administration; in short he reconsolidated the state and sultanate. Furthermore, the Anglo-Ottoman Commercial Treaty of 1838, which also proved to be an inspiration for similar agreements with other states, became the foundation for free trade based on low import and export duties, thus allowing British merchants to conduct business throughout the empire and oblige the Ottoman state to rescind all monopolies. The economic liberalism adopted by the state was expressed in politics by the imperial reform edict of 1839, declared under the rule of new sultan, Abdulmecid I. Despite its liberal themes, the decree strictly confined itself to sharia law and constantly underlined the compatibility of new laws with sharia. The main items of the decree were safeguarding life, safeguarding honor and property, tax assessment, military recruitment, and the duration of the military service.[60] The Edict of Reorganization of 1839 dealt with certain fundamental rights such as the guarantee of life, property and honor

---

58 Tuncer Baykara. "II. Mahmud'un Islahatında İç Temeller: 1829-1839 Arasında Anadolu." *Tanzimat'ın 150. Yıldönümü Uluslararası Sempozyumu.* Ankara: Atatürk Kültür, Dil ve Tarih Yüksek Kurumu (1994): 264.

59 Findley, *Turkey*, 36.

60 *ibid.* 36-44.

for all subjects.[61] The decree was full of religious terminology and its compatibility with sharia law was underlined many times over.[62] Yet it should also be noted that the decree and the ensuing regulations limited the sovereignty of the caliph-sultan in favor of governmental authority, both in theory and practice.[63]

The Reform Edict of 1856, on the other hand, had fewer allusions to Islamic law. The edict aimed at restricting the Sultan's sovereignty and partially separating religious authority from the emerging and centralizing modern bureaucracy. The edict not only confirmed the rights granted in the Edict of 1839, it also furthered those rights by tapping a more secular vein when articulating its core concepts.[64] As such, the Reform Edict of 1856 was based on the fundamental premises of the Edict of 1839 with a more secular outlook.

The missionaries were the intellectual and religious avant-garde of their times and they were progressive liberals fighting against slavery, for women's emancipation, and for legal and social equality.[65] By selectively referring to the Western or 'modern' elements of the Tanzimât era, they saw a new potential for expansion. The ongoing process of centralization and modernization proved them right because in the following decades the missionary establishment flourished. At the same time, however, the centralizing state gradually saw a rival and a fully grown enemy in the missionaries. What had been a contest between the missionaries and local groups had slowly been transported to a new realm, in which the state decided to have more authority.

---

61 Nurullah Ardıç. "Islam, Modernity and the 1876 Constitution." *The First Ottoman Experiment in Democracy*. Eds: Christoph Herzog, Malek Sherif. Würzburg: Ergon (2010): 9.

62 *ibid.* 91-93.

63 *ibid.* 91.

64 *ibid.* 93-94.

65 Hans-Lukas Kieser. *Nearest East: American Millennialism and Mission to the Middle East*. Philadelphia: Temple University Press (2010): 14.

5.2.2 Civilization, 'Civilisation,' Medeniyet

When Mustafa Reşit Pasha was appointed as emissary to Paris by Sultan
Mahmud II in 1833, one of the first things he noticed was the persistence of
the European public in its negative attitude towards the Ottoman Empire,
which it had adopted during the Greek revolution.[66] To change that opinion
became one of his main aims. He used the French word 'civilisation' in his
correspondence instead of its Ottoman Turkish counterpart 'medeniyet' because medeniyet was used to define city-dwellers as opposed to desert no-
mads. It did not denote the conceptual realm that 'civilisation' embraced.
Mustafa Reşit Pasha defined 'civilisation' as "the education of people and
the realization (implementation) of regulations (terbiye-i nâs ve icray-ı ni-
zamat)." In order to propagate this in the Ottoman Empire, he acquired a
newspaper, *Courrier Français*, and hired a columnist on a regular salary to
respond to the criticism against the Ottoman Empire in the press. The gist
of his propaganda was that Turkey had adopted the path of 'civilisation'
and Sultan Mahmud's reforms were in accord with the necessities of 'civilisation.' Mustafa Reşit Pasha was one of the masterminds behind the preparation and implementation of Tanzimât reforms, so his perceptions of
Western civilization were crucial.[67]

The invention of the new concept of medeniyet by the Ottoman elites
aimed at differentiating civilization from its cultural-religious vein.[68] As
such, the terms signified a superior social order, moral fabric, proper etiquette, progress, and contented living in opposition to ignorance, inertia,
and backwardness.[69] In the second half of the nineteenth century the notion
of medeniyet was gradually accepted as the main axis of national achievement by the elites.[70] From the beginning of the reform era, the state asserted
itself as the primal force to achieve the ideal of medeniyet, and the term
was used to evaluate the state of society by attributing medeniyet a central

---

66 Enver Ziya Karal. "Gülhane Hatt-ı Hümayûnu'nda Batı'nın Etkisi." *Belleten*,
    Vol. 28, No.112 (1964): 592.
67 *ibid.* 592-594.
68 Karpat, *Politicization*, 11.
69 *ibid.* 11.
70 *ibid.* 11.

role in identity formation.[71] The state claim to a monopoly on the medeni-yet project brought the bureaucracy and state-affiliated intelligentsia to the fore as the prime agents of modernization, which resulted in the legitimization of their political supremacy.[72]

Unlike the Ottoman state, the missionaries had a clear understanding and a well-defined notion of civilization. Articulating the postmillennialist ideas of material progress and echoing the theology of Hopkins and Bellamy, they rejoiced that various nations seemed to have agreed to invest in agricultural development, increasing their wealth and population, and enjoying "the blessings of science and civilization."[73] Besides having a developed theory of civilization, the missionaries were well equipped with the tools to implement it as a project. The Foreign Missionary School in Connecticut, responsible for the education of the youth picked from various parts of the world, was founded so as to educate these youngsters in such a way that they could be "employed in the work of civilizing and evangelizing the people of their respective countries [...]."[74] The tools that would raise the uncivilized nations to the league of civilized ones were "teaching husbandry, mechanic arts, household manufactures and economy, reading and writing so that they can be transformed into a civilized and Christianized, a wealthy and virtuous happy people," like American Christians. The Missionaries would bring these improvements to the Near East, "the land whence the light of immortality first shone upon the darkened nations."[75]

The contrast between the Ottoman and American Evangelical articulations of the notion 'civilization' is striking. While the missionaries had a clear idea, the Ottomans were struggling to define the term and only afterwards half-heartedly tried to fulfill its demands. Hence, the first half of the nineteenth century can be understood as a period in which the seeds of rivalry were sown between two powers in the domains of modernity and civi-

---

71 *ibid.* 11.

72 *ibid.* 11-12.

73 "Present Encouraging Aspects of the Unevangelized Parts of the World." *The Missionary Herald*, February (1820): 55.

74 "Address of the Prudential Committee of the American Board of Commissioners for Foreign Missions." *The Missionary Herald*, March (1820): 135.

75 "Report of the Prudential Committee." The Missionary Herald, January (1821): 10.

lization. Both sides had a claim to transform society and improve the administration, and both had a vision of the future. The fight was not over the past, it was for the future.

Moreover, the concept of civilization was not understood from a mutual point of view by the Muslim and Christian populations of the empire. Following the Edict of 1856, the notion of Ottomanism gained ground as the edict and the subsequent reforms regarded the subjects of the Sultan as equal citizens in principle.[76] Christian citizens, however, saw their connection to civilization not via Ottomanism, equal citizenship or medeniyet, but through Christianity.[77] They considered Christianity as their main bond with Western civilization, and by considering themselves as part of Western civilization many Christians saw themselves superior to Muslims.[78] In point of fact, Ottomanism was slowly transformed into a Muslim identity, first in attempts to create a common identity among the dominant group in the empire, namely the Muslims, during the Hamidian era, and secondly in its identification with Turks in the Young Turk era.[79]

The difference of opinion on the concept of civilization was not limited to Muslim-Christian opposition. As the idea became popular among the Muslim middle classes after 1880, a new rift became apparent between the defenders of economic liberalism, and state-sponsored progress.[80] The former group was in favor of civil initiative and agricultural investment with the aim of attaining the level of medeniyet, while the latter group, consisting of certain intellectuals and members of the central bureaucracy, advocated government guidance.[81] Yet despite major differences in opinion, both parties shared medeniyet as a common goal.[82] In short, social, economic, and political changes and identity formations in the second half of the nineteenth century were affected by the old and new ideas alike, and the concept that stood for this blend was medeniyet.[83]

---

76 Karpat, *Politicization*, 12.
77 *ibid.* 12.
78 *ibid.* 12.
79 *ibid.* 12.
80 *ibid.* 105.
81 *ibid.* 104.
82 *ibid.* 104-105.
83 *ibid.* 328.

The Ottoman notions of medeniyet and missionary civilization were not totally exclusive. The idea of proper etiquette, and particular individual qualities were inherent aspects of the missionary project of civilization, along with its transgenerational social prospects and technological infrastructure. Missionary reports from the beginnings of the mission repeatedly point to particular habits among indigenous peoples, such as table manners (sitting on the ground or using hands rather than utensils), house interiors in regard to furniture, the way women rode horses in contrast to 'American ladies,' personal relations, individual privacy, and personal hygiene. Such observations did not stem from peripheral concerns. In the great scheme of history, they might look trivial; in the making of a mission they turned out to be central. Before Eli Smith and H. G. O. Dwight started their tour of Anatolia and Armenia in 1830, the Board demanded that they investigated the incidence of polygamy, the position of females in society, whether the 'family government' was appreciated, whether lewdness, drunkenness, profaneness and casual sexual intercourse were frowned upon, the industriousness of the people, the moral integrity of merchants, and the political integrity among the rulers.[84]

5.2.3 Dark Clouds

Since "the spirit of political and legal reform prevailing during the first half of the Tanzimât [...] changed the ABCFM's attitude toward Ottoman power," the missionaries took advantage of the new political atmosphere.[85] The favorable climate started to change when the missionaries interpreted the new Ottoman Reform Edict of 1856 as legally enabling proselytism among Muslims. The case is thoroughly examined in the previous chapter. Suffice it to say that the Porte almost crushed the mission in Istanbul after a long period of meticulous observation and evaluation.

After the recognition of the Protestant community as a legal entity in 1850, Abraham Ütücüyan, a converted Armenian, was chosen as head of

---

84 "Views and Proceedings in Reference to This Mission." *The Missionary Herald*, March (1830): 77.

85 Kieser, *Nearest East*, 46.

the Protestant community.[86] The decree that recognized the Protestant community covered the regulations of the community's internal affairs, tax collection, marriage, and posts pertaining to community administration.[87] In 1851, the Protestants assembled a people's assembly in Istanbul to elect an executive board and the head of the Protestant community.[88] The community prepared a bylaw and presented it to the executive board. The bylaw and the acts of the executive board were open to civil inspection. Moreover, the head of the community was chosen from among the laity. The community based its administrative principles on democratic representation.[89] Finally, on March 12, 1878, the state promulgated the Protestant Community Constitution (Protestan Cemaati Nizamname-i Esasîsi).[90]

The edict of 1856 also granted non-Muslim communities the right to open schools. In 1869, the Regulation of Public Education imposed legal restrictions on this right and schools were classified as either public or private, required official licenses to operate, and had to present their curricula for examination by the Ministry of Education.[91] These regulations could hardly be enforced but in 1877 an inspectorate of non-Muslim and foreign schools was set up, in 1880 implementation was made mandatory by the local educational commissions, and in 1894 Turkish language teaching was made obligatory.[92]

The severity of the precautions in the 1880s and 1890s had to do with administrative change. With the coming of Sultan Abdulhamid II to power, a new era began that effectively ended Tanzimât. The Hamidian regime was so concerned with the American mission on Ottoman soil that the precautions taken against missionaries constituted an important aspect of im-

---

86 Gazi Erdem. *Osmanlı İmparatorluğunda Hıristiyanların Sosyal ve Dini Hayatları: 1856-1876.* Ankara: Ankara Üniversitesi (2005): 183 (Unpublished PhD dissertation).

87 *ibid.* 183.

88 *ibid.* 184.

89 *ibid.* 184.

90 *ibid.* 187.

91 Akşin Somel. "Christian Community Schools During the Ottoman Reform Period." *Late Ottoman Society: The Intellectual Legacy.* Ed. Elisabeth Özdalga. London: Routledge Press (2005): 268.

92 Deringil, *Well Protected Domains,* 105.

perial policy. Wary as he was of Western interventionism, Abdulhamid accused Christian leaders of fostering biases against Islam while promoting ideas of broadmindedness and fairness for civilization.[93] His accusations were based on real events such as the French missionaries' attempts to incite Maronite peasants against Druse landlords, the fight over the control of holy sites in Jerusalem, and a one-sided report by an American missionary on Bulgarian events in 1876.[94] One of his priorities during his reign was the union of the Muslim communities in the empire, and he implemented a series of regulations to achieve that end.[95] Although the main aim was chiefly to realize the unity of the Sunni majority, his efforts soon covered a wider span. The state took steps in an attempt to transform the marginalized Yezidi and Nestorian peoples into a constituent of the Ottoman Muslim Union. The government opened mosques and schools in Yezidi villages and sent Sunni *ulema* (religious scholars) to acquaint the Yezidis with orthodox Islam. Moreover, group leaders were systematically honored with titles and medals. Schools and mosques were built in Nestorian villages as well, and many Nestorians from the districts of Antakya, Latakia, and Alexandria were thus converted.[96]

Abdulhamid's policy was not a series of unrelated precautions against Western influence. The authorities prohibited the distribution of unapproved versions of the Koran and in 1897, an overall prohibition was passed so that only copies of the Koran published by the state were allowed on the market.[97] In effect, measures for building schools and printing the Koran were supported by the introduction of travelling *ulema* in Iraq, Syria and Cyprus.[98] In 1892, Mehmed Rauf Pasha, the governor of Damascus, advised that the travelling ulema policy should be continued and recommended that the *ulema* be sent to the countryside during the holy month of Ramadan in order to counterbalance the missionary presence in Syria.[99]

---

93 Karpat, *Politicization*, 173.

94 *ibid*. 173.

95 *ibid*. 199-204.

96 *ibid*. 205.

97 *ibid*. 231.

98 Benjamin C. Fortna. *Imperial Classroom*. Oxford: Oxford University Press (2002): 93.

99 *ibid*. 94.

Likewise, local notables and officers from Cyprus asked for new schools, and for 300 hundred copies of the Koran to be distributed, and for members of the *ulema* to cross the countryside and prevent the Christianization of the island.[100] During this era, conversion to Islam from other sects was encouraged and converts were offered financial help as a reply to Western missionary work.[101] Yet, the state never officially urged Christians to convert.[102] Abdulhamid believed in the importance of unity among the Muslims of the empire and the importance of education and scientific progress. He was convinced that the alienation of Muslim pupils from their religion and culture was due to lack of religious education and the influence of Western schools. As a result, the state attempted to restrain Muslim children from attending missionary schools since local authorities were unable to prevent missionary work.[103]

Abdulhamid's displeasure was based on hard facts. The missionary schools surpassed the public and community schools by far in terms of quality and quantity.[104] Missionary magazines and newspapers published for the Western audience influenced the public view about the Ottoman Empire. These publications shaped public attitudes and molded public opinion on foreign policy issues.[105] Thus, together with the internal conflict on educating and transforming the Sultan's subjects, there was an ongoing problem of internal representation of the Empire. Abdulhamid's administration was aware of the degree and content of the manipulative influence that the missionaries had on Western public opinion. During this period, excerpts from *The Missionary Herald* were translated into Turkish by state officials; Ottoman diplomatic emissaries sent information, including the report of Münci Bey warning the sultan about the political interests of missionary activity in Ayvalık. The local authorities were constantly warned to monitor missionary activities in their areas.[106] In an attempt to counterbalance missionary representations, Abdulhamid sent a photo album of 1,824

---

100 *ibid.* 95.
101 Karpat, *Politicization*, 231.
102 *ibid.* 232.
103 *ibid.* 232.
104 Fortna, *Classroom*, 50, 116.
105 Reed, "Foreign Policy," 232.
106 Deringil, *Well Protected Domains*, 125-127.

photographs representing his empire and a collection of Ottoman stamps to the Library of Congress in Washington in 1893. A collection of janissary costumes was sent to the World's Fair in Chicago for exhibition the same year.[107]

Retaining the Tanzimât policy for centralization and spreading education, Abdulhamid abandoned the policy of equality and made the Sunni Hanefi sect the official sect of the Empire.[108] For him the missionaries were "the most dangerous enemies of the social order." His new policy included entrusting conversion to the Hanefi sect. In a memorandum dated April 8, 1892, Süleyman Hüsnü Pasha, Governor of Bagdad, suggested the foundation of Daîler Cemiyeti, a Sunni Hanefi missionary organization. The Ottoman state was establishing its own missionary network to challenge western missionaries.[109] Abdulhamid and his cadre studied their lessons well. There was a mutual learning process between the state and the missionaries and Abdulhamid was trying to catch up with the latter. An explanatory note written by Cevdet Pasha on request of the sultan in 1893 represents the retrospective and comprehensive attitude the Hamidian regime assumed on the matter of education. Cevdet Pasha was critical of Tanzimât reforms as facilitating the growth in number of foreign schools and he regarded private schools opened or sponsored by foreigners as a threat to the social order.[110] In a memorandum, written by Zühtü Pasha, Minister of Education in 1893, the number of foreign schools, information on how they were founded, their aims and programs, and the issue of inspection were covered in de-

---

107 Selim Deringil. "II. Abdülhamid Döneminde Osmanlı Dış İlişkilerinde 'İmaj' Saplantısı." *Sultan II. Abdülhamid ve Devri Semineri.* İstanbul: Edebiyat Fakültesi Basımevi (1994): 153, 156.

108 Selim Deringil. "The Invention of Public Image in the Late Ottoman Period, 1808 to 1908." *Comparative Studies in Society and History,* Vol. 35, No. 1, January (1993): 13.

109 *ibid.* 13, 14, 19.

110 Yahya Akyüz. "Cevdet Paşa'nın Öğretim ve Tanzimat Eğitimine İlişkin Bir Layihası." *OTAM (Osmanlı, Tarih, Araştırma ve Uygulama Merkezi Dergisi),* No. 3, Jan. (1992): 85-114.

tail.[111] Şakir Pasha, the inspector general of the Eastern Anatolian provinces, wrote a similar explanatory note in 1898. The note included suggestions on measures to be taken against foreign, especially missionary schools, the detrimental activities of these schools, and the need to establish high quality public schools including vocational schools for boys and girls in order to prevent Christian economic supremacy in Anatolia.[112] Abdulhamid's policy soon caused a humanitarian and diplomatic crisis. During the years 1894-1896, massacres swept Anatolia, particularly the six eastern vilayets. Thousands of Armenians were killed by Hamidian light cavalry, civilians and paramilitaries. The missionary reactions to the massacres have been examined in the fourth chapter.

The above account is the broader background of missionary narrative examined in this study. The Ottoman-missionary encounter and the missionary narrative can be fully understood in this context. The historical events and periods evaluated in the previous chapters took place in this setting and the missionary narrative was created during the long century of modernization.

---

111 Yahya Akyüz. "Abdülhamit Devrinde Protestan Okulları ile İlgili Orijinal İki Belge." *Ankara Üniversitesi Eğitim Bilimleri Fakültesi Dergisi*, Vol. 3, No. 1 (1970): 122-126.

112 *ibid.* 126-128.

Conclusion

This study set out to explore the conceptual metaphor networks inherent to the official missionary discourse of the ABCFM, how that discourse constituted a narrative, and the place of those metaphor networks in the narrative structure. It was proposed that the conceptual metaphorical formations *systematically* contributed to the formation of a missionary narrative, and that they would provide invaluable insight into how missionary investments, actions, activities and purposes were defined and depicted, how the 'other' was depicted and consequently a valid institutional sense-making mechanism was created, and how all these reflections were brought together in a coherent missionary narrative by the help of a conceptual basis.

In short, there is an institutional narrative and one of its most important elements is its conceptual background. The conceptual background is based on conceptual metaphors and those conceptual metaphors are expressed in the texts as linguistic metaphors. This conceptual background is crucial for the institutional missionary perception of the outside world, the past, the present, and the future. The missionary text is considered to be a narrative, more specifically first and foremost travel writing, in a narratological sense. Therefore, the texts are evaluated in terms of the well-established story-discourse distinction in narratology. The conceptual metaphors contribute to the narrative and by tracing them one can identify a systematic formation.

The missionary narrative also relies on an already established narrative source, namely the Bible. Biblical parables and allusions to the Kingdom of God and eschatology had a fundamental impact on the narrative created by the missionaries of the ABCFM. Their parables and references were also the main source for conceptual metaphors. Thus, as one conceptual domain is projected onto another conceptual domain, as is the case in conceptual metaphors, stories and narratives originating from the Bible are projected onto other, real life stories by the missionaries. Since the conceptual metaphors mainly referred to a more general parable and story background related to the Millennium and the Kingdom of God, the eschatological parabolic background likewise constituted a background for metaphors. To examine the process of projection, how one story is projected onto another story, conceptual blending theory was applied.

The projection of one conceptual domain, such as cultivation, onto another one, such as propagation, produces a conceptual metaphor; in this case **Encouraging Beliefs is Cultivating a Plant**. This projection is one-sided, positive, and moves from one domain to the other unidirectionally. Yet the majority of metaphors allude to parables and parabolic stories from the Bible. These parables and parabolic structures are also projected onto other stories, creating mental spaces and producing a blend. Such a projection is multidirectional. Thus, the Biblical parables and parabolic stories can be projected onto real life events or reflections from the nineteenth century. And the nineteenth century story domain is projected onto the parabolic stories as well. As such, the missionaries reflected their experiences, thoughts and plans through a systematic and coherent discursive structure and created a specific narrative. Parabolic narrative structures were, by their very nature, already projected onto other stories. The mental space created by those reflections in Christian history was projected onto another reality occurring in the nineteenth century. This process created a similar but original blend. Conceptual metaphor networks hold these narrative structures together via linguistic metaphors which are related to Biblical eschatological parabolic narratives.

In the third chapter, a close reading of missionary texts displayed how this metaphoric narrative construction functioned. Furthermore, the link and interconnection between the projection of conceptual domains in the case of conceptual metaphors, and the projection of stories in the case of conceptual blending was teased out and presented. The scrutinized texts were the missionary writings in *The Missionary Herald* magazine from the first ten years of the Ottoman mission. They were considered representative of missionary discourse and its conceptual vein. The relationship between the narrative and the conceptual background was displayed and narrative elements that are conceptually represented were detected. Moreover, the way that multilayered parabolic narrative structures were built up on the conceptual basis was also shown.

Five groups of conceptual metaphors were identified. These are: metaphors of cultivation, metaphors of war, metaphors of light and darkness, metaphors of way/path/road, and metaphors of door/opening. The metaphors predominantly originated form Biblical sources. The main context was the Kingdom of God and the Millennium in postmillennialist terms. All of the conceptual metaphorical formations were related to missionary discourse. These metaphors and their linguistic expressions constitute the discourse part of missionary narrative. The discourse is how the narrative was told. The metaphors and their linguistic expressions referred to the outer world, past, and future. They are the story part of the missionary narratives. Story is what is told in the narrative.

The missionaries came to a new land, started looking for openings and doors to enter (opportunities), wanted to walk on the right path leading to the final destination (the Millennium and finally the second coming), looked for a fertile ground and favorable climate to sow their precious seed, conducted a spiritual warfare against the enemies of 'truth,' and while they were the enlightened ones, the rest was in darkness. All these metaphorical formations originated from a Biblical background. They are related to Christian eschatology and thus to the Kingdom of God. By using these metaphors, the missionaries constantly alluded to that source of parables, parabolic structures and Biblical stories. As the stories were already related to the Kingdom and consequently to the purposes of the Board, the use of conceptual metaphors created an easily understandable, compact, condensed, and coherent narrative. The original stories and parables were stories projected onto other stories. By alluding to them, the missionaries used the original mental space created in the first projection. Moreover, by projecting them onto their reality, they created a new mental space and a new line of projection that were still in connection with the original conceptual and parabolic background.

The fourth chapter dwelled on the continuity of these discursive formations in later missionary writings. For this purpose, two case studies were presented. The first case study focused on the failed attempt at starting a mission to the Muslims between 1856-65. The second study is on the missionary responses to the Armenian Massacres of 1894-96. The choice of case studies is based on the high importance of those momentous events for the missionaries.

In the first case study, metaphors of doors and openings made up the majority of metaphorical expressions. Metaphors of cultivation, metaphors of war, metaphors of light and darkness were used as well. Metaphors of way/path/road were missing. Seeing new opportunities in a new era after the Edict of 1856, the missionaries interpreted the political atmosphere in their favor. They started to see new opportunities for a new mission field which hitherto was closed. But there were several setbacks. Firstly, since they had confined their activities mainly to the Christians, the missionaries lacked important knowledge that could have been to their advantage for embarking on successful missionary work among the Muslims. They had limited knowledge of the Muslim culture and the ways people lived. Moreover, they learned Turkish spoken by the Armenian community, which was not sufficient to communicate efficiently with Muslim Turks. Secondly, despite their claims that the Muslims were ready for their call, the Muslims did not readily accept their call. Thirdly, and most importantly, the state did not evaluate the Edict of 1856 as permitting missionary work among Muslims. As a consequence of these obstacles, mission work for Muslims could not develop and the number of converts remained rather small. Due to the small scale of this mission work, the missionaries also narrated stories of single individuals. Under these circumstances, the missionaries used metaphors of door and opening as a reference to possible opportunities. Their future expectations were depicted by metaphors of cultivation. As the frictions between the authorities and the missionaries became clear, the dichotomy was expressed by metaphors of light and darkness, and their fight against government persecution found its expression in metaphors of war. The missionaries could not start a full throttle mission for the Muslims. Government pressures and public reaction were so great that after 1865 they did not try to recommence it either. The failure is the reason for the lack of metaphors of way/path/road in this case, because they could never enter the road that would bring them to the final destination.

The Armenian massacres elicited a more structured and thorough response from the missionaries. Although the missionaries were caught off guard at the beginning, after the first shock, they analyzed the situation rationally and a highly effective narrative gradually replaced the initial responses of perplexity, confusion and dismay. The missionaries not only used all five conceptual metaphorical fields that were detected in chapter 3, but also created a coherent, powerful and effective narrative to address the immediate problems they encountered. The situation was so drastic that metaphors of light and darkness were frequently used, and they also appeared in the special case of adverse weather condition and storm metaphors referring to the massacres and the ensuing chaos. The missionary narrative repeatedly referred to 'God's hand' and God's intervention in order to provide the readers with a positive and easily understandable actor of agency. In addition, the missionaries also used metaphors of cultivation. In a special case, when confronted with the loss of many lives they referred to the blood of martyrs as the seed of the church and developed a discourse dealing with the issue of martyrdom. When the chaos abated, they were able to reflect on the future of the missions in the region and their narrative comprehensively dwelled on plans and opportunities that had arisen from the unfavorable conditions. Metaphors of doors and opening, together with metaphors of way/path/road became abundant during this phase. Target oriented, the missionaries were looking for openings and opportunities. It was a war between light and darkness, but they were to occupy the field. Orphans, desolate Armenian Apostolic Church members, people in need of help were cherished as opportunities to further the cause of 'Christian faith.' The leitmotif of the narrative was the Kingdom and the Millennium. Eschatological goals were constantly repeated and brought back to the readers' minds. The narrative also tried to persuade the readers of *The Missionary Herald* in the United States that past mission work had been conducted for good reason and that there was an even more urgent and deeper need for further missionary activity.

From the very beginning, the missionaries used a network of interrelated conceptual metaphors that originated from Biblical sources. The combination of conceptual and parabolic projection as a part of depicting what they encountered constituted a narrative. In the case of starting a mission to the Muslims, the narrative could not be articulated with the utmost effectiveness. The missionaries were short of the necessary evaluation skills, mainly as a result of their lack of knowledge about their target groups and their failure to interpret the political atmosphere. The external conditions were too strong to overcome and they could not utilize their conceptual background properly. Their projections were insufficient in number, and as a result of their failure to commence the new mission they could not effectively use conceptualizations and projections they had about the future, eschatology, and purposeful activity. The Armenian massacres, on the other hand, triggered a strong response. Although in the immediate aftermath of the massacres the missionary narrative displayed the dismay and perplexity prevailing among the missionaries, they soon applied their complete conceptual toolkit to evaluating the situation. The Kingdom was a central concept, and metaphors and a parabolic background were put to work. They expressed their teleological ideas via a strong institutional discourse, which resulted in a strong institutional sense making, positive feedback, legitimization of future mission work for themselves and their readers, and opportunity seeking. The missionary narrative was produced in the turbulent atmosphere of the nineteenth century Ottoman Empire. The paradoxical stance of missionaries towards modernization – as in the cases of expressing a universal Christian identity with a distinct Americanness, providing excellent secular education together with religious education, celebrating scientific and technological innovations but preferring rural settings – gradually clashed with the interests of a modernizing and centralizing Ottoman state.

The conceptual metaphorical discursive formations of the ABCFM missionaries in the Ottoman Empire are an excellent example of the convergence of text and the outer world. The missionary narrative is not only a testimony to the special way the missionaries developed learning strategies and found their orientation in a new setting, it was also a response to the challenges posed by modernization, motion and mobility of people, and the encounter with the 'other.' Work on missionary texts is a door that opens onto American and Ottoman political, religious and cultural history, the issue of modernity, globalization, as well as other non-fictional and fictional narratives dealing with the same era. The texts are suitable sources for a comparative perspective which can facilitate work on different writings dealing with the time period and geographical locations. Furthermore, the explication of a vast network of conceptual metaphors and an interconnected parabolic Biblical narrative shows the range of application of Conceptual Metaphor Theory and Blending Theory, and how they can be applied to historical texts. Above all, the study of missionary narrative is an enriching and enjoyable mental journey to bygone times, countries and people.

Bibliography

PRIMARY SOURCES

"A Martyred Preacher in Turkey." *The Missionary Herald*, February (1897): 80-84.

"Address of the Prudential Committee of the American Board of Commissioners for Foreign Missions." *The Missionary Herald*, March (1820): 134-141.

"Annual Meeting of the Board." *The Missionary Herald*, November (1864): 329-351.

"Annual Survey." *The Missionary Herald*, November (1897): 432-442.

"Annual Survey." *The Missionary Herald*, November (1898): 439-453.

Barnum, Herman N. "Eastern Turkey: Letter from Mr. Barnum." *The Missionary Herald*, January (1862): 22-26.

——. "The Outlook in Turkey." *The Missionary Herald*, April (1896): 146-149.

Bird, Isaac. "Extracts from the Journal of Mr. Bird." *The Missionary Herald*, February (1829): 47-50.

——. "Letter from Mr. Bird to the Assistant Secretary." *The Missionary Herald*, November (1824): 344.

——. "Palestine Mission: Journal of Mr. Bird." *The Missionary Herald*, October (1827): 302-305.

——. "Syria: Journal of Mr. Bird." *The Missionary Herald*, April (1829): 111-114.

Bird, Isaac; William Goodell, Eli Smith. "Departure of Missionaries from Beyroot." *The Missionary Herald*, November (1828): 348-350.

Bird, Isaac; William Goodell. "Journal of Messrs. Goodell and Bird." Missionary Herald, (1824): 236-242.

——. "Mission to Palestine: Beyroot." *The Missionary Herald*, September (1825): 271-273.

Brewer, Josiah. "Mission to Western Asia: Communications of Mr. Brewer." *The Missionary Herald*, March (1828): 70-74.

Brewer, Josiah; Elnathan Gridley. "Extracts from the Communications of Messrs. Gridley and Brewer." *The Missionary Herald*, August (1827): 233-240.

Browne, John K. "Modern Martyrdom in Armenia." *The Missionary Herald*, February (1896): 84-88.

"Central and Eastern Turkey Mission." *The Missionary Herald*, May (1897): 191-192.

"Central Turkey Mission." *The Missionary Herald*, August (1896): 333-335.

"Central Turkey Mission." *The Missionary Herald*, December (1898): 507-508.

"Central Turkey Mission." *The Missionary Herald*, January (1898): 24-26.

"Central Turkey Mission." *The Missionary Herald*, June (1897): 236-237.

"Central Turkey Mission." *The Missionary Herald*, May (1896): 206-208.

"Death of Mr. Fisk." *The Missionary Herald*, April (1826): 128-132.

"Destruction of the Turkish and Egyptian Fleets at Navarino." *The Missionary Herald*, January (1828): 19-20.

Dwight, H. G. O. "Northern Armenians: Letter from Mr. Dwight." *The Missionary Herald*, June (1857): 185-189.

——. "The Northern Armenians: Letter from Mr. Dwight." *The Missionary Herald*, October (1860): 311-313.

Dwight, H. G. O.; Eli Smith. "Mediterranean: Letters from Messrs. Smith and Dwight." *Missionary Herald*, December (1830): 375-378.

"Eastern Turkey Mission." *The Missionary Herald*, August (1897): 315-317.

"Eastern Turkey Mission." *The Missionary Herald*, August (1898): 314-316.

"Eastern Turkey Mission." *The Missionary Herald*, February (1897): 59-62.

"Eastern Turkey Mission." *The Missionary Herald*, July (1897): 275-278.

"Eastern Turkey Mission." *The Missionary Herald*, July (1898): 276-278.

"Eastern Turkey Mission." *The Missionary Herald*, June (1897): 237-241.

"Eastern Turkey Mission." *The Missionary Herald,* March (1896): 106-107.

"Eastern Turkey Mission." *The Missionary Herald,* March (1897): 113.

"Eastern Turkey Mission." *The Missionary Herald,* September (1897): 353-354.

"Editorial Paragraphs." *The Missionary Herald,* February (1898): 62-64.

"Editorial Paragraphs." *The Missionary Herald,* April (1896): 133-142.

"Editorial Paragraphs." *The Missionary Herald,* April (1897): 129-136.

"Editorial Paragraphs." *The Missionary Herald,* April (1898): 125-131.

"Editorial Paragraphs." *The Missionary Herald,* April, (1896): 133-142.

"Editorial Paragraphs." *The Missionary Herald,* August (1897): 297-303.

"Editorial Paragraphs." *The Missionary Herald,* December (1898): 485-491.

"Editorial Paragraphs." *The Missionary Herald,* February (1896): 45-50.

"Editorial Paragraphs." *The Missionary Herald,* January (1896): 1-8.

"Editorial Paragraphs." *The Missionary Herald,* January (1897): 1-9.

"Editorial Paragraphs." *The Missionary Herald,* July (1898): 253-260.

"Editorial Paragraphs." *The Missionary Herald,* June (1896): 221-227.

"Editorial Paragraphs." *The Missionary Herald,* March (1896): 89-96.

"Editorial Paragraphs." *The Missionary Herald,* March (1897): 85-94.

"Editorial Paragraphs." *The Missionary Herald,* May (1896): 177-184.

"Editorial Paragraphs." *The Missionary Herald,* May (1897): 169-176.

"Editorial Paragraphs." *The Missionary Herald,* October (1898): 377-384.

"Editorial Paragraphs." *The Missionary Herald,* September (1896): 347-352.

"Editorial Paragraphs" *The Missionary Herald,* July (1897): 257-265.

"Editorial Paragraphs" *The Missionary Herald,* November (1896): 435-440.

Everett, Joel S. "Constantinople: Letter from Mr. Everett." *The Missionary Herald,* January (1856): 14-15.

Farnsworth, Wilson A. "Northern Armenians: Letter from Mr. Farnsworth." *The Missionary Herald,* January (1860): 17-19.

——. "Some Results of Missionary Work in Turkey." *The Missionary Herald,* March (1896): 99-102.

——. "The Armenians." *The Missionary Herald,* February (1897): 55-59

——. "Western Turkey: Letter from Mr. Farnsworth." *The Missionary Herald,* March (1861): 73-74.

——. "What Shall the Missionaries in Turkey Do?" *The Missionary Herald*, February (1896): 57-59.

"Fifty Years of the Central Turkey Mission." *The Missionary Herald*, October (1897): 391-393.

Fisk, Pliny. "Palestine Mission: Extracts of a Letter from Mr. Fisk to the Corresponding Secretary." *The Missionary Herald*, April (1822): 111-112.

——. "Palestine Mission: Journal of Mr. Fisk." *Missionary Herald*, August (1824): 242-245.

——. "Palestine Mission: Journal of Mr. Fisk." *Missionary Herald*, October (1824): 305-311.

——. "Palestine Mission: Journal of Mr. Fisk." *The Missionary Herald*, September (1824): 269-275.

——. "Palestine Mission: Letter from Mr. Fisk." *Missionary Herald*, March (1825): 65-68.

——. "Western Asia: Letter of Mr. Fisk." *The Missionary Herald*, September (1827): 267-268.

Fisk, Pliny; Jonas King. "Journal of Messrs. Fisk and King from Cairo to Jerusalem, through the Desert." *The Missionary Herald*, February (1824): 33-42.

——. "Palestine Mission: Journal of Messrs. Fisk and King, in Upper Egypt." *The Missionary Herald*, December (1823): 375-378.

——. "Palestine Mission: Journal of Messrs. Fisk and King." *The Missionary Herald*, March (1824): 65-71.

——. "Palestine Mission: Journal of Messrs. Fisk and King." Missionary Herald, April (1824): 97-101.

——. "Palestine Mission: Journal of Messrs. Fisk and King, in Upper Egypt." *The Missionary Herald*, November (1823): 343-350.

Fisk, Pliny; Levi Parsons. "Letter from the Rev. Messrs. Fisk and Parsons." *The Missionary Herald*, June (1820): 265-267.

——. "Letter of Messrs. Parsons and Fisk to the Corresponding Secretary." *The Missionary Herald*, July (1821): 206-207.

——. "Letter from Messrs. Fisk and Parsons to the Corresponding Secretary." *The Missionary Herald*, June (1822): 178-179.

——. "Letters from Messrs. Parsons and Fisk." *The Missionary Herald*, April (1821): 102-105.

——. "Letters of Messrs. Parsons and Fisk to the Corresponding Secretary." *The Missionary Herald*, March (1821): 76-78.

——. "Palestine Mission: Journal of Messrs. Fisk and Parsons." *The Missionary Herald*, September (1821): 276-278.

——. "Palestine Mission: Journal of Messrs. Fisk and Parsons at Scio." *The Missionary Herald*, April (1821): 97-101.

——. "Palestine Mission: Journal of Messrs. Fisk and Parsons, During Their Tour in Asia Minor." *The Missionary Herald*, August (1821): 250-256.

——. "Palestine Mission: Journal of the Missionaries." *The Missionary Herald*, July (1821): 201-202.

——. "Palestine Mission: Letter from Messrs. Fisk and Parsons, to the Cor. Sec. of A. B. C. F. M." *The Missionary Herald*, April (1820): 173-174.

——. "Palestine Mission: Letter from Messrs. Fisk and Parsons." *The Missionary Herald*, January (1821): 19-20.

Goodell, William. "Extracts from Mr. Goodell's Correspondence." *The Missionary Herald*, June (1828): 171-175.

——. "Great Meeting of Armenians at Constantinople." *The Missionary Herald*, April (1827): 112-115.

——. "Letter from Mr. Goodell to the Corresponding Secretary." Missionary Herald, November (1826): 354-359.

——. "Letter from Mr. Goodell to the Corresponding Secretary." *The Missionary Herald*, January (1826): 11-14.

——. "Letter from Mr. Goodell." *The Missionary Herald*, July (1824): 214-216.

——. "Mediterranean: Letter from Mr. Goodell, Dated Malta, July, 1830." *The Missionary Herald*, December (1830): 373-375.

——. "Mediterranean: Letter from Mr. Goodell." *The Missionary Herald*, November (1826): 354-359.

——. "Mediterranean: Letter from Mr. Goodell." *The Missionary Herald*, December (1830): 373-375.

——. "Northern Armenians: Letter from Mr. Goodell." *The Missionary Herald*, April (1857): 120-121.

——. "Palestine Mission: Climate of Syria." *The Missionary Herald*, November (1825): 345-348.

——. "Palestine Mission: Communications from Mr. Goodell." *The Missionary Herald*, June (1827): 178-180.

——. "Palestine Mission: Journal of Mr. Goodell." *The Missionary Herald*, November (1824): 341-344.

——. "Palestine Mission: Journal of Mr. Goodell." *The Missionary Herald*, September (1824): 275.

Goodell, William; Isaac Bird. "Extract from the Journal of Messrs. Goodell and Bird." *The Missionary Herald*, July (1824): 213-214.

——. "Palestine Mission: Journal of Messrs. Goodell and Bird." *The Missionary Herald*, August (1824): 236-242.

Greene, Joseph K. "Western Turkey: Letter from Mr. Greene." *The Missionary Herald*, April (1865): 110-114.

Hamlin, Cyrus. "Northern Armenians: Letter from Mr. Hamlin." *The Missionary Herald*, December (1857): 390-391.

Herrick, George F. "Letter from Mr. Herrick." *The Missionary Herald*, August (1864): 305-311.

——. "Western Turkey: Letter from Mr. Herrick." *The Missionary Herald*, April (1862): 119-121.

——. "Western Turkey: Letter from Mr. Herrick." *The Missionary Herald*, November (1862): 353-355.

——. "Western Turkey: Letter from Mr. Herrick." *The Missionary Herald*, December (1864): 376-378.

——. "Western Turkey: Letter from Mr. Herrick." *The Missionary Herald*, January (1865): 16-17.

——. "Western Turkey: Letter from Mr. Herrick." *The Missionary Herald*, March (1865): 78-80.

——. "Western Turkey: Letter from Mr. Herrick." *The Missionary Herald*, October (1864): 305-311.

"Instructions to Mr. Temple." *The Missionary Herald*, October (1822): 335-336.

"Items of Intelligence." *The Missionary Herald*, August (1862): 237-240.

"Items of Intelligence." *The Missionary Herald*, February (1863): 39-41.

Kimball, Grace N. "Relief Work at Van, Eastern Turkey." *The Missionary Herald*, June (1896): 231-235.

King, Jonas. "Palestine Mission: Journal of Mr. King at Dar el Kamer." *The Missionary Herald*, July (1824): 211-213.

——. "Palestine Mission: Journal of Mr. King." *The Missionary Herald*, November (1825): 338-345.

——. "Palestine Mission: Journal of Mr. King." *The Missionary Herald*, December (1825): 369-377.

——. "Palestine Mission: Journal of Mr. King." *The Missionary Herald*, October (1825): 313-318.

——. "Palestine Mission: Journal of Mr. King." *The Missionary Herald*, October (1824): 311-315.

Leonard, Julius Y. "Northern Armenians: Letter from Mr. Leonard." *The Missionary Herald*, April (1859): 111-116.

"Mediterranean: Operations of the Church Missionary Societies Press at Malta." *The Missionary Herald*, November (1826): 359-361.

"Mediterranean: Views and Proceedings in Reference to this Mission." *The Missionary Herald*, March (1830): 73-78.

"Miscellanies." *The Missionary Herald*, June (1856): 181-185.

"Miscellanies." *The Missionary Herald*, May (1862): 162-165.

"Miscellany." *The Missionary Herald*, October (1858): 322-324.

"Mission to Palestine." *The Missionary Herald*, January (1823): 4.

"Monthly Summary." *The Missionary Herald*, January (1865): 24-29.

"Monthly Summary." *The Missionary Herald*, September (1864): 277-283.

Morse, Charles F. "Northern Armenians: Letter from Mr. Morse." *The Missionary Herald*, August (1858): 250-254.

"Northern Armenians: Station Reports." *The Missionary Herald*, September (1859): 268-277.

"Northern Armenians: Station Reports." *The Missionary Herald*, September (1860): 269-278.

"Palestine Mission." *The Missionary Herald*, April (1823): 212-213.

Parsons, Benjamin. "Northern Armenians: Letter from Mr. Parsons." *The Missionary Herald*, July (1857): 210-215.

——. "Western Turkey: Letter from Mr. Parsons." *The Missionary Herald*, August (1862): 242-244.

Parsons, Levi. "Letter from Mr. Parsons to the Corresponding Secretary." *The Missionary Herald*, February (1822): 44.

——. "Palestine Mission: Extract of a Letter from the Rev. Levi Parsons to the Treasurer of the A.B.C.F.M." *The Missionary Herald*, December (1820): 288.

——. "Palestine Mission: Journal of Mr. Parsons, While at Jerusalem." *The Missionary Herald*, February (1822): 33-44.

——. "Palestine Mission: Journal of Mr. Parsons." *The Missionary Herald*, January (1822): 16-19.

——. "Palestine Mission: Letter from Mr. Parsons to Mr. Cyrus Byington." *The Missionary Herald*, April (1822): 109-110.

Pratt, Andrew T. "Southern Armenians: Letter from Dr. Pratt." *The Missionary Herald*, May (1860): 151-153.

"Present Encouraging Aspect of the Unevangelized Parts of the World." *The Missionary Herald*, February (1820): 55-56.

"Printing Establishment for Western Asia." *The Missionary Herald*, March (1821): 80-82.

"Reasonable Expectations in Relation to the Palestine Mission." *The Missionary Herald*, July (1826): 212-214.

"Recent Intelligence." *The Missionary Herald*, June (1861): 187-189.

"Recent Intelligence." *The Missionary Herald*, November (1857): 379-382.

"Religious Denominations in Syria." *The Missionary Herald*, April (1826): 126.

"Report of the Prudential Committee." *The Missionary Herald*, December (1820): 553-556.

"Report of the Prudential Committee." *The Missionary Herald*, January (1821): 2-12.

"Report of the Prudential Committee." *The Missionary Herald*, July (1823): 203-208.

"Report of the Prudential Committee." *The Missionary Herald*, March (1821): 67-71.

"Report of the Prudential Committee." *The Missionary Herald*, March (1822): 65-71.

Schauffler, William G. "Mission to Western Turkey: Letter from Mr. Schauffler." *The Missionary Herald*, November (1860): 342-343.

Smith, Eli. "Extracts from a Letter of Mr. Smith to the Corresponding Secretary." *The Missionary Herald*, October (1827): 306-308.

——. "Extracts from the Journal of Mr. Smith." *The Missionary Herald*, June (1829): 176-180.

——. "Obstacles to the Growth of Evangelical Piety in Syria." *The Missionary Herald*, April (1828): 111-114.

——. "Syria: Communications from Mr. Smith." *The Missionary Herald*, August (1829): 241-245.

——. "Syria: Hints Respecting its Political State." *The Missionary Herald*, September (1829): 279-280.

——. "Western Asia: Letter from Mr. Smith to the Corresponding Secretary." *The Missionary Herald*, November (1827): 337-343.

Smith, Eli; H. G. O. Dwight. "Mediterranean: Extracts from Letters of Messrs. Smith and Dwight." *The Missionary Herald*, January (1831): 15-18.

"State and Progress of Palestine Mission." *The Missionary Herald*, April (1827): 103-112.

"Suggestions with Regard to Future Measures." *The Missionary Herald*, November (1828): 351-352.

"Survey of the Missions of the Board." *The Missionary Herald*, January (1861): 1-13.

"Survey of the Missions of the Board." *The Missionary Herald*, January (1862): 7-17.

Temple, Daniel. "Extract of a Letter from Mr. Temple to a Gentleman in Boston." *The Missionary Herald*, June (1822): 179.

——. "Mission to Palestine: Malta." *The Missionary Herald*, September (1825): 273-274.

"The Massacres in Turkey." *The Missionary Herald*, February, (1896): 54-57.

"The Outbreak at Van, Eastern Turkey." *The Missionary Herald*, September (1896): 353-356.

"Thoughts Suggested by the Preceding Journal." *Missionary Herald*, April (1821): 101-102.

"Thoughts upon the Printing Establishment in Malta." *The Missionary Herald*, July (1826): 211-212.

"To the Secretaries, Treasurers, and Collectors of Associations." *The Missionary Herald*, September (1825): 302.

"Triennial Statement Made by the American Board to the National Congregational Council, Portland, Oregon, July 11, 1898." *The Missionary Herald*, August (1898): 304-309.

Walker, Augustus. "Diarbekir: Letter from Mr. Walker." *The Missionary Herald*, November (1856): 331-333.

West, Henry S. "Western Turkey: Letter from Dr. West." *The Missionary Herald*, April (1861): 100-102.

"Western and Eastern Turkey Missions." *The Missionary Herald*, April (1897): 153-154.

"Western Asia: Proceedings of Messrs. Brewer and Gridley." *The Missionary Herald*, January (1828): 19.

"Western Turkey Mission." *The Missionary Herald*, April (1896): 154-155.

"Western Turkey Mission." *The Missionary Herald*, August (1897): 313-315.

"Western Turkey Mission." *The Missionary Herald*, January (1896): 22-23.

"Western Turkey Mission." *The Missionary Herald*, January (1898): 23-24.

"Western Turkey Mission." *The Missionary Herald*, March (1896): 105-106.

"Western Turkey Mission." *The Missionary Herald*, March (1897): 111-112.

"Western Turkey Mission." *The Missionary Herald*, March (1898): 110-111.

"Western Turkey Mission." *The Missionary Herald*, May (1897): 188-191.

"Western Turkey Mission." *The Missionary Herald*, October (1897): 396-398.

"Western Turkey: Station Reports." *The Missionary Herald*, September (1863): 268-273.

Wheeler, Crosby H. "Northern Armenians: Letter from Mr. Wheeler." *The Missionary Herald*, March (1859): 83-86.

White, George E. "The Supreme Aim." *The Missionary Herald*, April (1897): 141-142.

White, George H. "Southern Armenians: Letter from Mr. White." *The Missionary Herald*, October (1860): 309-311.

"Word of Cheer and Cries for Help." *The Missionary Herald*, June (1898): 176-182.

SECONDARY SOURCES

Abbott, H. Porter. *The Cambridge Introduction to Narrative*. Cambridge: Cambridge University Press (2003).

Abrams, M. H.; Geoffrey Galt Harpham. *A Glossary of Literary Terms*. Boston: Wadsworth (2009).

Ahlstrom, Sydney E. *A Religious History of the American People*. New Haven: Yale University Press (1972).

Akyüz, Yahya. "Abdülhamit Devrinde Protestan Okulları ile İlgili Orijinal İki Belge." *Ankara Üniversitesi Eğitim Bilimleri Fakültesi Dergisi*, Vol. 3, No. 1 (1970): 121-130.

——. "Cevdet Paşa'nın Öğretim ve Tanzimat Eğitimine İlişkin Bir Layihası." *OTAM (Osmanlı, Tarih, Araştırma ve Uygulama Merkezi Dergisi)*, No. 3, Jan. (1992): 85-114.

Anderson, Rufus. *History of the Missions of the American Board of Commissioners For Foreign Missions to the Oriental Churches, Volume I.* Boston: Congregational Publishing Society (1872).

Ardıç, Nurullah. "Islam, Modernity and the 1876 Constitution." *The First Ottoman Experiment in Democracy.* Eds: Christoph Herzog, Malek Sherif. Würzburg: Ergon (2010): 89-106.

Bal, Mieke. *Narrratology: Introduction to the Theory of Narrative.* Toronto: University of Toronto Press (1997).

Barnes, Albert. *Lectures on the Evidences of Christianity in the Nineteenth Century.* New York: Harper's (1868).

Barnett, S. J. *The Enlightenment and Religion: The Myths of Modernity.* Manchester: Manchester University Press (2003).

Barton, James Levi. *Daybreak in Turkey.* Boston: The Pilgrim Press (1908).

Baumgartner, Frederic J. *Longing for the End: A History of Millennialism in Western Civilization.* London: Macmillan (1999).

Baykara, Tuncer. "II. Mahmud'un Islahatında İç Temeller: 1829-1839 Arasında Anadolu." *Tanzimat'ın 150. Yıldönümü Uluslararası Sempozyumu.* Ankara: Atatürk Kültür, Dil ve Tarih Yüksek Kurumu, (1994): 263-270.

Beaugrande, Robert-Alain de; Wolfgang Ulrich Dressler. *Introduction to Text Linguistics.* London: Longman (1981).

Berk, Stephen E. *Calvinism versus Democracy: Timothy Dwight and the Origins of American Evangelical Orthodoxy.* Connecticut: Archon Books (1974).

Berman, Marshall. *All That is Solid Melts into Air.* London: Verso (1983).

The Bible: Authorized King James Version. Oxford: Oxford University Press (1997).

Bloch, Ruth H. *Visionary Republic: Millennial Themes in American Thought, 1756-1800.* Cambridge: Cambridge University Press (1985).

Blumenberg, Hans. "Light as a Metaphor for Truth." *Modernity and the Hegemony of Vision*. Ed. David Michael Levin. Berkeley: The University of California Press (1993): 30-62.

Booth, Wayne C. "Resurrection of the Implied Author: Why Bother?" *A Companion to Narrative Theory*. Eds. James Phelan, Peter J. Rabinowitz. Malden: Blackwell (2005): 75-88.

Braudel, Fernand. *The Mediterranean and the Mediterranean World in the Age of Philip II*. London: Collins (1973).

Brown, Ira V. "Watchers for the Second Coming: The Millenarian Tradition in America." *The Mississippi Valley Historical Review*, Vol. 39, No. 3, Dec. (1952): 441-458.

Buchenhorst, Ralph. "Einleitung: Das Fremde im Übergang." *Von Fremdheit lernen*. Ed. Ralph Buchenhorst. Bielefeld: Transcript (2015): 9-37.

Burke, Peter. *History and Social Theory*. Cambridge (UK): Polity (1992)
——. *What is Cultural History?* Cambridge (UK): Polity (2004).

Calinescu, Matei. *Five Faces of Modernity: Modernism, Avant-Garde, Decadence, Kitsch, Postmodernism*. Durham: Duke University Press (1987).

Cawardine, Richard J. *Evangelicals and Politics in Antebellum America*. Yale University Press: New Haven (1993).

Chatman, Seymour. *Story and Discourse: Narrative Structure in Fiction and Film*. Ithaca: Cornel University Press (1989).

Coakley, J. F. "Printing Offices of the American Board of Commissioners for Foreign Missions 1812-1900: A Synopsis." *Harvard Library Bulletin*, Volume 9, Number 1 (Spring 1998): 5-34.

Conforti, Joseph A. *Jonathan Edwards, Religious Tradition & American Culture*. Chapel Hill: University of North Carolina Press (1995).

Deringil, Selim. "'There Is No Compulsion in Religion': On Conversion and Apostasy in the Late Ottoman Empire: 1839-1856." *Comparative Studies in Society and History*, Vol. 42, No. 3, July (2000): 547-575.

——. "II. Abdülhamid Döneminde Osmanlı Dış İlişkilerinde 'İmaj' Saplantısı." *Sultan II. Abdülhamid ve Devri Semineri*. İstanbul: Edebiyat Fakültesi Basımevi (1994): 149-162.

——. "The Invention of Public Image in the Late Ottoman Period, 1808 to 1908." *Comparative Studies in Society and History*, Vol. 35, No. 1, January (1993): 3-29.

——. *The Well Protected Domains: Ideology and the Legitimation of Power in the Ottoman Empire 1876-1909*. London: I.B. Tauris & Co Ltd. (1998).

Dictionary of Mission Theology: Evangelical Foundations. Ed. John Corrie. Nottingham: Inter-Varsity Press (2007).

Dodd, Charles Harold. *The Parables of the Kingdom*. New York: Scribner (1961).

Dodge, Bayard. "American Educational and Missionary Efforts in the Nineteenth and Early Twentieth Centuries." *Annals of the American Academy of Political and Social Science*, Vol. 401, America and the Middle East, May (1972): 15-22.

Douglas, Roy. "Britain and the Armenian Question, 1894-7." *The Historical Journal*, No: 19, 1 (1976): 113-133.

Eisenstadt, S. N. "Multiple Modernities." *Daedalus*, Vol. 129, No. 1, Winter (2000): 1-29.

Elshakry, Marwa. "The Gospel of Science and American Evangelism in Late Ottoman Beirut." *Past and Present*, No. 196, Aug. (2007): 173-214.

Erdem, Gazi. *Osmanlı İmparatorluğunda Hıristiyanların Sosyal ve Dini Hayatları: 1856-1876*. Ankara: Ankara Üniversitesi (2005) (Unpublished PhD dissertation).

Erhan, Çağrı. "Ottoman Official Attitudes towards American Missionaries." *The United States and the Middle East: Cultural Encounters*. Eds. Abbas Amanat, Magnus T. Bernhardsson. New Haven: YCIAS (2002): 315-341.

Findley, Carter V. *Bureaucratic Reform in the Ottoman Empire: The Sublime Porte, 1789-1922*. New Jersey: Princeton University Press (1980).

——. *Turkey; Islam, Nationalism, and Modernity: A History, 1789-2007*. New Haven: Yale University Press (2010).

First Ten Annual Reports of the American Board of Commissioners for Foreign Missions, with Other Documents of the Board. Boston: Crocker and Brewster (1834).

Fortna, Benjamin C. *Imperial Classroom*. Oxford: Oxford University Press (2002).

Fuller, Robert. *Naming the Antichrist: The History of an American Obsession*. Oxford: Oxford University Press (1995).

Gillespie, Michael Allen. *The Theological Origins of Modernity*. Chicago: The University of Chicago Press (2008).

Goodell, William. *Forty Years in the Turkish Empire*. New York: Robert Carter and Brothers (1876).

Goody, Jack. *Capitalism and Modernity: The Great Debate*. Cambridge (UK): Polity (2004).

Grabill, Joseph L. *Protestant Diplomacy and Near East: Missionary Influence on American Foreign Policy, 1810-1927*. Minneapolis: University of Minnesota Press (1971).

Grady, J. E.; T. Oakley; S. Coulson. "Blending and Metaphor." *Metaphor in Cognitive Linguistics*. Eds. R. W. Gibbs and G. J. Steen. Amsterdam/Philadelphia: John Benjamins (1999): 101-124.

Greene, Joseph K. *Leavening the Levant*. Boston: The Pilgrim Press (1916).

Hanioğlu, M. Şükrü. *A Brief History of the Late Ottoman Empire*. Princeton: Princeton University Press (2008).

Harvey, Anthony Ernest. *A Companion to the New Testament: The New Revised Standard Version*. Cambridge: Cambridge University Press (2004).

Hatch, Nathan O. *The Democratization of American Christianity*. New Haven: Yale University Press (1989).

Herman, Luc; Bart Vervaeck. "Ideology." *The Cambridge Companion to Narrative*. Ed. David Herman. Cambridge: Cambridge University Press (2007): 217-230.

Himmelfarb, Gertrude. *The Roads to Modernity: The British, French, and American Enlightenments*. New York: Alfred A. Knopf (2004).

Karal, Enver Ziya. "Gülhane Hatt-ı Hümayûnu'nda Batı'nın Etkisi." *Belleten*, Vol. 28, No.112 (1964): 581-601.

Karpat, Kemal H. *The Politicization of Islam*. Oxford: Oxford University Press (2001).

Katz, Michael B. *Reconstructing American Education*. Cambridge (Mass.): Harvard University Press (1987).

Khalaf, Samir. *Protestant Missionaries in the Levant: Ungodly Puritans, 1820-60*. London: Routledge (2012).

Kieser, Hans-Lukas. *A Quest for Belonging: Anatolia Beyond Empire and Nation*. Istanbul: Isis Press (2007).

——. *Nearest East: American Millennialism and Mission to the Middle East*. Philadelphia: Temple University Press (2010).

Kövecses, Zoltán. *Metaphor: A Practical Introduction.* Oxford: Oxford University Press, (2002).

Kress, Gunther; Theo van Leeuwen. *Reading Images: The Grammar of Visual Design.* London: Routledge (1996).

Kuran-Burçoğlu, Nedret. "Turkey." *Imagology.* Eds. Manfred Beller; Joep Leerssen. Amsterdam: Rodopi (2007): 254-258.

Lakoff, George; Mark Johnson. *Metaphors We Live by.* Chicago: University of Chicago Press (2003).

Lakoff, George; Jane Espenson, Alan Schwartz. *Master Metaphor List, Second Draft Copy.* Berkeley: University of California Berkeley, Cognitive Linguistics Group (1991).

Maksudyan, Nazan. "Being Saved to Serve: Armenian Orphans of 1894-1896 and Interested Relief in Missionary Orphanages." *Turcica*, Vol. 42 (2010): 47-88.

Mayr, Ernst. "The Idea of Teleology." *Journal of the History of Ideas,* Vol. 53, No. 1 January - March (1992): 117-135.

Melson, Robert. "A Theoretical Inquiry into the Armenian Massacres of 1894-1896." *Comparative Studies in Society and History,* Vol. 24, No. 3 (1982): 481-509.

Memorial Volume of the First Fifty years of the American Board of Commissioners for Foreign Missions. Boston: Published by the Board (1863).

Merguerian, Barbara J. "'Missions in Eden': Shaping an Educational and Social Program for the Armenians in Eastern Turkey (1855-1895)." *New Faith in Ancient Lands: Western Missions in the Middle East in the Nineteenth and Early Twentieth Centuries.* Ed. Heleen Murre-van der Berg. Leiden: Brill (2006): 241-262.

Moorhead, James H. "Between Progress and Apocalypse: A Reassessment of Millennialism in American Religious Thought, 1800-1880." *The Journal of American History,* Vol. 71, No. 3, December (1984): 524-542.

Nell, Werner. "Innenansichten von der Außenseite: Befremdung und Marginalität als Erkenntnis-Chancen in einigen autobiographischen Texten aus dem 18- Jahrhundert." *Von Fremdheit lernen.* Ed. Ralph Buchenhorst. Bielefeld: Transcript (2015): 145-168.

Ortaylı, İlber. *Ottoman Studies.* Istanbul : Bilgi Üniv. Yayinlari (2007).

Perry, Arthur L. *Williamstown and Williams College*. New York: Charles Scribner's Sons (1899).

Pratt, Marie Louise. *Imperial Eyes: Travel Writing and Transculturation*. London: Routledge (2003).

Punter, David. *Modernity*. New York: Palgrave Macmillan (2007).

Quandt, Jean B. "Religion and Social Thought: The Secularization of Postmillennialism." *American Quarterly*, Vol. 25, No. 4, October (1973): 390-409.

Reed, James Eldin. "American Foreign Policy, the Politics of Missions and Josiah Strong, 1890-1900." *Church History: Studies in Christianity and Culture*, Vol. 4, Issue 02, June (1972): 230-245.

"Remarks of President Barack Obama at Student Roundtable," 2 May 2009, URL = http://www.whitehouse.gov [view date: 24 June 2015].

Richter, Julius. *A History of the Protestant Missions in the Near East*. New York: Fleming H. Revell Company (1910).

Rodogno, Davide. *Against Massacre: Humanitarian Interventions in the Ottoman Empire, 1815-1914*. Princeton: Princeton University Press (2012).

Routledge Encyclopedia of Narrative Theory. Eds. David Herman, Manfred Jahn. London: Routledge (2005).

Sağlık ve Eğitim Vakfı, URL = http://www.sev.org.tr/kurumlarimiz [view date: 21 January 2017].

Salt, Jeremy. *Imperialism, Evangelism, and the Ottoman Armenians, 1878-1896*. London: Cass (1993).

Schaeffer, Jean-Marie. "Fictional vs. Factual Narration." Paragraph 1. *the living handbook of narratology*. Eds: Peter Hühn et al. Hamburg: Hamburg University. URL = http://www.lhn.uni-hamburg.de/article/fictional-vs-factual-narration [view date: 21 January 2017].

Schmid, Wolf. "Implied Reader." Paragraph 5. *the living handbook of narratology*. Eds: Peter Hühn et al. Hamburg: Hamburg University. URL = http://www.lhn.uni-hamburg.de/article/implied-reader [view date: 21 January 2017].

Showalter, Douglas K. "The 1810 Formation of the American Board of Commissioners for Foreign Missions." *The Role of the American Board in the World*. Eds. Clifford Putney, Paul T. Burlin. Eugene: Wipf & Stock (2012): 1-10.

Smylie, John Edwin. "Protestant Clergymen and American Destiny: II: Prelude to Imperialism, 1865-1900." *The Harvard Theological Review*, Vol. 56, No. 4 Oct. (1963): 297-311.

Somel, Akşin. "Christian Community Schools During the Ottoman Reform Period." *Late Ottoman Society: The Intellectual Legacy*. Ed. Elisabeth Özdalga. London: Routledge Press (2005): 254-273.

Stone, Frank Andrews. *Academies for Anatolia*. California: Caddo Gap Press (2005).

Strong, William E. *The Story of the American Board*. Boston: The Pilgrim Press (1910).

Swift, David Everett. "Conservative versus Progressive Orthodoxy in Latter 19th Century Congregationalism." *Church History*, Vol. 16, No. 1, March (1947): 22-31.

Said, Edward W. *Orientalism*. New York: Pantheon Books (1978).

Toolan, Michael. "Coherence." Paragraph 1. *the living handbook of narratology*. Eds: Peter Hühn et al. Hamburg: Hamburg University. URL = http://www.lhn.uni-hamburg.de/article/coherence [view date: 21 January 2017].

Turner, Mark. *The Literary Mind*. Oxford: Oxford University Press (1996).

Tuveson, Ernest Lee. *Redeemer Nation: The Idea of America's Millennial Role*. Chicago: University of Chicago Press (1968).

Wilson, Ann Marie. "In the name of God, civilization, and humanity: The United States and the Armenian massacres of the 1890s." *Le Mouvement Social*, No: 227 (2009/2): 27-44.

Youngs, Tim. *The Cambridge Introduction to Travel Writing*. Cambridge: Cambridge University Press (2013).

Yücel, İdris. "An Overview of Religious Medicine in the Near East: Mission Hospitals of American Board in Asia Minor." *Journal for the Study of Religions and Ideologies*, Vol. 14, Issue 40, Spring (2015): 47-71.

Zürcher, Erik J. *Turkey a Modern History*. London: I.B. Tauris & Co Ltd (1993).

Historical Sciences

Gesa zur Nieden, Berthold Over (eds.)
Musicians' Mobilities and Music Migrations in Early Modern Europe
Biographical Patterns and Cultural Exchanges

2016, 432 p., 34,99 € (DE),
ISBN 978-3-8376-3504-1
E-Book: 34,99 € (DE), ISBN 978-3-8394-3504-5

Klaus Weinhauer, Anthony McElligott, Kirsten Heinsohn (eds.)
Germany 1916-23
A Revolution in Context

2015, 266 p., 39,99 € (DE),
ISBN 978-3-8376-2734-3
E-Book: 39,99 € (DE), ISBN 978-3-8394-2734-7

Jörg Rogge (ed.)
Recounting Deviance
Forms and Practices of Presenting
Divergent Behaviour in the Late Middle Ages
and Early Modern Period.
In Collaboration with Kristina Müller-Bongard.

2016, 208 p., 29,99 € (DE),
ISBN 978-3-8376-3588-1
E-Book: 26,99 € (DE), ISBN 978-3-8394-3588-5

All print, e-book and open access versions of the titels in our entire list
are available in our online shop www.transcript-verlag.de/en!